The Twenty-First Century Catholic

James Kinn

RESOURCE PUBLICATIONS, INC.
San Jose, California

www.rpinet.com

Reprint Department
Resource Publications, Inc.
160 E Virginia Street, Suite #170
San Jose, CA 95112
(408) 286-8505
(408) 287-8748 fax

Library of Congress Cataloging-in-Publication Data

Kinn, James W., 1931-
  The twenty-first century Catholic / James Kinn.
     pages cm
  ISBN 978-0-89390-763-1 (pbk.) -- ISBN 0-89390-763-4 (pbk.)
  1. Catholic Church--Doctrines. 2. Spiritual life--Catholic Church. 3.
Christian life--Catholic authors. I. Title.
  BX1754.K5196 2013
  282.09'051--dc23
                                        2013012049

Printed in the United States of America
13 14 15 16 17 | 5 4 3 2 1

Design and Production: Patty Sweet

Copyeditors: Barbara Mellen and Caroline Thomas

APPRECIATION

I am deeply grateful to three friends who reviewed this book and greatly improved its contents and style: Roger O'Brien for his careful and professional critique of the entire contents; Mary Lou Larkin, BVM, for her valued comments and careful corrections of my style; Donald Stalzer for his observations and suggestions. My thanks also to Carol Elsholz who created the insightful reflections at the end of each chapter.

ACKNOWLEDGMENTS

Acknowledgment is made to Oxford University Press, N. Y., the publisher of the *New American Bible,* Donald Senior, general ed. Copyright © 1986 by the Confraternity of Christian Doctrine, Washington, DC. All the Scripture texts are taken from this version.

Quotations from *The Future Church: How Ten Trends Are Revolutionizing the Catholic Church* by John L. Allen, Jr., copyright © 2009 by John L. Allen, Jr. are used by permission of Doubleday Religion, an imprint of the Crown Publishing Group, a division of Random House, Inc. Any third party use of this material, outside of this publications, is prohibited. Interested parties must apply directly to Random House, Inc. for permission. Most of the statistics of my chapter 17, "Upside-down Church in 2050," are taken from his book.

Extracts from the *Documents of the Second Vatican Council* are the author's own translation.

Quotations from ON BEING A CHRISTIAN by Hans Kung, copyright © 1976 by Doubleday, a division of Random House, Inc. Used by permission of Doubleday, a division of Random House, Inc. Any third party use of this material, outside of this publication, is prohibited. Interested parties must apply directly to Random House, Inc. for permission.

Quotations reprinted by permission of the publisher from WHAT HAPPENED AT VATICAN II by John W. O'Malley, pp. 307, 311, Cambridge, Mass.: The Belknap Press of Harvard University Press, Copyright © 2008 by the President and Fellows of Harvard College.

Quotations from *The Collected Works of St. John of the Cross*, translated by Kieran Kavanaugh and Otilio Rodriguez, Copyright © 1964, 1979, 1991 by Washington Provice of Discalced Carmelites ICS Publications 2131 Lincoln Road, N.E. Washington, CD 20002-1199 U.S.A. www.icspublications.org.

Quotations from *Christianity; Essence, History and Future* are printed with permission from the Continuum International Publishing Group, © Kung, 1996.

CONTENTS

PART II: CATHOLICS

INTRODUCTION

The last fifty years have seen more changes in the Catholic Church than any other similar period, except for the first hundred years after Christ and the time of the Protestant Reformation. Vatican Council II and the opening up of Scripture to modern methods of criticism were the two dominant events of these amazing years in a church that many inside and outside of the Church were sure would never happen.

Twenty years after the council, Raymond Brown, an outstanding American Scripture scholar, made this observation:

> If Vatican Council II may be looked upon as an inner Roman Catholic reformation, I wish to ask whether in these next twenty years a continuation may not produce what Christians on all sides might wish to achieve: a truly reformed Catholic Church. … Roman Catholicism has made a tremendous start toward self-reform, and the machinery and forces are there to continue it. I recognize that this ongoing reform is not going to be smooth ….[1]

The last phrase, "ongoing reform is not going to be smooth," was prophetic.

Two years later, in 2003, Monika Hellwig added a further historical perspective:

> These four decades [since the Vatican Council] have seen a breaking open of the scriptures for the people of God in ways that had not happened within the Catholic Church for long centuries. These have been decades of rediscovering our spirituality traditions, decades of liturgical blossoming,

---

1   Raymond Brown, *The Critical Meaning of the Bible* (NY: Paulist Press, 1981), pp. 114-15.

1

decades of a whole new … sense of the social justice
concerns integral to the lived gospel of Jesus Christ. … Of
course, this has not been like a triumphal march, a simple
forward progression of a church with a shared vision and
purpose.[2]

The clause, "this has not been a triumphal march," is also quite
accurate historically.

The first thing I hope to do in this book about twenty-first
century Catholicism is to describe honestly what has happened
in these fifty years since Vatican Council II. These have been
turbulent years of reform and, sometimes, Roman control of
the reform. There are deep divisions in the Church, not only in
Rome, but also all over the world. There has been a weakening
of the Church in Europe and the United States, at least in terms
of regular church attendance; yet there are countries in Africa
where the Church is thriving as never before.

In America, many conservative Catholics are distressed by
the changes in the Church, while many progressive Catholics
are troubled by signs of Roman retrenchment. If we admit all
these diverse concerns and struggles going on in our American
Church, what does all that bode for us in the twenty-first
century? Some of my friends argue that there is no way we can
be realistic about the present situation in the Church and still
be positive about the future. I also felt that way for some time.
But now I believe that we can be entirely realistic and, at the
same time, positive about the American Church in the twenty-
first century. That is my primary goal in writing this book: to be
realistic about this very human Church, yet also very hopeful
and **optimistic** for Catholics in this new century.

The audience I have in mind for this work is the ordinary
intelligent Catholic. I have tried to avoid technical terms
throughout; those that are retained are explained immediately

---

2   Monika Hellwig, "A Note on Vatican II in Historical Perspective" in *Catholic Theology Facing the Future,* Dermot Lane, ed. (NY: Paulist Press, 2003), pp. 125-26.

in the text and also in the glossary. My own sense of the people I have known in various parishes in the last fifty years is that the majority of our people have adapted quite well to the changes in our Church since Vatican II, and they have shown great forbearance and tolerance for the human failures of our bishops and priests. Yet I have seen so many Catholics who have given up on the practice of their religion or who have simply drifted away from the faith, for many different reasons. These are the Catholics I particularly want to reach. I want to present this Church of Christ in a realistic way and show them the renewed appeal of Jesus and his way, which the advances of Scripture and the reforms of the council have offered us all.

Part I, Catholicism, concentrates on the teachings of our faith and on the institutional Church. The first two chapters describe the two dynamic changes in the twentieth century that began a revolution in our Church: Vatican Council II and the advances in Scripture study. These two profound developments in our Church affect us all dramatically in this century; the entire view of our faith in this century depends greatly on these two elements. Chapters 3-8 describe some of the doctrinal questions that theologians will continue to investigate in this twenty-first century regarding Jesus Christ, the Trinity, ecumenism, and other teachings of the Church. Some readers may find these chapters difficult and theological, yet these are some of the main issues for theological study in this century. Chapters 9-18 are about the institutional Church: the pope, the Curia, the bishops, and the theologians. Our focus here is on how they dealt with the changes proposed by Vatican II. Studying the elements of any institution is not easy or inviting. I have tried to make these chapters more appealing by adding engaging events and interesting stories. Chapter 15 deals with the interplay of culture and religion; chapter 16 considers the interplay of evolution and faith; chapter 17 surveys the demographic changes that are turning our world and our Church "upside down;" chapter 18 takes a hard look at the divisions in the Church.

Part II, Catholics, focuses on the faith and life-style of Catholics in this new century. The title of this book indicates that our primary concern is the individual faith-life of Catholics, rather than the institutional Church. Chapter 19 starts our discussion of twenty-first century Catholics by emphasizing our personal faith in Jesus as the unique and central inspiration of our Christian life. Chapter 20 suggests elements of an authentic lay spirituality based on the ordinary lives of lay people. The following chapters center on the human Jesus, who is our way, our truth, and our life. This concentration on Jesus Christ as our human model is the heart of our vision for this new century. Such a spirituality, centered on Jesus, will hopefully continue to drive our Church in this new century.

Let me conclude this introduction with my dream for our Church, despite all her obvious faults. Here is my vision for the American Church in the twenty-first century. I see Catholics in America today to be much like the early settlers in America, who left the settled areas of the East and went in covered wagons to reach and settle in the West. The East represents the Church of the last century, which had a vertical form, with law and order and a settled theology. To varying degrees, we are willing to leave the settled areas of the East, with its definite authority and familiar church groups. The West represents the Church of the twenty-first century that seeks a more horizontal Church, with more need for group sharing, more freedom, and new ways of spirituality. We have been slowly crossing the great plain for an extended time. Our progress is aided by a new outlook and by some understanding of where we are heading. But we still don't know what to expect, and we know that we have to cross those Rocky Mountains. Besides that, our multitide is strung out for hundreds of miles. Many are stopping and looking back East. Some of those, who were our leaders back East and reluctantly joined us on this journey, want us all to turn around and go back where things were more familiar and secure. Still others are unhappy with some of the changes they already made on this journey; they were more comfortable just following along, rather than having to make difficult decisions and trying to find a new way. As we approach those mountains, we are uncertain how to get over them. Even our adventurous leaders cannot assure us that everything will go well. And they certainly don't know exactly what lies on the other side of the mountains.

But some of us have been scouting ahead; we reached a pass through the mountains and looked over. What we saw on the other side was not clear and distinct, but it looked like a beautiful valley that stretches out for hundreds of miles and looks green and fertile. If we are going to settle there, we will need to form strong communities and a new way of life — a life of acceptance of differences; a life of real love and concern for all, without needless rules; a life of authentic human meaning, not legalistic or intellectual ideals; a life of responsible interdependence and creativity. It is our job, now, to get over these mountains and make a new way, together with our companions on this journey. Never before have we had such an opportunity—to find a new land, a new Church. We feel encouraged by the Spirit who moves us forward, toward that new Church that is aborning. It is our challenge and our privilege to bring it to birth.

PART 1: CATHOLICISM

CHAPTER I

Vatican Council II:
Aggiornamento

One seed of twenty-first century Catholicism was Vatican Council II, 1962-1965. Yet this transforming event in the Church was so unlikely and extraordinary that it almost didn't happen. One story describes how improbable this event was. In 1950, Yves Congar published *Vraie et fausse reforme dans l'Eglise.*[3] *(True and False Reform in the Church*; though it was never translated into English.) Many scholars thought his book—the very idea of reform in the church—was a provocation. When the papal nuncio in Paris, Archbishop Angelo Roncalli, read the book, he inscribed in his copy, "A reform of the Church—is it possible?" A few years later, Archbishop Roncalli became Pope John XXIII. The idea of reform in the Church—or renewal—became a driving question for him. Meanwhile, Congar's other two books on the Church[4] became popular as well as controversial. These three books introduced the ideas that would dominate the agenda for Vatican II: 1) *Ecclesia semper reformanda (*the Church always in need of reform); 2) the Church as the people of God; 3) a form of ecumenism acceptable to Catholics.[5]

Besides Yves Congar, in the twenty years leading up to Vatican II, there were several other theologians in France and

---

3   Yves Congar, OP, *Vraie et fausse reforme dans l'Eglise* (Paris: Cerf, 1950).

4   Yves Congar, OP, *Chretiens desunis* (Paris, Cerf, 1937); translated as *Divided Christendom: A Catholic Study of the Problem of Reunion* (London: Centenary Press, 1939); and then *Jalons pour une theologie du laicat* (Paris: Cerf, 1953); translated as *Lay People in the Church* (Westminster, MD: Newman Press, 1965).

5   Cf. Fergus Kerr, *Twentieth-Century Catholic Theologians* (Malden, MA: Blackwell Publishing, 2007).

Germany who were part of the New Theology. This New Theology was not a new system of theology, but an effort by a wide range of scholars to enter into dialogue with contemporary thought. Such theologians as Henri de Lubac, Jean Danielou, and Marie Dominique Chenu in France, Karl Rahner and Otto Semmelroth in Germany, and Hans Urs von Balthasar in Switzerland attempted to return to the biblical, patristic, and liturgical sources that enriched the Church in the first millennium. The approach of these scholars differed from the more abstract and systematic theology of Thomas Aquinas, because it relied greatly on the biblical and historical sources.

In January 1959, Pope John XXIII astonished everyone by announcing a full-scale council, Vatican Council II, in order to reform the Church. In July 1960, Congar was among the first appointed by the pope to draft the texts for the council's consideration. John XXIII took this bold step despite strong resistance from the Curia. When the council started in October 1962, it became apparent that it had many distinguishing and even unique characteristics:

- It was most likely the largest religious meeting in the history of the world: 2,860 council fathers attended part or all of the four sessions, 64% of the bishops were from outside Europe.

- Non-Catholic observers were admitted for the first time to the body of the council.

- The mere spectacle of this huge council made it so newsworthy that it was covered by radio and television around the world.

- The scope of the council in general, and especially of the Constitution on the Church in the Modern World, was directed to the entire world.

- The main purpose of this council was not to define any doctrines, but to bring the teaching of the Church up to date (*aggiornamento*); its purpose was pastoral—to proclaim the faith more clearly for today's world.

By giving birth to this council, Pope John XXIII ushered in a new era in the Catholic Church. He opened up in the Church the way to renewal (*aggiornamento*); to a profound respect for the Bible in worship, theology, and church life; to the Church's affirmation of human rights, including an affirmation of the freedom of religion and conscience for all; to an ecumenical attitude toward Judaism and Islam; to openness to the modern world with a positive attitude toward science and democracy; and to a proclamation of the gospel in keeping with the time.[6] This council "represented an epoch-making and irrevocable turning point" of the Catholic Church.[7]

Two major tuning points for the council happened very quickly. The first occurred only twenty minutes into the first general meeting. As soon as the list of committee chairmen, prepared by the Curia, was presented for approval, two cardinals suggested that a recess be granted so that they could consider the candidates. The 2,700 council fathers quickly realized what this suggestion implied, and they slowly broke into a thunderous applause so that no vote needed to be taken on the motion. After the recess, a quite different list of committee chairmen was suggested by the full council. "Suddenly, dramatically, effective institutional power in Roman Catholicism had swung from the Curia to the Council of Bishops."[8]

The second turning point occurred on November 20. "[After] days of bitter exchanges ... the majority of the Council fathers voted **against** the draft text *de fontibus revelationis,* on 'the sources' of Christian revelation, the work of a team of (mostly) Roman university theologians, presided over by

---

6   Cf. Hans Kung, *The Catholic Church* (New York: Modern Library, 2003), p. 181.

7   Ibid. p. 182.

8   Michael Novak, *The Open Church* (New York: Macmillan Company, 1963), p. 9.

Cardinal Ottaviani ….."[9] The vote fell short of the two-thirds majority needed to reject a text, but John XXIII intervened on the side of the majority, so that a new commission could be formed to compose a fresh text on revelation.

Curial theology tended to emphasize the doctrinal teaching of the Church throughout history more than Scripture. However, this new commission put more emphasis on Scripture, insisting that "[t]here is one source of God's Word: Scripture, as interpreted by Tradition, by the living Church."[10] This decision permitted the Council members and theologians to make proper use of the recent advances of scriptural exegesis such as literary and historical criticism, following Pope Pius XII's encyclical, *Divino Afflante Spiritu* (By the Divine Inspiring Spirit), in 1943.[11] This move toward greater emphasis on Scripture "was the turning point, not only [for] the defeat of the Holy Office theologians; but, as many saw at the time … with delight or dismay, the close of an age – in principle, at least."[12] Throughout the council, then, Scripture was the primary foundation and source for their work. What follows in the rest of this chapter is a brief summary of six of the major documents of Vatican II, and then some comments on what they meant for our Church.

A. DOGMATIC CONSTITUTION ON THE CHURCH (*LUMEN GENTIUM*)

Robert Outler asserts that the Dogmatic Constitution on the Church might be considered the masterpiece of Vatican II. First, because this is the first fully developed **conciliar** exposition of the doctrine of the Church in history, and second, because of its truly pastoral tone and ecumenical spirit.[13] Avery

---

9   Fergus Kerr, p. 37 (emphasis added).

10   Michael Novak, p. 11.

11   Cf. Chapter 2, below.

12   Fergus Kerr, p. 37.

13   See Albert Outler in *The Documents of Vatican II*, Walter Abbott, SJ, gen. ed. (New York: American Press, 1966), p. 102.

Dulles calls this constitution the most imposing achievement of Vatican II.[14] Yet, probably no other document of Vatican II underwent more **drastic revisions** between the first schema and the finally approved text. That is because the first schema resembled the traditional treatise on the Church found in most theological manuals published for generations, placing heavy emphasis on the hierarchical and juridical aspects of the Church, including the supremacy of the Pope. But the council fathers saw the need for a radically different vision of the Church, more biblical, more historical, more ecumenical, and more people-centered. This constitution was debated and reworked over three sessions of the council. Despite many revisions and vigorous debate, the council fathers voted overwhelmingly (2,156 to 5) to affirm the Church as the biblical **People of God**, who possess the dignity and freedom of sons and daughters of God with Christ as their head. So this dramatic new vision of the Church begins with the definition of the Church as the **People of God**.[15] That is, "the Church" is not primarily defined by the hierarchy but rather by all the People of God.

B. THE CHURCH IN THE MODERN WORLD (*GAUDIUM ET SPES*)

The longest document of the Council, *Gaudium et Spes*, is extraordinary for three reasons. First, it addresses not only Christians or Catholics, but also the entire modern world. It focuses on how the Church relates to the "whole of humanity... and how it conceives of the presence and functions of the

---

14　See Avery Dulles, SJ in *The Documents of Vatican II*, p. 13.

15　*Acta Apostolicae Sedis (AAS), 1965, p. 20, Lumen Gentium,* 9. Chapter II is entitled "The People of God." Only then, in Chapter III, does *Lumen Gentium* consider the hierarchical structure of the Church. **NOTE: All the quotes taken from the Documents of Vatican II will be from the *Acta Apostolicae Sedis (AAS).*** There are four books published in the U.S. that contain the English translations of the documents of Vatican II. But all of them refuse to grant permission to quote from their copyrighted material. So the only way to legally quote those important documents is to rely on the official Latin documents found in the *Acta Apostolicae Sedis* (1964-1966). My translation from the Latin is not an "official" translation, but it is reliable.

Church in the world today."[16] No other council of the Church, apparently, has deliberately addressed the entire world.

Second, it departs from the usual language of earlier councils. Often the language of earlier councils was judicial, legislative, argumentative, and condemnatory. In this document, especially, the language is much more that of dialogue and affirmation. Third, this document is unique in its positive attitude to the world; thus, it asserts, "nothing genuinely human fails to raise an echo in [Christian] hearts …. That is why [the Church] realizes that it is truly and intimately linked with the human race and its history."[17] That is, the Church now wants to engage in conversation about modern questions, such as the current trends of our world today, the role of human beings in our universe, the profound and rapid changes around the world, the amazing progress of science, the endless political, social, racial, and economic disputes, and the ultimate destiny of humanity:

> [T]here is a growing awareness of the sublime dignity of human persons …. They ought, therefore, to have ready access for all that is necessary for living a genuinely human life: for example, food, clothing, housing, the right freely to choose their state of life … the right to education … to their good name, to respect … to freedom, including freedom of religion.[18]

Throughout this document, the Church exhibits a positive attitude toward this world: its sciences, its psychological search, its historical studies, its industrialization, and its increasing forms of communication. It admits that methodical investigations into every branch of learning, if done in a genuinely scientific manner and in accord with moral norms, never conflicts with faith. And it rejects the attitude of some Christians who do not appreciate the rightful independence

---

16   *AAS*, 1966, p. 1026; *Gaudium et Spes, 2.*
17   *AAS*, 1966, p. *1025; Gaudium et Spes, 1.*
18   *AAS*, 1966, p. 1027; *Gaudium et Spes, 26.*

of science.[19] This is another unusual, clear affirmation of the value of every branch of human learning. It shows the Church's willingness to learn from the world as well as to speak to it.

C. CONSTITUTION ON THE SACRED LITURGY (*SACROSANCTUM CONCILIUM*)

It was appropriate that the first completed work of Vatican II was this Constitution on the Sacred Liturgy. For "the liturgy is the summit toward which the activity of the Church is directed…[and] at the same time, it is the fount from which all its power flows."[20] So this constitution seeks to reform the very life of the Church. In fact, it sought to totally transform every facet of Catholic liturgy.

Let me explain from my personal experience just how thorough and unexpected was the reform. When I was in the seminary during the 1950s, the liturgy we experienced had remained basically unchanged for several hundred years. The Mass was in Latin; the priest had his back to the people; he was the lone celebrant of the Mass; the servers and congregation responded only a few times during the entire Mass. Throughout our years in the seminary, we had many discussions about possible changes in the liturgy of the Church. Among us, there were some liberal-minded classmates who envisioned minor liturgical changes that might happen during our years as priests. But no one ever suggested that the liturgy should be in English, that the altar would be turned around, that the people would participate in the liturgy as lectors, commentators, communion ministers, leaders of song, and coordinators of liturgy. Yet, by the time we were priests for just a few years, all those changes happened throughout the universal Church.

The Constitution on the Liturgy based all these amazing changes on several principles: First, the constitution insisted

---

19   See *AAS*, 1966, p. 1055; *Gaudium et Spes*, 36.
20   *AAS*, 1964, p. 102; *Sacrosanctum Concilium*, 10.

that the Mass was not a private devotion, but a celebration of the local Church acting as a community of the People of God. Second, there should be active participation by all the faithful, who contribute according to their liturgical functions. The priest would still be the presider, but all the People of God would be celebrants in union with Christ. Third, there was to be an increased emphasis on Scripture that is "of paramount importance in the celebration of the liturgy;"[21] therefore, there were to be more readings from Scripture with more variety, so that much more of the Scriptures would be proclaimed throughout the three-year cycle. Fourth, the liturgy should be accommodated to modern times and to the various cultures of the people. The council "has no wish to impose a rigid uniformity … [but] fosters … the gifts of the various races and peoples."[22]

As the first reform resulting from the Council, it was quickly carried out in most parishes throughout the world and became the concrete experience of renewal for all the Church (*aggiornamento).* The Council quickly ceased to be something remote to most Catholics and made a dramatic difference in their lives very quickly. Seldom in the history of the Church had there been such an immense effort of teaching, educating, training, and parish accommodation in order to understand and adjust to major change.

D. DOGMATIC CONSTITUTION ON DIVINE REVELATION *(DEI VERBUM)*

This constitution has a dramatic history of development; in the early days of the Council, it constituted a turning point for all the Council Fathers, as indicated on page 8, above. The first chapter of the original schema was on the two sources of revelation, Scripture and tradition. This emphasis on tradition had been the distinctive way the Church responded to the

---

21   *AAS,* 1964, p. 106; *Sacrosanctum Concilium,* 24.

22   *AAS,* 1964, pp. 107-08; *Sacrosanctum Concilium,* 37.

Protestant Reformation norm of *sola scriptura* (Scripture alone as the one source of revelation). The final form of this constitution moderated this distinction: "Sacred tradition and sacred Scripture form one sacred deposit of the word of God."[23] This solution was definitely a compromise; it did not agree to the Protestant norm of *sola scriptura,* but it did affirm that Scripture and its transmission through history (tradition) were treated as the singular source of revelation and faith.

The Council insists that all the books of the Bible are sacred and canonical because they were written under the inspiration of the Holy Spirit. But the actual writing of these books depends primarily on the limited abilities of the human authors, so that "due attention must be paid to the customary and characteristic styles of perceiving, speaking, and narrating which prevailed at the time of the sacred writer and to the customs men normally followed at that period ...."[24] In keeping with the groundbreaking encyclical of Pius XI in 1943, *Divino Afflante Spiritu* (By the Divine Inspiring Spirit), the council noted that scholars and ordinary readers of Scripture should "have regard for 'literary forms'."[25] It taught, therefore, that truth is expressed in various forms, such as prophesy, moral stories, parables, sermons, poetry, metaphor, and proclamation history, and it depends on the ability and limits of the human authors. Both Pius XI's encyclical and this constitution formed the foundation for the great explosion of our knowledge and interpretation of Scripture throughout the rest of the twentieth century.

E. DECLARATION ON RELIGIOUS FREEDOM (*DIGNITATIS HUMANAE*)

Over a period of two years, five modified versions of the Council's first draft on religious freedom appeared in print. During this time, 120 speeches were made in public debates

---

23 *AAS,* 1966, p. 822; *Dei Verbum,* 10.

24 Ibid. 12.

25 Ibid. p. 120.

and 600 written interventions were sent to the secretariat. In fact, the greatest argument on religious freedom in church history occurred in the council chambers.[26] Fr. John Courtney Murray of the U.S. was the person primarily responsible for developing this document. He explains that it contains three doctrinal tenets: 1) the ethical doctrine of religious freedom as a human right; 2) a political doctrine with regard to the functions and limits of government in matters religious; 3) the theological doctrine of the freedom of the Church.[27]

This was the most controversial document of the whole council. Together with the Constitution on the Church in the Modern World *(Gaudium et Spes)*, it opened up a new era between the Church and the world. According to this new approach, the Church does not have a double standard in dealing with the secular order—freedom for the Church when Catholics are a minority, but privilege for the Church and intolerance for others when Catholics are in the majority.[28] Rather, this constitution

> declares clearly that the human person has a right to religious freedom. This freedom means that all men are to be immune from coercion on the part of individuals or social groups and of any human power, in such wise that in matters religious, no one is to be forced to act in a manner contrary to his own beliefs ….[29]

This principle of religious freedom has long been recognized by civil, constitutional law in many countries, even though it was not always practiced by some of those countries. However, Catholic canon law has been slow to acknowledge this principle, especially in terms of the freedom of all religions. Because of

---

26　See John Courtney Murray, SJ on p. 672 of *The Documents of Vatican II*. Fr. Murray was the American scholar most responsible for this unexpectedly clear and forthright statement of the Church on human and religious freedom.

27　See ibid.

28　See ibid. p. 673.

29　*AAS, 1966*, p. 930; *Dignitatis Humanae, 2.*

that, this statement of the council is really a milestone for the Church.

F. DECREE ON ECUMENISM
(*UNITATIS REDINTEGRATIO*)

The Decree on Ecumenism could well mark the beginning of a new era in the relation of the churches to one another— an era that may truly be called ecumenical.[30] Certainly the terminology of this decree goes beyond previous positions by the Church. That is, instead of dogmatically insisting that other churches return to Rome as the only possible move toward unity, this decree is concerned with a movement toward Christ for all churches.[31]

Contrary to the language sometimes used in earlier documents, in this decree the Church's attitude toward Christians in other churches is decidedly positive and respectful.

> [T]he Catholic Church accepts them with fraternal reverence and love. Those who believe in Christ and have been properly baptized attain a certain communion … with the Catholic Church …. [So that] all who have been justified by faith in baptism are incorporated into Christ; they have a right to be called Christian and be accepted as brothers or sisters in the Lord.[32]

The decree describes various activities that will foster this ecumenical movement: 1) every effort to eliminate words, judgments and actions, which make mutual relations among Christians more difficult; 2) dialogue between competent experts from different churches; 3) cooperation in projects, which work for the common good; 4) prayer together for unity among the churches; 5) examination of their own faithfulness

---

30   See Samuel McCrea Calvert in *The Documents of Vatican II*, p. 367.

31   See id.

32   *AAS*, 1965, 93; *Unitatis Redintegratio*, 3.

to Christ and undertaking the task of renewal.[33] This decree makes special note of the Eastern Churches and other separated Christians.

A much shorter document of the council needs to be mentioned here: Declaration on the Relationship of the Church to Non-Christian Religions *(Nostra Aetate)*. This declaration speaks positively about Hinduism, Buddhism, Judaism, and Islam. The attitude of the Church to these major faiths is expressed clearly and encouragingly:

> The Church ... reproves, as foreign to the mind of Christ, any discrimination against people or any harassment of them on the basis of their race, color, condition in life or religion. Accordingly, this Sacred Council ardently begs the Christian faithful ... 'to be at peace with all peoples and in that way to be true sons and daughters of the Father' [see Rom 12:18].[34]

Chapter 6, below, will consider ecumenism more thoroughly. After chapter 2 describes some of the advances in our understanding of Scripture, we will have a better view of ecumenism according to Scripture and the mind of Christ.

* * * * *

We began this study of Vatican II with the story about Yves Congar and his positive influence on Pope John XXIII. Congar was one of the first French theologians associated with the new theology, *"la nouvelle theologie."* Jean Danielou, Henri de Lubac, and Marie-Dominique Chenu also wrote extensively about *"la nouvelle theologie."* Rome was quick to censure these writers, and they were all removed from their teaching positions for a time. Nevertheless, the new theology continued to grow. In 1951,

---

33 See *AAS,* 1965, 94; *Unitatis Redintegratio,* 4.

34 *AAS,* 1966, 744; *Nostra Aetate,* 5.

Jean Danielou published his book, *Bible et liturgie,*[35] in which he explained his new theology and its approach to theology, which was called *"ressourcement,"* literally meaning a return to the sources. This term and theological approach became a rallying point for much of Vatican Council II. In general, such a theology not only encompassed the great mysteries of our faith in an intellectual way, but also sought to provide spiritual nourishment by drawing its inspiration from a return to the three great interlocking sources—the Bible, the ancient liturgy, and the early Fathers of the Church. *Ressourcement* involved a return to the patristic sources of the early Church, and, in addition, sought the texts that had relevance for one's spiritual life. This adaptation of patristic outlook was seen as a major improvement on the overly intellectualizing theology prevalent in the Church. Because patristic theology originated in pastoral settings and was embedded in sermons or occasional treatises, it sought to touch hearts and minds, in order to win inner assent and lead to spiritual commitment to Christ.

This adaptation of patristic outlook and language became widespread among younger theologians of Europe. Then, just before the beginning of Vatican II, Cardinal Frings of Cologne sent a memorandum to Cardinal Amleto Cicognani concerning the first seven documents the council fathers had received for discussion in the opening weeks of Vatican II. He argued that the texts should avoid the style of textbook theology and "speak instead the vital language of Scripture and the Church Fathers." The author of Frings' memorandum was Joseph Ratzinger![36]

When Vatican II began, then, Pope John XXIII did not reject *ressourcement* as a valid approach and even accepted several French theologians as *periti* for the council. As we noted above, the bishops at the council quickly voted to change the

---

35   Jean Danielou, *Bible et liturgie* (Paris: Cerf, 1951); English translation, *The Bible and the Liturgy* (Notre Dame, IN: Notre Dame University Press, 1956).

36   See Jared Weeks, "Six Texts by Professor Joseph Ratzinger as *Peritus* before and during Vatican Council II," in *Gregorianum*, 89 (2008).

committee chairmen and the working outlines prepared by the Roman theologians. As a result, Pope John XXIII's plan for *aggiornamento* was open to the approach of *ressourcement*. That is, "bringing the Church up to date" would not rely exclusively on the present-day theological teachings, but would also concentrate on the three great interlocking sources of the Bible, the ancient liturgy, and the early Fathers of the Church. In order to understand how all this works, let us consider now how *ressourcement* influenced some individual council documents.[37]

Regarding the Constitution on the Sacred Liturgy, *Sacrosanctum Concilium,* the fundamental principle of the liturgical reform was the participation of the whole assembly in the sacred action, a principle derived from ancient liturgical practices. Also, the restoration of the first part of the Mass, the Liturgy of the Word, was similarly derived from historical liturgies.

Regarding the Constitution of the Church, *Lumen Gentium,* the council rejected the juridical, political, and canonical language of speaking about the Church and substituted the more rhetorical and poetic language similar to that of the first millennium. Also, the definition of the Church as "the People of God" was contrary to the recent theological and hierarchical language about the Church, and more in keeping with early Church attitudes.

Regarding the Constitution on Divine Revelation, *Dei Verbum,* the council did not entirely accept the *sola scriptura* terminology, but did tone down the two-source doctrine of Scripture and Tradition, which the Church had so strongly emphasized since the Protestant Reformation. It also, more strongly than previously, encouraged the reading of Scripture.

---

37   Cf. John O'Malley, *What Happened at Vatican II* (Cambridge, MA: The Belknap Press of Harvard University, 2008). In this careful historical study of Vatican II, O'Malley describes the importance of *ressourcement* for the entire council. My development here, on pages 17-19, is based on his description on pp. 301-02.

With the Declaration on Religious Freedom, *Dignitatis Humanae,* the council refashioned the old teachings on the free character of the act of faith and on the primacy of conscience in moral decision-making. It accepted the groundbreaking work of John Courtney Murray on freedom of religion for people of all nations.

The Decree on Religious Life, *Perfectae Caritatis,* strongly encouraged that the up-to-date renewal of religious life [as] a constant return both to the sources of Christian life and to the primitive inspiration of the institutes and their adaptation to the conditions of our time.

The Decree on Ecumenism, *Unitatis Redintegratio,* began with hope for the "restoration" of Christian unity that prevailed before the Reformation of the sixteenth century. The entire decree did not insist that other Christian churches should rejoin the Catholic Church, but rather that they all work together for greater unity in Christ. The tone was not superior toward other churches but rather respectful and gentle.

Ressourcement was central to the notion of collegiality of the bishops in the Church. This single issue was at the heart of the battle between the center (Rome) and the periphery (the rest of the Church). Historically the Church had never officially defined collegiality; but in the first millennium, it had often practiced it as its normal mode of operation. Then, from the eleventh century, the Western Church increasingly sidelined the collegiality of the bishops (together with the pope). Papal primacy developed incrementally in a steady line until the nineteenth century, when it actually accelerated even more. In that century, the Roman congregations, in consort with the pope, increased their practical authority even over the bishops, and the pope himself took over the appointment of bishops; and finally, Vatican I defined papal primacy and infallibility. So, by the time the decree on the Pastoral Office of the Bishops of the Church was taken up at Vatican II, the issue was intensely and hotly debated. Nevertheless, when the actual decree was published, it failed to express any of the strong feelings of the bishops. Although it did manage to present a positive proposal for real collegiality, it was far from expressing the forceful opinions of the council fathers. It did recommend international synods of bishops together with the pope, and national conferences of bishops that would be able to address regional issues. But this positive result was only apparent, as we will see later on.

The decrees On the Life and Ministry of Priests and On the Apostolate of the Laity encouraged diocesan councils and senates of priests as collaborators with their bishops, and also provided for parish and diocesan councils of the laity. Such collaboration by priests and laity was another outgrowth of *ressourcement*. Without *ressourcement* and the constant emphasis on the Bible, the liturgy, and early teachings of the Church Fathers, Vatican Council II would not have fulfilled so much of the dream of Pope John XXIII's dream of *aggiornamento*.

Here are two different evaluations of the significance of Vatican II. First, in 2003, Fr. John Markey, OP, made this assessment of the council:

> Vatican II was a revolution …. It was the most fundamental shift in self-understanding by the church in 1,500 years. It fundamentally altered the structures that no one could have foreseen or planned. It is a revolution because it is not over yet. We now realize we are in the middle … of a transformation that takes years to complete and is beyond the power of anyone to control or stop.[38]

Fr. Hans Küng offered this evaluation in 2001:

> … I maintain my overall verdict: for the Catholic Church this council represented an epoch-making and irrevocable

---

38   John Markey, OP, quoted by David Gibson in his *The Coming Catholic Church* (NY: HarperCollins Publishers, 2003), p. 13.

turning point…. There was a clear affirmation of freedom of religion and conscience and of human rights generally…. There was … a positive turn toward Judaism … [and] a new constructive attitude to Islam and the other world religions. … There was a new, fundamentally positive attitude to modern progress … and to the secular world, science, and democracy generally.[39]

* * * * *

Finally, let me add a personal note about the council. Throughout the years before the council, I was in the seminary studying theology and Scripture that were taught in Latin and in the traditional fashion. All of us kept to the required textbooks and spent almost all our study-time on them. One of my classmates, who was very smart and inquisitive, often read the works of non-traditional theologians. One of our professors came to his room one day and noticed his eclectic choice of theological texts. He immediately commented, "You don't need to read such books; just concentrate on the regular texts." That attitude was not something that depressed us, but it did clarify for us how we should direct our studies. We just limited our studies to the traditional Latin texts. Nevertheless, we still thought that we had received a solid foundation in traditional theology and were well prepared for ministry.

By the time I finished my doctoral studies, Vatican II was about to begin. Within a few short years, we had to ingest a new view of Church as the People of God, as well as dramatic changes to the liturgy, including Mass in English, an explosion of Scripture knowledge, and a realization that there really was salvation outside the Church. We did not adjust to all of that immediately, because it took years to change our entire way of theological and practical thinking. The adjustment was even more difficult for older priests, who had spent their entire priesthood in the pre-Vatican II Church. By 1970, many young

---

39   Hans Kung, *The Catholic Church*, pp. 182-84.

priests and a good number of older priests were quite caught up in the vision of Vatican II and realized what a dynamic new view of Church it presented. The people in our parishes felt divided in their attitude toward the changes that they experienced. For much of the 1970s and beyond, we all had a sense of living in two Catholic worlds; the division between the pre-Vatican view and the post-Vatican view was huge for a time. But our people gradually warmed up to the changes and realized that they had an active part to play in the Church as the People of God. Perhaps by 1990, most of our people either were delighted to be a part of the new Church or were at least compliant with the changes. Personally, I was filled with enthusiasm for the vision and real development flowing from Vatican II.

REFLECTIONS

After each chapter, I am adding a couple reflection questions. My hope is that they may lead to your personal observations or reactions to the chapter, or they may lead to discussions with a group of people.

1. Yves Congar introduced these three ideas into the agenda of Vatican II: 1) The Church is always in need of reform; 2) The Church is defined as the People of God; 3) A new form of ecumenism. Which of these three ideas do you think has influenced the Church most at the parish level?

2. What were some of the unique characteristics of Vatican Council II? Why do you think some of these came about?

3. List some examples to show how the Eucharistic Liturgy is a celebration of the "People of God" in contrast to a purely private devotion.

CHAPTER 2

New Approach to Scripture

In 1943, Pope Pius XII issued his encyclical, *Divino Afflante Spiritu* (By the Divine Inspiring Spirit), which formally advocated the historical-critical method of interpreting Scripture. That is, he insisted that Scripture should be interpreted according to its literal sense to ascertain the mind of the author. He did not intend fundamentalist literalism but rather the real, religious meaning of the Word of God. That meant that biblical scholars:

> … ought to endeavor to determine the character and circumstances of the sacred writer, the age in which he lived, his written or oral sources, and the forms of expression he employed. History, archeology, and other sciences should be employed to understand more perfectly ancient modes of writing.[40]

This encyclical finally gave Catholic approval to recognizing different types of literature or different literary forms in the Bible. Formerly, too many books of the Bible were thought to be history in the strict sense; now it could be shown that many of these books (or parts of them) were not intended as history, or they were not history in the modern sense of documented history. Often the authors made use of other forms of literature, such as poetry, prophecy, parables, metaphors, legends or moral stories. For decades, Protestant and Jewish interpreters of the Scriptures had used this proper form of interpretation. Now Catholic interpreters also had an intelligent and honest way of facing up to the obvious historical problems present in Scripture. This emphasis in recognizing the different literary

---

40   Raymond Brown, SS, "Church Pronouncements," 22. This is found in *The New Jerome Biblical Commentary,* edited by Raymond Brown, SS, Joseph Fitzmyer, SJ and Roland Murphy, O. Carm. (Englewood Cliffs, NJ: Prentice Hall, 1990), p. 1170.

forms of the Bible is the greatest contribution of Pope Pius XII in *Divino Afflante Spiritu.*

The second important document on biblical interpretation was the "Instruction on the Historical Truth of the Gospels" by the Pontifical Biblical Commission in 1964. Its central point was that interpreters of the Gospels were encouraged to pay attention to **three stages** of the development of the Gospels. The first stage comes from Jesus himself, who first explained his doctrine according to the mentality of his listeners. The second stage is that of the apostles, who, after Jesus' resurrection, reflected on his life and words with greater understanding and then preached and explained his words, taking into account the needs and circumstances of their listeners. They used various modes of speaking: catechesis, stories, testimonies, hymns, doxologies, and prayers. In the third stage, the gospel writers committed to writing what had been passed down orally first, and then in pre-gospel writings. They adapted what they narrated to the situation of their readers and to the purpose they had in mind. They did not always report the sayings of Jesus literally, but retained the sense of his sayings. Their main purpose was not modern-type history but rather the proclamation of the historical Jesus to offer the Church a basis of faith.

One year later, in 1965, Vatican II published its Constitution on Divine Revelation. The presentation was largely positive, repeating the three stages mentioned in the "Instruction on the Historical Truth of the Gospels." In chapter 2, this constitution considered the disputed theological question of whether we should speak of two sources of revelation (Tradition and Scripture) or only one source (Scripture alone, as interpreted by Tradition). It did not agree with the Reformation idea of *sola scriptura* (Scripture alone), but chose a middle ground: That Scripture and Tradition merge into a unity and tend toward the same end. It added that the teaching office of the Church authentically interprets the Word of God; it is not above the Word of God, but serves it. Chapter 3 deals with inerrancy; it affirms "We must profess that the books of Scripture teach firmly, faithfully, and without error the truth which God, for the sake of our salvation, willed to be confided to the sacred writings."[41] But the sense of this affirmation is that God uses human authors who write in human fashion and make mistakes about precise history or science, so that the writing is "truth without error" only to the extent that it involves the salvific purpose of God. That means that the Bible is not always accurate in terms of scientific matters and historical facts, but it is inerrant only to the extent that it teaches what God intends for our salvation. Let me conclude with how the council describes the primary significance of Scripture; it "provides support and strength to the sons and daughters of the Church ... [and] food of their souls. It is the pure and perennial fount of their spiritual life ... [and] the soul of sacred theology."[42]

Catholic scriptural scholarship has advanced dramatically in the last fifty years. The average Catholic has not been offered many opportunities to learn about these new insights into the Bible. This chapter offers a summary of seven of the major advances in our knowledge of Scripture that are most significant for our faith.

First, consider the major problem about **the historical Jesus** that dominated much of the twentieth century scholarship. The last several years have seen tremendous strides in our effort to understand the life and ministry of Jesus from a modern, strictly historical viewpoint. After previous studies questioned almost every deed or spoken word of Jesus, recent studies have come to recognize the essential historical facts of his life, along with his proclamation of the Kingdom of God.[43] That is, we

---

41   *AAS*, 1966, p. 823; *Dei Verbum*, 11.

42   *AAS*, 1966, p. 828; *Dei Verbum*, 21.

43   See the two volume work by John P. Meyer, especially volume 2: *A Marginal Jew* (NY: Doubleday, 1994).

know historically that Jesus was the eschatological prophet or end-time preacher of God's Kingdom through his powerful preaching, miracles, and ministry. His death and resurrection were the completion of his ministry along with his promise of everlasting life with God.

Second, the Pontifical Biblical Commission, in 1964, settled many questions regarding the **historical truth of the gospels.** Their instruction affirmed that the gospels are substantially historical, but are not literally true in every word or detail. They explained that, before being written down, the gospel material passed through three stages of development that thoroughly modified it. First, Jesus spoke and acted in the context of his time and place; he explained his doctrine in his own Jewish language, adapting it to his listeners. Second, the apostles, with their fuller understanding of Christ and his teaching after the resurrection, proclaimed Jesus' message to the people of their time (the second third of the first century, 33-67 CE).[44] They adapted his message according to the circumstances of their listeners, and they translated it into Greek. Third, the sacred authors of the gospels committed to writing what had been passed on orally at first and then in pre-gospel writings. They also arranged the materials they had according to their own purposes in writing. Thus, the evangelists sometimes expressed the saying of Jesus not literally but differently; nevertheless, they retained the sense of these sayings.

Third, the **authors** of the gospels were not apostles. In the past, it was assumed that the New Testament and the apostolic era were coterminous; that is, the books of the New Testament were written by apostles themselves. The axiom we heard was: Revelation was closed with the death of the apostles. Today we believe that most of the New Testament was written after the death of the last known apostle. Thus, Peter and Paul

---

44   CE stands for the "common era"; it is the modern equivalent of AD (*annoDomini,* "in the year of our Lord"). The abbreviation, CE, is more acceptable to people who are not Christians.

likely died in Rome in the 60s and James (the leader of the Jerusalem Church, not one of the twelve) also died in the 60s. So, with the exception of the undisputed letters of Paul, the rest of the New Testament was written in the last one-third of the first century (67-100 CE), which is now designated the "sub-apostolic period," a period in which the N. T. authors wrote without using their own names but rather the names of apostolic forebears. And the authors of the gospels were not eyewitnesses of the ministry of Jesus, but rather second-generation Christians, drawing their knowledge from the earlier apostolic generation that had personally experienced Jesus.

Fourth, consider **the synoptic problem**, which deals with the sources of the four gospels. In the twentieth century, scholars generally agreed that Mark was the first written gospel. When they compared both Matthew and Luke to Mark, they realized that they used Mark as a source for much of their gospels. But they also found much material common to Matthew and Luke and yet not found in Mark. The scholars surmised that this **common material** came from another source, which they named the "Q source" (Q stood for the German word, *Quelle,* meaning source). They concluded that there were two major sources for Matthew and Luke: Mark and Q; this is called the two-source theory and is now almost universally accepted. Of course, in addition to the two sources of Mark and Q, Matthew had special material of his own, as did Luke.

Fifth, we take note of some **conclusions about John's Gospel**. Raymond Brown, who is the premier Johannine scholar today, suggested that three or more writers contributed to the final gospel, one of them being the Beloved Disciple. He also brilliantly described the division in the Johannine Church into the followers of the Beloved Disciple and the "separatists." The separatists based their entire faith on the words of Jesus in the Gospel, such as: "Whoever believes in the Son has eternal life ..." (Jn 3:36). From such gospel sayings, they concluded that a Christian was saved simply by faith in Jesus Christ, meaning they did not have to live according to the Ten Commandments at all, nor did they see the need for any authority in the Church. This group, then, separated from the rest of the Johannine Church. Brown then explains that the twenty-first chapter of John's Gospel (very soon added to the gospel) and the First Epistle of John are a concerted effort to refute their position.

Sixth, recent scholarship has carefully delineated **four different types of "Jewish/Gentile Christianity"**: 1) Those who insisted on the full observance of the Mosaic law; they were the ultraconservatives centered in Jerusalem (see Acts, chapters 11-15); 2) Those who did not insist on circumcision but required converted Gentiles to keep some Jewish observances; they were moderately conservative and included Peter, the Apostle (see Acts 15 and Gal 2); 3) Those who did not require Jewish observances, especially those concerning "kosher" food laws; they were liberals and had Paul as their strong leader (see Gal 2 and 1 Cor 8); 4) Those who did not require Jewish regulations nor even Jewish cult or festivals; they were radicals for whom Christ replaced the O. T. festivals (see John's Gospel, chapters 5-10 and Hebrews).

Seventh, scholars are generally in agreement now regarding the **authorship of the Pauline Epistles**. After centuries of discussion about the thirteen Pauline Epistles, there is general agreement that only Romans, Galatians, 1 and 2 Corinthians, Philippians, 1 Thessalonians, and Philemon are authentically written by Paul; while 2 Thessalonians, 1 and 2 Timothy, and Titus are not authored by Paul, and Ephesians and Colossians are probably not authored by him. All thirteen of these epistles make up the Pauline corpus. (The Letter to the Hebrews is neither written by Paul nor belongs to the Pauline corpus.) Since Paul is the most prolific writer of the New Testament, this conclusion about authorship is significant. It is often important to separate the authentic epistles of Paul from the rest of the

Pauline corpus, especially when we are trying to be accurate about the exact teaching of Paul.

These seven major advances in Scripture study are only summarized here. They are generally accepted by all mainline Christian churches. Along with other recent developments in scriptural study, they establish the basic principles for interpreting Scripture. They clarify the historical authors of the Scriptures and the time the books were written. They are faithful to the diverse forms of literature found in Scripture. They properly distinguish truths about God's salvation from incidental scientific and historical matters that are not part of revelation. They indicate four different types of Jewish/Gentile Christianity, which were only gradually reconciled. They show the interdependence of the synoptic writers and their sources. And they carefully separate the authentic epistles of Paul from those written by others. Future chapters, especially chapters 3-7, will give a better view of how Scripture influences our theology today. And much of part II will present our Catholic life-style as thoroughly grounded on the historical Jesus as found in Scripture.

My own life experience might offer some simple clarification of what has happened to our appreciation of Scripture. When I was in the seminary in the 1950s, our Scripture professor was Fr. William Dowd, S. J. The textbook we used was in Latin. Studying Scripture in Latin was tough enough, but this text had the most complex Latin of all our texts; the style of the Latin was equivalent to the difficult English of Shakespeare. Even Fr. Dowd did not want to teach Scripture in Latin; he had appealed to his superiors to permit him to use English in the classroom, but his appeal was denied. And, finally, the content of the text was entirely based on the strictly literal approach that had prevailed for hundreds of years, not the historical-critical approach of *Divino Afflante Spiritu*.

This lack of updating in the approach to Scripture study in

the 1950s was perhaps not reprehensible, for the new approach to Scripture was just in its infancy. But this situation was compounded because our theological study was also affected by it. Our approach to the doctrines of the Church still followed the following classical pattern in use since the thirteenth century. That is, each thesis began with the approach of St. Thomas Aquinas; first presenting the objections to the doctrine, then adding the definitions of the Church, followed by the evidence from Scripture, and finally, giving his refutations of the objections. Each thesis was given a theological note; that is, it was declared to be defined dogma, or it was given a lesser note, such as *proxima fidei* (close to being defined), or common and certain, or merely most probable. In such a method of developing a thesis, Scripture was more of a handmaiden of theology, rather than the heart of theology.

Today, our theology flows from Scripture, so that solid biblical criticism is the primary source of all theology. That is, theologians begin with the original meaning of the relevant Scripture text in keeping with the best modern commentaries. Then they explain any relevant definitions of the Church and compare them to Scripture. That seems to be the way to make Scripture the heart of our theology.

The volume of scholarship that has been published in the last sixty years is immense; it represents a veritable explosion of our knowledge of Scripture. It has invigorated the study of Catholic theology, providing it with a profound biblical basis. For many reasons in the past, ordinary Catholics have not been able to update their knowledge of Scripture. But in recent years, there is a great wealth of Scripture scholarship available that is able to open up the Bible for us and to deepen our faith in Jesus. All the Scripture commentaries mentioned throughout this book are worth reading. Many fine parish programs, such as RENEW and Scripture study groups, exist in our parishes today; they offer fine group studies of individual books of the Bible. For some individuals who would appreciate a few suggestions, let me offer a short list of books that I found most helpful.

- **EASY COMMENTARIES AND STUDIES**

    1. Karris, Robert, OFM, gen. ed., *Collegeville Bible Commentary*. Collegeville MN: Liturgical Press, 1983. These are individual pamphlets for each book of the Bible, offering a good and easy commentary.

    2. Brown, Raymond, SS, *Jesus God and Man*. Milwaukee: Bruce Publishing Co., 1967. A fine overview of what the New Testament tells us about Jesus

    3. _____. *An Introduction to New Testament Christology*. NY: Paulist Press, 1994. Different approaches to Christology in the New Testament.

    4. _____. *The Churches the Apostles Left Behind*. NY: Paulist Press, 1984. Seven New Testament views of the Church and the People of God.

- **INTERPRETATION OF SCRIPTURE AND THEOLOGY**

    1. Fitzmyer, Joseph, SJ, *The Interpretation of Scripture*. NY: Paulist Press, 2008. Guidelines for interpreting Scripture according to Vatican II and the Biblical Commission.

    2. _____. *A Christological Catechism*. NY: Paulist Press, 1991. Questions and answers regarding the history of Jesus, his teachings and deeds.

    3. Brown, Raymond, SS, *Biblical Exegesis and Church Doctrine*. NY: Paulist Press, 1985. Historical-critical interpretation of the Bible and the development of Church doctrine.

    4. _____. *The Critical Meaning of the Bible*. NY: Paulist Press, 1981. The human word in the Bible and biblical scholarship. What the Bible meant and what it means.

    5. O'Collins, Gerald, SJ and Kendall Daniel, SJ, *The Bible*

for Theology. NY: Paulist Press, 1997. Ten principles for the theological use of Scripture.

- **SINGLE VOLUME COMMENTARIES**

  1. Brown, Raymond, SS, Fitzmyer, Joseph, SJ, and Murphy, Roland, OCarm, editors, *The New Jerome Biblical Commentary.* Englewood Cliffs, NJ: Prentice Hall, 1990. An excellent Catholic commentary of the entire Bible plus superior articles on various biblical topics.

  2. Barton, John and Muddiman, John, editors, *The Oxford Bible Commentary.* Oxford: Oxford University Press, 2001. An excellent ecumenical commentary of the entire Bible plus some introductory essays.

- **ADVANCED COMMENTARIES**

  1. Albright, William and Freedman, David, gen. editors, *The Anchor Bible Commentaries.* New York: Doubleday. 78 volumes by leading ecumenical scholars throughout the world. My preferences are volumes numbered 28 and 28A (Luke), 29, 29A (John), 31 (Acts of the Apostles) and 33 (Romans).

  2. Keck, Leander, et al, editors, *The New Interpreter's Bible.* Nashville: Abingdon Press. 12 volumes by leading ecumenical scholars throughout the world.

* * * * *

One of my all-time favorite movies was *Bridge over the River Kwai.* Not everything in this movie was historical, but the following story by Ernest Gordon is. Gordon wrote *Through the Valley of the Kwai,* in which he documented what happened in a Japanese prison camp during World War II. In just a couple years, 12,000 prisoners had died of disease and the brutality of their guards, while building a railroad bridge for their captors. Men were forced to work in heat that sometimes reached 120 degrees. Bareheaded and barefooted, they built the entire bed for the railroad from dirt and stone carried in baskets on their backs. Their only clothes were dirty rags; their only bed was the bare ground. But their worst enemy was not their hard lives exactly but their own selves. The fear of the Japanese made the prisoners paranoid. The law of the jungle became their law. They stole from one another just to stay alive; they distrusted one another; and they informed on one another. The guards laughed at how they treated one another.

Then something incredible happened. Two prisoners organized others into Bible study groups. Through their study of the gospel, the prisoners gradually discovered that Jesus understood their situation, because he too had been hungry, bone-weary, betrayed and persecuted. Everything about Jesus— what he was, what he did, what he said—began to make sense and come alive for them. The prisoners stopped thinking of themselves as the victims of some cruel tragedy. They stopped informing on one another and destroying one another. Slowly the camp went through a transformation that amazed not only the Japanese but also the prisoners themselves. What had changed these desperate men was the experience of Jesus as they found him in the words of Scripture.

REFLECTIONS

1. Which of the seven examples of the advances in Scripture most impressed you?

2. Are you comfortable with the recent explanations that the gospels are not exact history but rather proclamation history, which went through various stages of development before they received their final form?

3. Explain the following idea in your own words: "The Bible is not always accurate in terms of scientific matters or historical facts, but it is inerrant to the extent that it conforms to the salvific purpose of God."

CHAPTER 3

Jesus, the Image of God

In the next few chapters, we want to discuss some of the results of Vatican II as well as the advances in modern Scripture study. First, we will take up four major dogmas of our faith: 1) Christology (How is Jesus God and man?); 2) Trinity (How is God three and one?); 3) Soteriology (How is Jesus our Savior?), and 4) Ecumenism (How to relate our Catholic religion and the other religions?).

Throughout most of our 2,000-year history, Christology was expounded principally on the basis of the early creeds and the early councils of the Church. Some modern theologians maintain that Christology today **should begin with the study of the New Testament**:

> By 1970 … for Schillebeeckx among many others, it no longer seemed possible to expound Christology solely on the basis of the classical creeds and conciliar definitions. A half-century of historical research … needed to be incorporated. Christology could begin, not from the doctrine of the Incarnation, as Thomas Aquinas does, but from the New Testament narratives, the story of how the man Jesus is discovered as Lord, scrutinized in the light of the best modern critical exegesis.[45]

There are many Christological questions that engage theologians in this twenty-first century, such as: 1) Exactly how is Jesus united to the Word of God? 2) How could the Son of God suffer? 3) What exactly did he know about the end of the world? 4) In what sense is he the founder of the Church? 5) Which sayings of his in Scripture are his exact words? 6) Exactly how did Jesus redeem us and open the gates of heaven for all

---

45   Fergus Kerr, *Twentieth-Century Catholic Theologians*, p. 59.

people? 7) Is Jesus the cause of all grace for humanity? But in this chapter, I want to narrow our focus on only one aspect of Christology: **how is Jesus God** according to Scripture and the early councils of the Church.

A. JESUS AS GOD IN SCRIPTURE

Modern scripture scholars offer two clear answers as background to this question: 1) Nowhere does any Scripture writer indicate that **Jesus** explicitly claimed to be God;[46] 2) For all of Israel's history, God was one and unique; in the monotheistic setting of Jesus' time, it would have been impossible for a Jew like Jesus to proclaim, "I am God."[47]

When we ask whether **Scripture** ever called Jesus "God," we need to carefully distinguish four groups of Scripture passages. For the first three groups, we will rely on the incisive development of Raymond Brown, SS, in *Jesus, God and Man* and *An Introduction to New Testament Christology.*[48]

First, several passages **distinguish** between Jesus and God; that is, they seem to imply that the title "God" was not used for Jesus. 1) Mark 10:18, "Why do you call me good? No one is good but God alone." 2) John 17:3, "… the only true God, and the one whom you sent, Jesus Christ." 3) 1 Timothy 2:5, "/For there is one God. /There is also one mediator between God and the human race, /Christ Jesus, himself human …." 4) John 14: 28, "[T]he Father is greater than I." 5) Mark 13:32, "[O]f that day … no one knows, … nor the Son, but only the Father." 6) 1 Corinthians 15:28, "[T]hen the Son himself will [also] be subjected to [God the Father]…" 7) Ephesians 1:17, "[T]he God of our Lord Jesus Christ, the Father of glory …." 8) 1 Corinthians 8:6, "[F]or us there is /one God, the Father, / from whom all things are and for whom we exist, /and one

---

46   See Joseph Fitzmyer, SJ, *A Christological Catechism* (NY: Paulist Press, 1991), p. 97.

47   Ibid. p. 98.

48   Raymond Brown, *Jesus, God and Man* (Milwaukee: Bruce Publishing Co., 1967) and *An Introduction to New Testament Christology* (NY: Paulist Press, 1994).

Lord, Jesus Christ, ….." In each of these passages, Jesus is somehow inferior to God the Father, as human, as a mediator or subject, or unequal in knowledge, goodness, or status.

Second, in the **early years** of the New Testament (perhaps up to 80 AD), Jesus was **not called "God."** That is, in the monotheistic setting of the Hebrew Scriptures, "God" was a title too unique to be applied to Jesus: "For there is **one God. /** There is also one mediator between God and the human-race, / Christ Jesus, **himself human** …." (1 Timothy 2:5-6; emphasis added). Therefore, especially in the early years of the Christian Scriptures, the monotheistic terminology inherited from the Hebrew Scriptures dominated the use of the term "God;" it simply could not be attributed to Jesus. Thus, the Synoptic Gospels never call Jesus "God;" and none of the sermons in the Acts of the Apostles ever speak of Jesus as "God." Nevertheless, the early writers did proclaim Jesus as the "**Son of God**," which term referred to Jesus' unique relationship to God as Messiah, the Davidic king whom God treated and protected as son. This Messiah acted with divine authority and power as the chief agent of God's gift of salvation.

Third, in the **later years** of the New Testament, Jesus was called God in some sense. That is, he was not only called "Son of God" but actually **"God" understood in a broader sense,** meaning that God had been so revealed in Jesus, that the designation "God" somehow had to include both Father and the Son of God. There is one isolated instance in Paul's writings in which Paul **might** have called Jesus "God": "… from [the Israelites], according to the flesh, is the Messiah. God who is over all be blessed forever." (Rom 9:5; this probably dates from 58 AD) This is the only instance in the main Pauline corpus, and it has been subjected to more discussion than any verse in the Christian Scriptures.

Around 90-100 AD, the usage of the term "God" in the broader sense becomes common. Thus, in the Pastoral Epistles,

Jesus is called "God and Savior": "… the appearance of the glory of the great God and of our savior Jesus Christ" (Titus 2:13). Similarly, 2 Peter 1:1, "… the righteousness of our God and savior Jesus Christ." Also, there are more examples in John's Gospel, such as John 1:18, "The only Son, God, who is at the Father's side, has revealed him." Finally, Hebrews 1:8-9, "[God addressed Jesus] the Son: /'Your throne, O God, stands forever and ever ….'" Such terminology seemed to have its origin in the worship and prayers of the community, particularly in the form of doxologies. Which means that such usage in not related to the ministry of Jesus but rather to the resurrected Jesus (as in Jn 1:18) or to the triumphant Jesus (Heb 1:8-9). This usage does not contradict the passages during Jesus' ministry in which he is pictured as less than God the Father (in the first group above).

We might summarize the significance of these first three groups of Scripture passages this way: 1) God revealed his sovereignty and lordship in, through, and by Jesus; 2) Jesus was sent by God as Savior, Messiah, and Son of God; and 3) he functions as God's agent on earth. What must be denied about these scriptural passages is that none of them could ever define Jesus philosophically, in terms of his essential being; it was not possible for Scripture to speak in the abstract categories of Greek philosophy such as person, nature, and substance. Such notions were unknown to all the Scripture writers.

The fourth category consists entirely of the beginning of John's Gospel: "In the beginning was the Word,/ and the Word was with God,/ and the Word was God…./ And the Word became flesh"… (Jn 1:1,14). This one passage became the central scriptural passage for the understanding of the person of Jesus throughout the early ecumenical councils of the Church. "No biblical text has had more influence on the development of christology than the Prologue to John's gospel."[49] "The prologue

---

49   Roger Haight, SJ, *Jesus, Symbol of God* (Maryknoll, NY: Orbis Books, 1999), p.173.

of the Fourth Gospel is the fullest and clearest statement of incarnational christology in the New Testament."[50] To solve the precise meaning of this passage would offer a tentative solution to the entire Christological problem.

We need to start with how the Hebrew Scriptures speak about word, wisdom, and spirit of God. These words do not refer to beings separate from God but rather **qualities** of the one God or the personification of God. For example: "[T]he **spirit** of the Lord fills the world ..." (Wis 1:7); "The Lord by **wisdom** founded the earth ..." (Prv 3:19); and "By the Lord's **word** the heavens were made ..." (Ps 33:6). Here "spirit," "wisdom," and "word" are **personifications** or attributes of God; they refer to God's spirit, wisdom, and word that act in our world, especially in creation. They are **figures of speech,** which say something about the person of God. They are not separate existing beings; in the quote from Proverbs, the "wisdom" does not materialize the wisdom of God and make it into a separate being; in the quote from the Psalms, the "word" is not a separate being but an attribute of God.

Accordingly, when John's Gospel describes the incarnation, "The Word became flesh," the Word could **not** have been an individual separate from God, because Scripture absolutely stops short of equating Jesus with God as a **second divine person.** The Word cannot be an hypostatization (a separately existing *hypostasis* or being), because the primary teaching of the Hebrew Scriptures is that Jahweh must be **one and unique**; it was absolutely not possible to posit a second god equal to Jahweh. Rather, "The Word became flesh" means that God himself made his presence known eminently in Jesus and that God is now present in human existence in the human person, Jesus. That is: the *Logos* (Word), as an **attribute** of God, can now be seen eminently in the human Jesus.

---

50   Robert Kyser, *John, the Maverick Gospel* (Atlanta: John Knox Press, 1976), p. 29.

B. JESUS AS GOD IN THE EARLY COUNCILS OF THE CHURCH

Because Scripture never used or even imagined Greek philosophical terminology, it never gave a clear ontological description of Jesus; it never defined him metaphysically (e. g., as one person with two natures). It took hundreds of years for the early Fathers of the Church to develop precise philosophical ways of defining Jesus as God and man. By the fourth century, there were two broad traditions of classical Christology.

Alexandrian or Eastern Christology was proposed by Greek theologians, such as Irenaeus, Athanasius, and Cyril of Jerusalem. The Alexandrian core description of Christ is that of the *Logos-sarx* (Word-flesh). That is, there is **one single subject** (*hypostasis)* in Christ, that of the Word (*Logos),* who is the eternal Son of God, who took on human flesh (*sarx)* for the space of a human lifetime. That means the conscious subject in Jesus is the *Logos,* which is continuous with its divine pre-existence, so that the incarnate divine nature is commingled with human flesh. Thus the principle of all activity in Jesus Christ is entirely the Word of God; there is no human initiative.

Antiochene or Western Christology was proposed by Latin theologians, such as Anselm and Theodore of Mopsuestia. The Anthiochene core description of Christ is that of the *Logos-anthropos* (Word-human being). That is, Jesus is an historical figure who bore **two distinct natures**. Thus, the human Jesus was indwelt by the Word (*Logos),* so that in Jesus both the divinity and the humanity are held together or united so as to make up one person. He is a human being in whom the *Logos* dwells.

The First Ecumenical Council of Nicea (325) was called by Emperor Constantine to settle whether and how Jesus is both God and human. It also needed to respond to Arius who taught that the Son, Jesus Christ, was distinct from the Father and **not**

equal to God. Contrary to Arius, Nicea affirmed that Jesus is consubstantial with the Father, meaning that he is of the same essence as the Father, equal to the Father in divinity. In order to reach this conclusion, Nicea did not start with the description of Jesus as found in Scripture (i.e., Christology "from below"). Rather it began with speculating about the transcendent God, whose Word became flesh in Jesus (i.e., Christology "from above"), so that Jesus is the Son of God enfleshed, the image of God and truly God in some way. It was struggling to explain how one person, Jesus, could at the same time be both God and man. Nicea never tried to explain from Scripture how Jesus could be one in being with the one God, Jahweh.

Nicea did not succeed in stamping out Arianism, nor did it end the argument about Jesus as both God and human. In a few years, Nestorius proposed a different solution: Jesus is one person who unites in himself two radically different **modes** of being, divinity and humanity, each possessing all the characteristics of these natures complete and intact. The Fourth Ecumenical Council of Chalcedon (351) was called by Empress Pulcheria and her husband, Marcian, to respond to Nestorius. Chalcedon taught that the one person, Jesus Christ, possessed a duality of **natures** in such a way that the property of each nature was preserved without confusion in one person, Jesus. Again, this council seemed to compromise the concrete, human history of Jesus found in the New Testament.

The Christology taught in both of these councils considered the *Logos* or Word to be present in Christ. Alexandrian Christology spoke of the *Logos* becoming **incarnate** in Jesus, while Antiochian Christology spoke of the *Logos* **dwelling** in Jesus. That is, both of these classical Christologies understood "the Word became flesh" as referring to the Son of God, **separate from God, the Father.** The critical fault in both Christologies was that they clearly departed from the way that "word, spirit, and wisdom" were used in the Hebrew Scriptures. That is, they did not understand the *Logos* (Word) as **a figure**

of speech, a personification, describing the one God, Jahweh. Instead, they understood the *Logos* (Word) in a philosophical and literal way as an **hypostatization** of the Word, as a being separate from God. Once the classical theologies understood the prologue of John's Gospel according to this model, that interpretation became the controlling paradigm for all the conciliar arguments and decisions. This conception of the *Logos* (Word) as an hypostasis created a problem that defied a solution.

Throughout these councils, the Eastern Greek bishops and the Western Latin bishops were far from agreeing on the full-scale theological explanation of the doctrine they proposed. All they could agree on was the bare bones statement that Jesus is true man and true God (*vere homo, vere Deus)*. Nevertheless, from that time on, Christianity embraced the teaching of the "hypostatic union" of God and man in Jesus Christ. By hypostatic union they meant that Jesus is somehow one person with two integral natures. Despite this lack of clarity, the Christological formula of Chalcedon, "true man and true God," became the constant, accepted teaching. As Hans Kung observed recently:

> [T]he christological formula found at Chalcedon (*vere homo – vere Deus)* gave a lasting dogmatic foundation to both the Byzantine and the Western Church … so … in christology there was a formula which could be accepted only as a "mystery"inaccessible to reason. But this formula by no means ended the struggles.[51]

Karl Rahner agrees that we have not reached the end of this Christological argument. He explains the problem this way:

> The official teaching of the church does not **explain** the essence of this substantial union and unity with the divine hypostasis of the Logos any further. It simply **clarifies**

---

51   Hans Kung, *Christianity* (NY: Continuum, 1995), pp. 192-93.

it by saying that it allows and requires as an ontological presupposition that the human be truly and genuinely predicated of the Logos himself. Attempts were made to develop more exact theories of the hypostatic union in the Middle Ages and in baroque theology, but they did not find universal acceptance, nor werethey incorporated into the official teaching of the church….[52]

Yet, I believe there could be a clear solution to this Christological problem. The core of this solution is found in the way that the Hebrew Scriptures speak about the Word of God. As explained above, whenever the Hebrew Scriptures refer to the word, spirit, or wisdom of God, they are referring to God himself or to an attribute of God. So that "The Word became flesh" means that the Word of God indwells Jesus, so that the Word of God, the revelation of God himself, becomes part of human existence in the human Jesus. This is the connection that John's prologue means to convey by saying "The Word became flesh."

The rest of John's Gospel never again speaks of the Word becoming flesh in Jesus. Rather, it uses different terminology about Jesus that helps us understand the entire connection between Jesus and God the Father. Throughout John's Gospel, Jesus is described as having a unique relationship to God: as the supreme revelation of God, as the human expression of God, as the truth about God, as the one who speaks and acts for God in human form. This special relationship to God is expressed in several ways. First, Jesus claims divine authority and power as the **chief agent** of God's gift of salvation. In Jesus' own words: "[J]ust as the Father raises the dead and gives life, so also does the Son give life to whomever he wishes. Nor does the Father judge anyone, but he has given all judgment to his Son" (Jn 5:21-22). Thus, salvation is made possible because of the revelation of God by his Son, who has divine

---

52   Karl Rahner, *Foundations of Christian Faith* (NY: The Seabury Press, 1978), p. 287.

authority and power as the chief agent of God's gift of salvation. Second, whoever **hears** Jesus' words, hears the words of God: "[W]hoever hears my word and believes in the one who sent me has eternal life …" (Jn 5:24; see also Jn 12:47-50). Third, to **see** Jesus is equivalent to seeing the Father: "[W]hoever sees me sees the one who sent me." (Jn. 12, 45; see also Jn 14, 9). Fourth, Jesus asserts that **belief** in him equals belief in the Father: "Whoever believes in me believes … also in the one who sent me …" (Jn 12:44).

This oneness of Jesus with the Father is directly related to the mission of Jesus. It certainly is based on the *saliah* concept, meaning that the one who is sent is the total representative of the one who sends him. But Jesus' union with God is much stronger than that, because Jesus is the Son of God who "say[s] only what the Father taught [him]" (Jn 8:28) and who does nothing by himself (see Jn 12:49-50). That means that the words and deeds of Jesus are not his own, but are intimately related to the Father. Thus, in John's Gospel, Jesus, the Son of God, is presented as the unique, historical being who expresses God present in history, who has the power and authority to lead people to salvation, and in whom people see and hear God the Father. Nevertheless, Jesus is never presented as one who is absolutely equal to God (a second god), but rather, as the one who expresses and reveals God and acts as his unique agent.

To summarize, then, all the complications regarding this sublime Johannine affirmation, "The Word became flesh," can be clarified by means of this one distinction. The "Word" is a figure of speech, a personification of God's own being or power. The phrase "became flesh" means that God's creative Word now dwells in the human person, Jesus Christ, so much that whoever sees Jesus sees God, whoever hears Jesus hears God, and whoever believes in Jesus believes in God. Certainly Jesus is the Son of God, the Lord and Messiah, and the Savior of all. All of these descriptions of Jesus, found constantly in Scripture, mean that Jesus is God's supreme expression, God's most profound revelation. In Jesus, we have the closest thing to God on earth, we encounter God himself, we have a vision of God in human form, we see the image of God.

REFLECTIONS

1. Some theologians claim that many Christians are almost Docetists, who taught that Jesus was God who only appeared to be human. Would you agree with them?

2. Fr. Roger Haight teaches that "Jesus is the concrete symbol of God." When Jesus proclaims, in the synoptic gospels, "[T]he Kingdom of God is among you." (Lk 17:21), how does that relate to himself?

3. In John's Gospel, what do you understand by Jesus' claims such as, "Whoever has seen me has seen the Father" (Jn 14:9)?

CHAPTER 4

One God but Triune

Chapter 3 concluded with the effort to further clarify Christology. In terms of this book's title, then, we can expect to see continued efforts to explain Christology during this twenty-first century. The topic of this chapter, the Trinity, should also receive careful scrutiny in this century. Karl Rahner asserts that such an effort is still very necessary: "[W]e still have to admit that the assertions about the Trinity ... are almost unintelligible to people today, and that they almost inevitably occasion misunderstandings."[53] Roger Haight adds that, "The doctrine [of the Trinity] is a product of historical development over centuries; that development is confusing, but it is no mystery; **God is a mystery, doctrines are not**."[54] And he offers the explanation of Catherine LaCugna:

> By mystery theologians mean the incomprehensibility of God as God. The term is never used to refer to a provisional state of knowledge. Therefore, while it is true that God is (absolute) mystery, it is *not* true that a doctrine is a mystery. Doctrines are simply doctrines, that is, human formulations which are meant to shed light on religious experience.[55]

In fact, the problems we saw regarding the christological problem also have some relevance for the nature of the Trinity. For the fundamental Jewish and early Christian tradition of monotheism insist that God is one and unique: "For there is one God. /There is also one mediator between God and the human race, /Christ Jesus, himself human..." (1 Tm 2:5-6). Such monotheism was essentially unable to allow a second God in any sense of real parity; that is, monotheism absolutely rules

---

53   Karl Rahner, *Foundations of Christian Faith*, p. 134.

54   Roger Haight, SJ, pp. 479-80 (emphasis added).

55   Catherine LaCugna, "Philosophers and Theologians on the Trinity," *Modern Theology* 2, no. 3, p. 175.

out a separate God equal to Yahweh. In the final analysis, the development of Christology has a bearing on the nature of God, for there are two contrary solutions to the problem of Christ being equal to God. That is, either Jesus is equal to God in the strict sense or he is not equal to God. In the first case Jesus is presented as a second God; in the other case Jesus is definitely subordinate to God. If, according to **high Christology**, Jesus is declared God, then monotheism (God is unique) is threatened. One way to save monotheism would be to affirm that Christ, the *Logos,* is not really distinct from God. But such a solution would seem to imply **Modalism**—that Father and Son are not two gods but only different **modes** of the one God. If however, according to **low Christology**, Jesus has a subordinate status to the Father, then Jesus is not strictly God. That solution is called **Subordinationism**—that Jesus is **subordinate** to the Father—and so does not interfere with monotheism.

Thus, the doctrine of the Trinity is **logically** derivative from the place that Jesus Christ plays in Christian theology. For the divinity of Christ generates the differentiation within the Godhead, meaning that if Jesus is God, then there must be two "gods;" also, the doctrine of the Trinity is **historically** dependent on Christology, for it grew out of centuries of endless discussion in the early councils about the nature of Jesus Christ.[56]

Historically, no theologian intended a tritheistic concept of God (that there are three separate gods, Father, Son and Holy Spirit); rather, all theologians wanted to preserve the monarchy of God (there is only one God). So the first point of the doctrine of the Trinity is that God is single and one, which affirms monotheism. The evident historical progress of the doctrine of the Trinity started with Jesus as the divine Savior. The Fathers of the Church began with the evidence of Scripture, which used terms such as Son of God and presented Jesus, in

---

56   See Roger Haight, p. 479.

John's Gospel, as very close to God (God in a wide sense, if you will). Over 200-300 years, the certainty grew that Jesus was the agent of divine salvation, and then that the Holy Spirit, closely allied with Christ and the Father, was also involved with divine salvation. Thus, the *Logos* and the Spirit of God eventually were somehow fully divine. Never did the Fathers or councils give up on the unicity of God; whatever they affirmed about the Son and the Spirit of God could never compromise the oneness of God.[57] The fundamental and guaranteed datum in Trinitarian theology is the oneness of God.

Karl Rahner, then, suggested a tentative solution for understanding the doctrine of the Trinity:

> Insofar as the **modes** of God's presence for us as Spirit, Son and Father do not signify the same modes of presence, insofar as there are true and real differences in the modes of presence for us, these three modes of presence for us are to be strictly distinguished. ... But insofar as these three modes of presence of one and the same God for us may not nullify the real self-communication of God as the one and only and same God, the three modes of presence of one and the same God must belong to him as one and the same God .... We are only trying to indicate here an initial approach towards an understanding of the Christian doctrine of the Trinity.[58]

Rahner's solution sounds a lot like Modalism, at least that's what some theologians claim. Nevertheless, I find it a promising new explanation of the doctrine of the Trinity, though not acceptable to the magisterium. Walter Kasper comes close to Rahner's solution in this quote: "The three persons of the Trinity are ... pure rationality; they are relations in which the one nature of God exists in three distinct and non-interchangeable ways. They are subsistent relations."[59] However,

---

57   See Roger Haight. p. 482.

58   Karl Rahner, *Foundations of Christian Faith*, pp. 136-37 (emphasis added).

59   Walter Kasper, *The God of Jesus Christ* (NY: Crossroad, 1986), p. 309.

Kasper would not likely agree that his explanation is closely allied to Modalism.

A third solution is offered by Edward Schillibeeckx. It begins with the human Jesus as the Son of God who expresses God for us:

> [O]nly if we start with Jesus is God's unity in its fullness (not so much a *unitas trinitatis* but a *trinitas unitatis*) [not a unity of trinity but a trinity of unity] to some extent accessible to us. Only in the light of Jesus' life, death and resurrection can we know that the Trinity is the divine mode of God's perfect unity of being.[60]

What he means is that, if we begin "from above," with the Trinity as our starting point separate from Christology, as soon as we posit Jesus as somehow divine, we end up with either Modalism or Subordinationism. But if we begin "from below," with the historical life of Jesus as the Son of God and expression of God, then we can come to know God's mode of existence as Trinity with a perfect unity of being.

These three solutions, just mentioned, will likely continue to be debated in this century. The underlying difficulty for understanding both doctrines, Christology and Trinity, lies in the endless confusion of the many terms such as person, nature, substance, hypostasis, *prosopon, homoousion,* and *homoiousion.*[61] Not only were these terms understood differently in the Eastern and the Western Church in the early centuries, but the concepts "person" and "nature" have quite different connotations in modern philosophy.

---

60   Edward Schillebeeckx, *Jesus,* p. 658. Piet Soonenburg clearly agrees with Schillebeeckx that we can only start with Jesus who is the self-communication of God in history, and not with the Trinity; see his quote in Roger Haight, *opus cit.* p. 471.

61   These terms are defined in the glossary at the end of the book. They are various Greek words or translations of Greek philosophical terms introduced to explain two natures in one person (Christ) or three persons in one nature (Trinity).

Roger Haight concludes his treatment of the Trinity by reminding us of the intimate connection between Jesus as the symbol of God and the doctrine of the Trinity:

> Trinity is a centering doctrine because it structures the creed and sums up the full Christian vision. But at the center of this center is the historical figure of Jesus who is the bearer and revealer of God in the Christian community. Thus at the literal center of the Christian vision of reality lies Jesus symbol of God.[62]

In conclusion, in a very practical way let me show how the doctrine of the Trinity is a "centering doctrine...[that] sums up the full Christian vision." The heart of our faith is found in this claim: in Jesus of Nazareth, God has communicated and revealed himself once and for all, uniquely and completely. Jesus is the image, revelation, and manifestation of God for us. In him is found all that we know about God and all that he intends to reveal to us: "Whoever has seen me has seen the Father" (Jn 14:9). The cross of Jesus and his resurrection are not only the source of our redemption, they also suggest the fundamental idea of God for us: "... God is love. In this way the love of God was revealed to us: God sent his only Son into the world so that we might have life through him" (1 Jn 4:8-9). Here, John's Gospel defines God as self-communicating love, and the concrete evidence of that is Jesus' life, death, and resurrection. That is, the entire history of salvation is also God's revealing to us who he is: the one who saves us and communicates his love to us completely in Jesus. Jesus Christ, then, is God in his self-revelation; he is God inasmuch as he reveals himself. **The revelation of God is a person, Jesus Christ:** "[I]n him dwells the whole fullness of the deity bodily ..." (Col 2:9).

But God also dwells in each of us by the Holy Spirit: "... [T]he way we know that [God] remains in us is from the Spirit

---

62   Roger Haight, p. 491.

that he gave us" (1 Jn 3:24). The Spirit is the agent of God's love: "… [T]he love of God has been poured out into our hearts through the holy Spirit that has been given to us" (Rom 5:5). The Spirit is the principle of all Christian life and activity: "… [N]o one can say, 'Jesus is Lord,' except by the holy Spirit" (1 Cor 12:3). That is, the Holy Spirit is the source of everything in our life relating to God; the Spirit is the cause of all grace, faith, and love that we possess. The Holy Spirit, then, is the truth and love of God within us; the Spirit is the source of our personal relationship to God. That is, **the possession of God is a person, the Holy Spirit**. God in us is called Spirit.

This is why the doctrine of the Trinity "sums up the whole Christian vision." The entire creed we believe in, all that we are as Christians, and our entire Christian life and hope are found in God—Father, Son, and Holy Spirit.

REFLECTIONS

1. The early councils of the Church defined the Trinity in terms of Greek philosophical terms such as person and nature. Today, "person" and "nature" do not have the same connotations as they did then. Would you like to see a better contemporary way of explaining the Trinity?

2. The doctrine of the Trinity (not the mystery) depends on 2,000 years of Church councils trying to understand the historical Jesus. As a teaching tool, preachers and teachers often use shamrocks and triangles to explore the doctrine of the Trinity. Think of the difference between doctrine (expressing in words a complex theological dogma) and mystery (the incomprehensible God). What does this distinction tell us about the way we express dogmas?

3. How can the mystery of the Trinity become a part of your life? Does making the sign of the cross help? Will praying to God as Creator, Redeemer, or Sanctifier help?

CHAPTER 5

How is Jesus Savior?

Soteriology is the study of Jesus precisely as Savior. We are Christians because we acknowledge and experience Jesus as Savior. We believe Jesus is the bringer of God's salvation. If we were asked to explain what that work of salvation consists of, we could give a general description of it but might hesitate to define exactly what it is. The reason for this is that there is a plurality of ways that salvation is conceptualized. In fact, the Church has never formulated a conciliar definition of salvation, probably because no single definition of salvation can capture the amplitude of this most fundamental of all Christian experiences. St. Paul describes how Jesus redeemed us and reconciled us to God in several ways. Some people in our modern world may find his terminology offensive, even harmful to faith. For example, they would resist describing that Jesus saves us:

- by freeing us from the bondage of original and personal sin
- by releasing us from the Devil's chains
- by ransoming us from slavery to sin
- by making satisfaction to an offended God
- by substituting his sinless person for all sinners
- by appeasing God's wrath for his disobedient creatures

Images such as bondage, slavery, paying ransom, and appeasing God's wrath seem inappropriate ways of describing Jesus' glorious work of salvation. Critical minds might admit that some of these modes of expression are only metaphors, but would still insist that they are far removed from our modern sense of God's salvation. Their sincere question might be: Aren't there ways of expressing how Jesus saves us that are more engaging and closer to our own actual human experience?

We will try to answer that question using Scripture itself. We begin with Paul's various descriptions of Jesus' saving work. Then, we will consider how other Scripture writers express the experience of Jesus as Savior. Finally, we will point to various positive descriptions of salvation that might be more appealing to today's Christians.

Paul uses several words to describe the effect of the Christ event. Let us consider five classic terms: salvation, justification, reconciliation, expiation, and redemption. "[The gospel] is the power of God for the salvation of everyone who believes …" (Rom 1:16; cf. 1 Cor 15:2). According to the plan of God, we are destined "… to gain salvation through our Lord Jesus Christ" (1 Thes 5:9). Jesus actually saves us by the power of his cross (1 Cor 1:18). Paul often describes Jesus' work as that of salvation; he asserts that God's salvation is mediated through the person of Jesus. It is not too much to affirm that for Paul the essence of Christian faith is that Jesus is the bringer of salvation from God. This is Paul's overarching description of the entire work of Jesus and the center of his Christology. All the other terms Paul uses in his letters for the Jesus-event might be seen as **variations of this general term: salvation**.

The image that Paul uses most frequently to express the effect of the Jesus-event is **justification**: "[All] are justified freely by [God's] grace through the redemption in Christ Jesus" (Rom 3:24). The direct cause of our justification is the death and resurrection of Jesus: "… [Jesus our Lord] was handed over for our transgressions and was raised for our justification" (Rom 4:25). What Paul means is that by his passion, death, and resurrection, Jesus brought it about that the Corinthians now stand before God's tribunal acquitted or justified; that is, though previously they were sinners, "… now … you were sanctified, you were justified in the name of the Lord Jesus Christ …" (1 Cor 6:11).

Another frequent Pauline term is **reconciliation**. "[God] … has reconciled us to himself through Christ and given us the ministry of reconciliation ..." (2 Cor 5:18). When Paul speaks this way he means that God has reconciled sinners to himself through the work of Jesus, so that they are brought from a status of enmity toward God to friendship with God. Paul points to the death of Jesus as the main cause of our reconciliation with God: "... if, while we were enemies, we were reconciled to God through the death of his Son, how much more, once reconciled, will we be saved by his life" (Rom 5:10). This reconciliation that Jesus has accomplished is the essence of the permanent peace that he brings to those who believe in him. That is, because Jesus has permanently reconciled us to God, we are at peace with God our Father. As Paul notes in the beginning of this chapter in Romans: "...   [S]ince we have been justified by faith, we have peace with God through our Lord Jesus Christ ..." (Rom 5:1; cf. also Eph 2: 14-18).

Paul describes another effect of the Jesus-event as **expiation:** "[All are justified] ... through the redemption in Christ Jesus, whom God set forth as an expiation ... by his blood" (Rom 3:24-25; cf. 1 Jn 2:2). Here Paul is reflecting the Old Testament Day of Atonement ritual (Lv 16:12-15), so that Jesus, by his death and shedding of blood, has achieved for humanity once and for all what the Day of Atonement ritual symbolized each year for Israel. At times, when Paul speaks about Jesus dying to expiate our sins, he mentions the "wrath" of God; for example: "How much more then, since we are now justified by his blood, will we be saved through him from the wrath" (Rom 5:9). Paul inherited this "wrath of God" quality from the Old Testament (e.g. Is 30:27-28), where it expresses God's negative reaction to **evil and sin**, not an anthropomorphic emotion of anger. Notice also that Paul actually contradicts the idea of "wrath" in God in v. 8: "...God proves his **love** for us in that while we were still sinners Christ died for us" (emphasis added). Paul's sense of expiation is that Jesus' blood, shed for the forgiveness of sin, removed the sins that alienated us from God. He adds that the initiative for this action is the graciousness of God and the love of Jesus. It is **not** Pauline teaching that God willed Jesus' death to satisfy the debts owed to God by sinners. Rather, Paul is offering vivid metaphors not theological insights.

Surprisingly, Paul only rarely describes the effect of the Jesus-event as **redemption.** He very clearly connects justification and redemption in Romans: "[All who believe] are justified freely by his grace through the redemption in Christ Jesus ..." (Rom 3:24). The New Testament notion of redemption seems to reflect the Hebrew Scriptures' use of the word, *lytron,* indicating a payment of **ransom** for slaves. But this same word was very often used in the metaphorical sense of **liberation,** and especially for God's liberation of his people Israel, **not** by paying a ransom but by the power of his mercy (as in Dt 7:8; 13:6; 6:15; 24:18; 2 Sm 4:9; 7:23; 1 Kgs 1:29; Pss 29:22; 44:27; 74:2). In the gospels and non-Pauline epistles, the word, redemption, is not often used; it is not a primary New Testament word to describe the saving work of Jesus. Yet, paradoxically, redemption has become a technical term in later theology and in modern popular language as the **most common way** to describe the saving work of Jesus.

Paul uses the word, redemption, in one other place: "... [Y]ou are in Christ Jesus, who became for us wisdom from God, as well as righteousness, sanctification, and redemption ..." (1 Cor 1:30). Here Paul simply ties together four ways of describing the saving work of Jesus without bothering to differentiate them. His approach here suggests that for him there is not a great difference among these terms.

St. Paul uses other terms to describe his experience of Jesus our Savior, such as **freedom, transformation, new creation, and glorification**. Often he speaks about the freedom won for us by the death and resurrection of Christ; by that he means a multifaceted freedom (e.g., see 2 Cor 3:17), which includes freedom from sin (e.g., Rom 5:19-21), from slavery (e.g., Rom 6:6), from the Mosaic Law (e.g., Rom 7:4-6), and from death as a final end (e.g., Rom 6:23). Other images of salvation that Paul uses are that of transformation (e.g., 2 Cor 3:18), and new creation (e.g., 2 Cor 5:17), and ultimate glorification (e.g., Rom 8:18-21). Any of these images of Jesus as Savior might add to our individual appreciation of his wondrous work of salvation, but perhaps the five above will be sufficient for our purposes here.

Our study of Paul offered several ways that Paul described his experience of salvation in Christ Jesus. His descriptions seem to reflect the experiences of the first Christians, and certainly provided the basis for the early Church to describe what Jesus accomplished by his ministry and passion. Later gospel writers used many of the same terms as Paul did, but they also described the saving work of Jesus in other terms, such as encounter with God, revelation of God, exemplar, and symbol of God's love. Some of these terms might be more effective and appealing for Christians of the twenty-first century.

Luke, in his Gospel, presents Jesus as filled with the Holy Spirit of God, so that those who heard him actually **encountered the Spirit of God in Jesus**. Luke attests that, from the beginning of his public life, Jesus is dominated by the Holy Spirit. At Jesus' baptism the Spirit descended upon Jesus as the permanent power dwelling in him, the Son and servant of God (Lk 3:22). Seventeen times in his Gospel, Luke continues to show the influence of the Holy Spirit on Jesus and his ministry. He wants us to recognize that the Holy Spirit is the power behind the whole work of Jesus. Then, at the end of the Gospel, he presents Jesus' charge to his disciples that "… repentance, for the forgiveness of sins, would be preached in his name to all the nations, …. You are witnesses of these things. And [behold] I am sending the promise of my Father upon you …" (Lk 24:47-49; "the promise of my Father" is the Holy Spirit, as indicated in Acts 1:8 and 2:33). Implied in this commission is that the saving work of Jesus—repentance and forgiveness preached to all the nations for their salvation—was to be carried out by his disciples through the power of the Spirit. Then Luke begins the Acts of the Apostles with the fulfillment of Christ's promise of the Holy Spirit: the disciples "… were all filled with the holy Spirit …" (Acts 2:4). On that day of Pentecost, Peter proclaims: "… [L]et the whole house of Israel know for certain that God has made [Jesus] both Lord and Messiah …" (Acts 2:36). And when his listeners asked, "What are we to do …?" he responded, "Repent and be baptized … in the name of Jesus Christ for the forgiveness of your sins; and you will receive the gift of the holy Spirit" (Acts 2:37-38).

The early believers encountered the Spirit of God in extraordinary ways (Acts 2:38-41; 10:44-46; 19:6). Throughout the Acts of the Apostles, individual missionaries were directed by the Spirit of God (Acts 8:29-39; 10:19-20; 11:12; 20:22). And the Council of Jerusalem was inspired by the Spirit (15:28). Thus, Luke presents the Holy Spirit as the source of life and growth in the early Church. This constant inspiration and guidance of the Spirit of God is the distinguishing feature of Luke's ecclesiology. In a word, the career of Jesus and the life of the Christian community give witness to the Spirit of God as present and immanent to human beings in power and love.

John begins his Gospel by describing the *Logos,* the Word; the prologue (Jn 1:1-14) begins: The Word was; the Word was with God; the Word was God; the Word became flesh. Here, John teaches that, in the incarnation, the Word did not just take on flesh or have a bodily appearance, but the Word became "flesh" in the Father's only Son. The Christology of this prologue is new and distinctive: "The prologue of the Fourth Gospel is the fullest and clearest statement of incarnational christology in the New Testament."[63] The rest of John's Gospel does not use the term, "Word," but it does continue to present Jesus as the definitive Wisdom and revelation of God. That is, the Wisdom of God, prominent in the wisdom books of the Hebrew Scriptures, is represented and even personified in Jesus and his teaching. Consider just one example: In speaking

---

63   Kyser, p. 29.

with Nicodemus, Jesus asserts that he is the truth people need to believe in for salvation, "… that everyone who believes in him … might have eternal life" (Jn 3:16), for he is "… the light [who] came into the world" (Jn 3:19; also see 3:34-36). In the Last Supper discourses, Jesus repeatedly affirms that he is the extraordinary revelation of God, the Father. In John, Jesus describes himself in profound metaphors. He is "the truth" (14:6), so that "If you know me, then you will also know my Father" (14:7). He declares that he is the image or visual experience of God: "Whoever has seen me has seen the Father" (14:9). Finally, John describes the purpose of all he has written: "… that you may … believe that Jesus is the Messiah, the Son of God, and that through this belief you may have life in his name" (20:31). This personification of the Word and revealed truth "is meant to emphasize the realism of God's presence in Jesus. And the realism of the incarnation in 'flesh' is meant to express dramatically the concrete visibility and availability of God's revelation in Jesus."[64]

John's Gospel also concludes that knowledge of God through the person and teaching of Jesus leads to salvation. He quotes Jesus: "Now this is eternal life, that they should know you, the only true God, and the one whom you sent, Jesus Christ" (17:3; see also 12:44-50 and 14:6). This leads to the awesome claim of Christian faith that **we come to know God through our encounter with the human Jesus**, and this knowledge leads to salvation.

The Letter to the **Colossians** begins with an early Christian hymn (Col 1:15-20) that presents Christ as the mediator of redemption:

[Christ] is the image of the invisible God,
    the firstborn of all creation.
  For in him were created all things in
      heaven and on earth, …

---

64   Roger Haight, *Jesus, Symbol of God*, p. 177.

all things were created through him
    and for him. …
[Christ] is the beginning, the firstborn from
    the dead,
  that in all things he himself might be
    preeminent.
For in him all the fullness was pleased
    to dwell,
  and through him to reconcile all
    things for him,
making peace by the blood of his cross ….

Here, "first born" designates a position of prominence among all creation. "Image" means a visible revelation, so that Jesus reveals the invisible God and that he himself is a part of God's being. "In him … through him … for him" mean that Jesus is the purpose and aim of creation. "In him all the fullness was pleased to dwell" proclaims that the presence of God exists now in all fullness in Christ. The fundamental conviction of this magnificent hymn is that Jesus is **the revealer of God, making God present to our human world.**

Colossians then continues to speak about…

[T]he mystery hidden … from generations past. But now it has been manifested to his holy ones, to whom God chose to make known the riches of the glory of this mystery among the Gentiles; it is Christ in you, the hope for glory. It is he whom we proclaim … teaching everyone with all wisdom, that we may present everyone perfect in Christ (1:26-28).

"The mystery hidden" is the message that Christ is the Messiah who is the hope of glory. "[P]resent everyone perfect in Christ" means that because the promise is identical with the Messiah, there is no human perfection except by unshakable trust in the Messiah and in faithfulness to him. This implies that Jesus is not only the premier revelation of God, but also the exemplar of what it means to be human. Though human existence is mysterious, its ultimate character and destiny are revealed in Jesus. He offers a model of what human life is for and where it is leading. Jesus himself shows us the way to actualize and fulfill our human potential. This conception of salvation as being embodied in the example of Jesus leads us to the practice of *imitatio Christi* (the imitation of Christ) as a formula for Christian spirituality: "… [P]ut on the Lord Jesus Christ …" (Rom 13:14); clothe "… yourselves with Christ …" (Gal 3:27); and "… put on the new self …" (Eph 4:24). Peter has this explicit invitation to imitate Christ: "… to this you have been called, because Christ also suffered for you, leaving you an example that you should follow in his footsteps" (1 Pt 2:21).

John presents his "miniature Gospel" in these famous words: "… God so loved the world that he gave his only Son, so that everyone who believes in him might not perish but might have eternal life" (Jn 3:16). Here, John proclaims the core of the Christian Gospel: namely, that the earthly life of Jesus our Savior flows from the fact that God loved the world so much that he gave his Son in order that the world might be saved. At the end of his prologue John tells us that, "No one has ever seen God. The only Son, God, … has revealed him" (Jn 1:18). That is, the purpose of Jesus' human life is to tell the story of God and his relationship to our world. Admittedly, the emphasis in this early part of John's Gospel is on the incarnation, not the redemption of Jesus. However, in John's first epistle, there is no doubt that the story of God's love is only expressed fully by the redemption of Jesus: "… **God is love.** In this way the love of God was revealed to us: God sent his only Son into the world so that we might have life through him. In this is love: … that he loved us and sent his Son as expiation for our sins" (1 Jn 4:8-10, emphasis added; also see 4:16). This is the closest the New Testament comes to telling us about the being of God. Because it connects the human existence of Jesus to eternal life, it expresses the high point of John's soteriology. That is, we know that "God is love" precisely **because** God "sent his Son as expiation for our sins" so that we might gain eternal life.

A logical conclusion to this "story of God" is a challenge for us to recognize in Jesus, the Son of God the Father, who has loved us in this amazing way. At the Last Supper, John presents Jesus' challenge to Philip: "Whoever has seen me has seen the Father. How can you say, 'Show us the Father'? Do you not believe that I am in the Father and the Father is in me?" (Jn 14:9-10). Finally, on the cross Jesus' last words imply that Jesus has brought to perfection this task the Father gave him—to make known God and his love to all the world: "It is finished" (Jn 19:30).

When discussing John's Gospel, we observed that Jesus brings salvation by **revealing God** to us. In this section, our topic is narrower; we focus on Jesus as the revelation of **God's love**. For me, this is the highpoint of all New Testament soteriology. That is, John's Gospel is simply the story of Jesus our Savior, who reveals our God as a God of love. Jesus, the Son of God, proves God's love by means of the greatest human example known to us: "No one has greater love than this, to lay down one's life for one's friends" (Jn 15:13). Why is this the greatest symbol of God's love? Because of the depth and intensity demanded of such an expression of love, and because it is the ultimate human sacrifice. In Jesus, God has come to us and has revealed a God committed to us in love. Like the early Christians, we know our God as a God of love: "In this is love: not that we have loved God, but that he loved us and sent his Son as expiation for our sins" (1 Jn 4:10).

The question addressed in this chapter is: What do we mean when we say that Jesus saved us and reconciled us with God? Studying Scripture, we find that the notions about God's salvation that some find repulsive are not actually found in Paul and the other Scripture writers. That is, Paul does not present our God as vindictive or wrathful. And other unappealing ways of describing God's salvation—such as offering a ransom or making satisfaction to an angry God—are actually metaphors, not literal theological notions. Our conclusion, then, is that Paul's way of describing how Jesus saves us is not inappropriate. Similarly, we highlighted other descriptions of God's salvation in Jesus that may be more satisfying and engaging descriptions of the work of Jesus our Savior.

As a final word, let me quote the wonderful insight of Jon Sobrino about the salvation wrought by Jesus:

> The New Testament's final word about Jesus' cross is that in it God's love was expressed. This language of love includes more than the language of "redemption," "salvation from sins." It includes these, but it goes beyond them …. **This is the New Testament's fundamental affirmation** … [:] **In Jesus' life and cross God's love has been displayed.** And God chose this way of showing himself, because he could not find any clearer way of telling us human beings that he really wills our salvation. … Not sparing the Son is the way of saying that there is no restraint on God's love for human beings.[65]

REFLECTIONS

1. Of all the terms that St. Paul uses to describe the effect of the work of Jesus, our Savior, which ones reflect your own preferences?

2. Which of the descriptions of the work of Jesus, our Savior, in John's Gospel are most appealing to you?

3. You have probably heard the question, "Have you chosen Jesus as your personal Savior?" As a baptized Christian, how can you answer this question?

---

65   Jon Sobrino, *Jesus the Liberator* (Maryknoll, NY: Orbis Books, 1993), p. 231 (emphasis added).

CHAPTER 6

Christianity and Other Religions

The driving force for all Christians who seek the unity of all Christian churches is Jesus' farewell prayer in John's Gospel: "I pray … for those who will believe in me … so that they may all be one, as you, Father, are in me and I in you, that they also may be in us, that the world may believe that you sent me" (Jn 17:20-21). His prayer is a constant challenge and driving force for all Christians to be united in a more visible way. And the horizon or backdrop for ecumenism in general is: "… God our savior, who wills everyone to be saved and to come to knowledge of the truth. /For there is one God. / There is also one mediator between God and the human race, /Christ Jesus, himself human, /who gave himself as ransom for all" (1 Tm 2:4-6; cf. also Acts 10:34-35). This horizon includes two parts: First, it affirms that God efficaciously wills **universal salvation**. Note that this saving will for all humankind is attributed to "God our savior" as the absolute element in the salvation of the world. That God's will knows no partiality was seen in the O. T. (Dt 10:17), and in Acts (10:34), and in Paul (Rom 2:11). Second, that Jesus is the one mediator for all. Just as throughout his life Jesus was completely related, directed, and centered on God, so also his function as mediator makes his bond with the Father one of total dependence. Also, during his ministry, Jesus did not condemn others who had **different forms of faith in God** (cf. Mt 11:22-24; 15:22-28; Mk 8:24-30; Lk 9:49-50). He recognized the positive value in God's eyes of the religious experience of other individuals by which they lived their faith in the one God.

There are two other Scripture quotes that seem to say that Jesus is the **exclusive** source of salvation, the only avenue of salvation. One is the most famous assertion of Jesus in John's Gospel: "I am the way and the truth and the life. No one comes to the Father except through me" (Jn 14:6). Here Jesus claims to be a unique "way" to God, the only avenue of salvation **for those who believe in him**; he does not rule out other "paths" to salvation through which Jesus' unique way may be secretly operative.

The other quote is found in Acts, in which Luke presents Peter as preaching: "There is no salvation through anyone else, nor is there any other name under heaven given to the human race by which we are to be saved" (Acts 4:12). This is the *textus classicus* for those Christians who claim that one must become a Christian in order to be saved. The problem with this interpretation is that it takes this quote out of context. The actual context is Peter speaking to the Sanhedrin and insisting that there is **only one name in the entire Jewish nation** throughout history leading to salvation. C. S. Song explains this historical context very well:

> ... [T]hose Christians who use the "no-other-name" text to assert the supreme role of the Christian church in the salvation of humankind and those who reject it as too restricted and exclusive are both in error. Both have failed to understand the central focal point of the story. ... We must keep in mind the political nature of the religious confrontation between the apostles and the religious authority. For Peter and the other apostles, there is only one name **in the entire Jewish nation,** past, present, and future, that can ... restore the true spirit of the Jewish religion. ... That name is Jesus.[66]

To sum up all this, these passages...

should not be understood in a way that leads to an **exclusivist** theology of salvation. The affirmation ... should be integrated into the entirety of the biblical message and interpreted in context.[67] In short, far from contradicting

---

66   C. S. Song, *Jesus in the Power of the Spirit* (Minneapolis: Fortress Press, 1994), p. 244 (emphasis added).

67   Cf. Acts 17:22–34, where Paul displays a very positive attitude toward Greek religiosity.

religious pluralism, faith in Jesus Christ requires acceptance and openness in dealing with it.[68]

So when we proclaim that the Christian Church has an irreplaceable function for salvation, it does not mean it has a monopoly on salvation and grace, but would admit that there are **other sources of grace and salvation** that are a part of God's plan of universal salvation offered to all.

Vatican Council II recognized the positive values of other faiths. In fact, the council established two important points: First, it affirmed clearly what had been cautiously taught previously in church documents— that God can lead **individuals** who, through no fault of their own, are ignorant of the gospel, to faith that leads to salvation. Thus, *Lumen Gentium* affirms clearly that "[t]hose also can attain to everlasting salvation who through no fault of their own do not know the Gospel of Christ ... but nevertheless seek God with a sincere heart and try in their actions to do his will ...."[69]

Second, the council touched on the salvific value of **other religions** as such. "In Karl Rahner's view, the council's main achievement consists of having looked beyond the question of the salvation of individual non-Christians to a positive relationship of the [Catholic] church with the **religions** as such."[70] To be clear, however, the council did not explicitly express the positive quality of non-Christian religions but only **suggests** it.

This first statement, above, about the salvation of **individuals,** is most significant for the history of the Church's stand on ecumenism. It boldly rejects the ancient tradition which seemed to deny salvation to those who do not belong to the Church. Beginning with early Fathers of the Church, such

68   Jacques Dupuis, SJ, *Christianity and the Religions* (Maryknoll, NY: Orbis Books, 2002), p. 39 (emphasis added).

69   *AAS.* 1966, 823; *Dei Verbum,*16.

70   Jacques Dupuis, p. 65.

as Origin, Cyprian, and Augustine, the Church taught "*Extra Ecclesiam nulla salus* (Outside the Church there is no salvation). The Fourth Lateran Council (1215) defined this as a **doctrine**. So, from the fifth to the sixteenth century this was the Church's accepted teaching. Then, in the seventeenth century, Rome indicated an apparent change to this position, when it condemned the Jansenist position: "*Extra Ecclesiam nulla gratia*" (Outside the Church there is no grace). Finally, Vatican II formally declared that **outside the Church there is salvation**. So, for the first time in its history, the Church expressed itself against such a narrow-minded absolutism, especially in terms of **individuals.**

The second statement, above, refers not just to individuals, but also to **other religions.** After Vatican II, Pope John Paul II published three separate encyclicals[71] indicating that, though Jesus is the universal mediator, there are various kinds of participated forms of mediation. Then, in 1991, a joint document of the Pontifical Council for Interreligious Dialogue and the Congregation for the Evangelization of Peoples went beyond anything said previously in church documents about the positive value of **other religions** for salvation:

> The mystery of salvation reaches out to [all men and women], in a way known to God. ... Concretely, it will be **in the sincere practice of what is good in their own religious tradition** and by following the dictates of their conscience that the members of other religions ... receive salvation in Jesus Christ, even while they do not recognize ... him as their Savior.[72]

What can we say, therefore, about the universal significance and **constitutive role** that Christianity attributes to Jesus

---

71 *Dominum et Vivificantem* (1986), *Redemptoris Missio* (1990), and *Tertio Millennio Adveniente* (1994).

72 This is found in Nuener and Dupuis, eds. *The Christian Faith in the Documents of the Church,* no. 1059 (emphasis added).

Christ? Theologians have maintained various positions in answer to this question, from the most exclusive to the most inclusive. The most reasonable position, I believe, is that of an **inclusive pluralism**. That is, having faith in Jesus Christ means that one has encountered God's offer of salvation in the person of Jesus of Nazareth, so that Jesus Christ is **the constitutive way of salvation for Christians**, in the sense that God has placed Jesus at the center of his saving plan for all who know him. It does not mean that Jesus is the constitutive way of salvation for all human beings, regardless of their time and place and their own experience of faith, because, humanly speaking, they have no effective connection with the historical Jesus. Thus, Jesus Christ is God's decisive revelation and constitutive Savior for all Christians. Nevertheless God's plan of salvation is also present and at work in other religious traditions—which are alternative and **effective historical manifestations of God.** That is the very way that God's salvific will is **at work everywhere.**

Similarly, what can we say about the **fullness of God's revelation to the world?** Vatican II affirms that Jesus Christ "completed and perfected revelation" and "is himself both the mediator of revelation and the fullness of revelation."[73] That means the very person of Jesus Christ—his deeds and words, his life, death, and resurrection—constitutes the fullness of revelation. In Jesus, God has uttered to the world his decisive word in a **qualitative** sense; that is, Jesus Christ is the pinnacle and the culmination of God's word: In Christ, God's revelation is of singular intensity, but does not exhaust the mystery of God. It does not exclude the continuation of divine revelation through prophets and sages of other religious traditions.

Nevertheless, if **God's universal salvific will** is to be really efficacious, then God must act in all of history through other **quantitative** ways, by which his universal love is discovered in a plurality of religions. For if God's love is to be truly **effective**

---

73   *AAS, 1966,* 819 and 818; *Dei Verbum,* 4 and 2.

for all people, then other religions, insofar as they expressly represent that love and hope, must be able to mediate God's love for them. To be entirely clear then, all the religions of the world—such as Judaism, Islam, Hinduism, Buddhism—are ways of expressing the truth about God and are able to mediate God's love. So they are an effective way to express God's universal salvific will.

We can understand this better, I believe, by considering that God's universal plan of salvation must refer to **all people**, even those who lived before the time of Christ and those who have never heard anything about Jesus even in our day. The Letter to the Hebrews leaves no doubt that "In times past, God spoke in partial and various ways to our ancestors through the prophets…" (Heb 1:1); that clearly refers to Jewish ancestors and might relate to other groups. In addition to that, our faith in the Holy Spirit seems to require that the Spirit was universally present and active **before** the time of Jesus and will always be active throughout **all parts of our world** for all of God's creatures as part of God's salvific will.

Let me summarize all that has been said so far about Jesus as savior and God who wills the salvation of all. Jesus Christ is the integral figure of God's salvation and the pinnacle of his revelation. But God's salvific will includes all humankind in the sense that all people are encouraged to seek and find God and his salvation by the inspiration of the Holy Spirit, as well as by the prophets and sages of the multitude of religions in our world today, and throughout all time. Almost all of the world's religions offer objective elements as a part of their traditions, such as sacred writings, moral norms of living, and symbolic or sacramental practices. These all help them to know God and worship him.

Karl Rahner has an insightful way of connecting God's salvific will, Jesus' unique mediatorship, and the Catholic Church:

… God's irrevocable promise of himself to human history has taken on historically concrete form as history that actually reaches its goal in God. … [In this sense, we understand Jesus] as God's promise of himself to the world and its history, a self-promise that is definitive, irrevocable, and establishes itself by the power of God himself …. If we assume that this irrevocable self-promise of God which has become historically concrete in Jesus must … be permanently present in history, then our statement also implies the historical continuance of a community of faith … [as] a permanent presence.[74]

What we often seem to overlook is that one of the primary purposes of the Vatican Council was to make progress toward the restoration of unity for all the Christian churches: "The restoration of unity among all Christians is one of the principal concerns of the Second Vatican Council …."[75] The decree laments that "… such division [among Christian faiths] openly contradicts the will of Christ, scandalizes the world, and damages the … preaching of the Gospel …."[76] As noted above, the decree on Ecumenism *(Unitatis Redintegratio)* marks the beginning of a new era in the relation of the churches to one another[77]

Many priests ordained before Vatican II, including myself, lacked a true spirit of ecumenism, for several reasons. First, they had been taught the traditional teaching that came from the early Fathers of the Church: *Extra Ecclesiam nulla salus* (Outside the Church there is no salvation). I'm embarrassed to admit that some of my strongest sermons as a young priest were on that subject. What drove such sermons was the literal understanding of passages such as Acts 4:12 ("There

---

74   Karl Rahner, *Theological Investigations, XXI,* (NY: Crossroad, 1989) p. 177.

75   *AAS,* 1965, 90; *Unitatis Redintegratio,* 1.

76   Ibid.

77   See Samuel McCrea Calvert in *Documents of Vatican II,* p. 367.

is no salvation though anyone else …"). Second, historical criticism of such passages was not yet the norm for interpreting Scripture. So priests did not realize how the historical context determined the meaning of such texts; they did not realize that Peter was speaking specifically to the historical group before him and telling the Jews that Jesus was really the Messiah, as well as telling Christians he was their unique Savior. Third, it would be several years before Pope John Paul II would publish his three encyclicals affirming that, though Christ is the universal mediator, there are various forms of participated mediators that are helps to salvation. And, finally, even though they were familiar with 1 Tm 2:4 ("… God … wills everyone to be saved …..") and believed it, still they did not have a clear understanding of how that was to be worked out in God's providence. Only after all these dramatic changes in the Church's approach to ecumenism could priests realize and teach that **outside the Church there is much salvation**, even for people who have never heard of Christ, in keeping with their human freedom and the efficacious will of God for the salvation of all.

In almost fifty years since the council, there have been many false steps and disappointments in the work of uniting the Christian churches. Nevertheless, there have been some notable ecumenical **advances** as well. Throughout these years there have been many high-level efforts to increase the unity of the churches. That is, leaders and theologians of two, three, or many churches have gathered together and struggled to find doctrinal agreements among the various churches. For example, in October 1999, representatives of the Lutheran and Catholic churches met in Augsburg, Germany. They signed a joint declaration of the doctrine of justification: "Together we confess: by grace alone in faith in Christ's saving work and not because of any merit on our part [we are justified]." That agreement meant that a new day had dawned in Lutheran-Catholic relationships, because they finally agreed on the central Lutheran teaching of "justification by faith alone."

Earlier in that same year, Anglican and Catholic leaders issued an agreement on authority in Christ's Church. Also, in 2000, there was a call to "common mission" agreement between Episcopalians and Lutherans, which allows both churches to share clergy and worship in some instances. Also, various other Orthodox and mainline Christian churches have come to agreements on several important theological doctrines. Clearly, we still have a long way to go to come closer to the expressed intention of Jesus our Savior, "… [T]hat they may all be one … in us …" (Jn 17:21). But I believe that we will see some surprising moves toward unity in this twenty-first century.

REFLECTIONS

1. Think about the meaning of an "exclusivist theology of salvation." What would such a theology imply for you, your family members, and your neighbors, who might be of another faith?

2. How would you explain the universal salvific will of God in terms of the religions of the world throughout history?

3. Give some reasons why Vatican Council II rejected the teaching: "Outside theChurch there is no salvation."

CHAPTER 7

Not Everything Is Defined

The last four chapters were concerned with four central dogmas of our faith. However, there are many teachings of the Church that are not proposed as dogmas but are taught authoritatively in encyclicals or *motu proprios* of the pope or by formal decisions of Vatican congregations. Within our Catholic tradition, we have always maintained that there is a hierarchy of truths; that is, besides dogmatic statements that are carefully defined by the pope of ecumenical councils, there are numerous doctrines in the field of scriptural exegesis, systematic theology, or moral theology that are taught **authoritatively** by the Church in various ways. Let us take a look at some of these teachings and come to grips with how we should assent to them.

A rather common rule in the past was that theologians and ordinary Christians should not speak publicly against such teachings. But if they have serious reasonable objections to any authoritative teaching, they should express these objections **privately**; for example, in theological journals or in professional gatherings of theologians or moralists. In the past, such a norm was more easily followed, because discussions among theologians in professional journals would generally remain **private.** Then, after their different insights, approaches, and objections were tested out among their peers, they could be published for Catholics in general in popular religious or secular periodicals. But that is not a very workable solution today, because today there is almost no forum for theologians to privately debate new insights or approaches, since even the most tentative or cautious testing of ideas is likely to be picked up by a Catholic periodical or by the secular press and reported as if it were a final doctrine that departs from the authoritative teaching of the Church.

The Church must find new ways to deal with this modern problem and find some creative ways for theologians to freely debate different ideas and objections without fear of scandalizing ordinary Catholics. More importantly, it seems that the Church must be more tolerant of honest dialogue and sincere testing of new positions by their theologians and moralists. For if such non-dogmatic teachings cannot be questioned and tested with sincere arguments of dedicated theologians, then, over time, the assent will not be rationally sound, and they will be teaching the People of God doctrines which they cannot explain rationally. The First Letter of Timothy cautions those who want to be teachers of the law that they must fully understand what they are teaching and rationally assent to it: "Some people … [want] to be teachers of the law, but without understanding either what they are saying or what they assert with such assurance" (1 Tm 1:7). Perhaps this might be a reasonable principle regarding questions and debates about authoritative, non-definitive teachings: The advance of Christian theology and morality requires **careful debate and professional testing** of ideas; otherwise, assent will not be rationally sound.

Here is one famous example of an authoritative moral teaching by the pope that led to deep discontent and endless confusion throughout the world. Pope Paul VI decided to separate the question of birth control from discussions of the Vatican Council. He wisely chose many experts from around the world, including moralists, doctors, and leading married couples. At the beginning of their discussions, most of them agreed with the traditional moral teaching. That traditional moral teaching declared that birth control was immoral, because it was contrary to the **biological** purpose of intercourse—the procreation of children. But the discussions went on for several months and also concentrated on the whole **human** purpose of intercourse—including the fostering of love between the spouses. They also took note of Vatican II's notable change regarding the ends and purposes of marriage. That is, instead of the traditional teaching that there is only one primary purpose of marriage—the procreation and education of children—the council spoke of two equal ends of marriage—the begetting of children and the fostering of conjugal love and union. After lengthy discussion, the great majority of the committee (64 out of 68) was in favor of changing the traditional teaching that all use of contraceptives was immoral. They came to the conclusion that birth control was moral and reasonable in certain circumstances (such as economic need, medical problems, or the need to foster marital love). Pope Paul VI received their conclusions and struggled with his own conscience for almost two years. Finally, one cardinal apparently convinced him that great harm would be done to the Church if he did not confirm the traditional teaching on birth control. So the pope, then, rejected the strong conclusion of his own special committee and published his encyclical, *Humanae Vitae*, as an authoritative moral teaching (though even the encyclical did not claim more than that). The whole world was amazed at his decision and many moralists could not understand the basis for his teaching, especially after the argument from the entire human purpose of intercourse, and from the change in the major ends of marriage. They were expected to accept his teaching simply on the basis of his authority, despite their rational objections and arguments. In addition, they were required not to teach anything contrary to the encyclical in public! This one issue became such a *cause celebre* that the laity began to lose confidence in this church teaching and did not find it credible.

Though most ordinary Catholics were not aware of their statement, Catholic theologians finally made a formal response to *Humanae Vitae* on July 30, 1968:

> … [A]s Roman Catholic theologians, conscious of our duty and our limitations, we conclude that spouses may responsibly decide according to their conscience that artificial contraception in some circumstances is permissible

and indeed necessary to preserve and foster the values and sacredness of marriage.[78]

Over a period of years these moralists were treated severely by Rome and many of them eventually left the priesthood.

Another moral teaching that has far-reaching consequences is that the human embryo has full humanity **from the moment of conception** and thus merits full protection. According to this teaching, as soon as the human sperm unites with the ovum, that new entity (properly called a zygote) is fully human. Biologists generally agree that about half of the fertilized ova (zygotes) never implant themselves in the uterus. This attaching to the uterus is called nidation or implantation. Without nidation in the uterus or in the ovarian tubes, the zygote dies. For some moralists, this nidation, which requires a few or several days, is the **critical moment for the beginning of human life.**

Apropos of this, here is a true story from the 1950s. When I was in the seminary, the most respected systematic theologian was Fr. Thomas Motherway, S.J. He was a conservative theologian, but, to the surprise of us seminarians, he proposed the following moral position: The critical moment for the beginning of human life is nidation. He presented two arguments for that position. The first argument was a general point about God's providence. Because biologists observe that more than half of the fertilized ova never nidate, that means that more than half of the embryos generated would die immediately. Theologians cannot imagine that, in God's providence, more than half of the human beings generated naturally would not survive more than a few hours; they argue that God would not so arrange human conception that most human beings would immediately die. Fr. Motherway's second argument dealt with the unique case of identical twins, who

---

78   Statement by Catholic Theologians, Washington, D.C., July 30, 1968. This is printed in Charles Curran and Richard McCormack, SJ, *Readings in Moral Theology, No. 8* (NY: Paulist Press, 1993), pp. 136-37.

are generated by a **single** fertilized ovum. That is, the single cell divides into two at a very early stage. But if human life begins as soon as the sperm unites with the ovum, that means it is **already one single person**, and it is impossible for such a single human person to suddenly become two human beings. Therefore, argued Fr. Motherway, the single fertilized ovum cannot immediately be an actual human being. It can only be human **after** its division into two separate cells. And it certainly has already divided into two cells by the time it nidates in the uterus; so only sometime **after** that division could the separate cells be twin human beings.

Some noted moralists would agree with that position and even extend the time of human individualization of the embryo to as much as fourteen days. Richard McCormick opted for the human status of the zygote only after implantation, which establishes individuality (up to fourteen days after fertilization). He argued that prior to this, the zygote could separate into two entities, each of which could develop into an infant or, conversely, two zygotes could fuse into a single embryo. And he also referred to the large number of fertilized ova that are lost prior to implantation, which wastage seems contrary to the wisdom and providence of God.[79] That argument seems to have merit. If it is at least probable, there are possible far-reaching conclusions that might be drawn regarding the morning-after pill and the use of embryonic cells for modern scientific advances.

In this early twenty-first century, there are many moral issues that need to be thoroughly discussed by moral theologians before they can come to common solutions. This need is most evident in the fields of medical ethics, just wars and weapons of war, human sexuality and fertility, divorce and remarriage, homosexuality, end of life ethics, and gene therapy for crops and animals.

---

79 Cf. *Moral Theology; Challenges for the Future*, edited by Charles Curran (NY: Paulist Press, 1990), p. 241.

But throughout this century, the greatest advances of science will probably be in the field of **genetics.** Now that scientists have mapped the entire human genome, geneticists will be increasingly able to improve certain genes, remove deleterious genes, and select or combine others. Eugenics will permit doctors to select certain genes, omit others, and recombine others already existing in the human gene pool. Genetic engineering will be able to change the genes in such a way as to eliminate certain deleterious types or improve the genotype. Thus, in terms of human embryos, doctors will be able to avoid human birth defects or switch on or off different genes. As this century proceeds, more and more chronic human diseases will be able to be treated or cured by gene therapy.

The future of this field of genetics seems almost unlimited, and it will involve questions we have never faced before. Certainly, there will be countless moral problems that will require moralists to thoroughly discuss and debate the morality of so many new procedures and to test moral choices and norms. The immense power that these procedures will place in human hands, and the complexity of these questions, will require a communitarian and social approach for scientists and moralists. Before any authoritarian decisions by the Church, there needs to be careful debate and professional testing of ideas. Only such careful sharing of ideas, testing of cases, and profound rational arguments will convince both scientists and Catholics of such complex moral choices. As Charles Curran recommends: "Since we have much greater power within this century, [in terms of scientific and genetic advancement] it is not too early to continue in a more structured way the dialogue which has already been initiated."[80]

REFLECTIONS

1. Contrast the teaching related to birth control in Pope Pius

---

80   Charles Curran, *Issues in Sexual and Medical Ethics* (Notre Dame, IN: University of Notre Dame Press, 1978), p. 132.

VI's encyclical, *Humanae Vitae,* and the formal response made by the Roman Catholic theologians in July 1968.

2. Reflect on your beliefs about abortion and the rational arguments in this chapter. If the fertilized ovum were not human until it is implanted in the uterus, how would that affect the morality of medical interventions immediately after rape or incest?

3. Apparently, the Church has never formally defined a single moral doctrine. Does that surprise you? Would you prefer that the Church define some moral issues or not?

Chapter 8

Changes in Church Law

Every civilized country requires laws for the order and safety of its citizens. Without civil laws, no nation can endure but would descend into chaos. Here in America, our system of civil laws is immense; every governing body has innumerable laws on the books. We have a constitution and a bill of rights; we have human rights laws, civil rights laws, tax laws, home ownership laws, voting laws, gun laws, driving laws, and endless other rules. In order to establish these laws and protect the common good, we have city councils, county boards, state legislatures, and a national congress. Each of these jurisdictions has hundreds or thousands of people whose job it is to pass the laws, to manage them, and to reform them.

Every institution and every church requires laws. Most of the laws of the Church are found in Canon Law. In 1918, the modern collection of all Canon Law was published. After Vatican Council II, many of those laws were reformed; then, in 1983, the new Code of Canon Law was published. Besides this Code of Canon Law, other regulations have been added by the Roman congregations, often in response to questions from bishops around the world.

During the twentieth century, some important changes were made regarding marriage laws, such as those regarding mixed marriage and annulments of marriage. Also, the index of forbidden books was dropped. Other welcome changes were in the form of the growing number of approved lay organizations: lay missionary societies, lay apostolic groups, Catholic Action, CFM, YCW, YCS, Marriage Encounter, the Charismatic Movement, Cursillo Movement, and many other groups. In addition, Vatican II encouraged the formation of parish councils, finance councils, archdiocesan councils, senates of priests, and national conferences of bishops. All of these changes during our lifetime are evidences of a constantly changing Church. Most of these changes were either instituted by Roman congregations or approved by them in some way. They are important facets of Church life and part of the discipline of the Church, but they are not generally connected with the essentials of our faith.

Because Rome instituted or approved them, it could also change them if it determined that certain laws or disciplines were more harmful than helpful for Catholic life. When Rome decided to change some of these regulations, they seemed to follow a prudent principle: As soon as a particular law or discipline causes more harm than good in the Church, it should be changed or modified. In our lifetime, the most familiar changes we witnessed were regarding the laws about fasting and abstinence; fish on Fridays, fasting during all of Lent, and fasting from midnight for communion. These seem to be good examples of applying that prudent principle.

But for most Catholics in the years after Vatican II, the first and most dramatic changes were in the liturgy. As Pope Paul VI said, "the liturgy was the first subject to be examined and the first too…in intrinsic worth and importance for the life of the Church."[81] In December 1963, almost immediately after this constitution was promulgated by the council, Catholics throughout the world experienced endless changes in the liturgy. The priest now faced the people; the Mass was in the vernacular; the entire congregation were active participants and celebrants of the Mass; and so many of the congregation were active as lectors, communion ministers, leaders of song, directors of parish liturgy, and members of parish liturgical committees. Within a few years, the rites of all the sacraments were revised, with varying degrees of effectiveness. This experience of change in the liturgy generally impressed the

---

81   This quote is part of C. J. McNasby's observations regarding the Constitution on the sacred liturgy. See *The Documents of Vatican II*, p. 133.

People of God throughout the world. Such dramatic change brought a sense of enthusiasm to the Church. It convinced the majority of Catholics that the council was indeed causing a revolution in the Church. Still, some bishops, pastors, and laity found these changes very threatening to the traditional lifestyle of the Church, and some Roman Curia members feared disruption of traditional order and authority. Thus, Archbishop Rembert Weakland, in 1973, while he was working in Rome, noticed that some members of the curia

> … were unhappy with the liturgical changes … and were insisting on more discipline and uniformity. It would not be wrong to say that the **changes in liturgy were the most divisive of all the issues Paul [VI] had to face. …** I could see the mounting opposition through my personal involvement in the post-conciliar liturgical reforms.[82]

Roman opposition to further changes in the liturgy also took the form of blocking regional adaptations to the universal Roman liturgy. That is, they frequently opposed opening the door to liturgical diversity in countries that are culturally very diverse from the European Church, such as China, Japan, and the countries of Africa and South America.

This opposition seemed to be contrary to *Gaudium et Spes* (The Constitution on the Church in the Modern World), which had spoken forthrightly about the openness to the diverse cultures of the modern world. The entire second part of this constitution was devoted to a prolonged discussion of the diversity of culture and how the Church might relate to this situation in terms of spreading the gospel:

> [T]he Church … has used the inventions of different cultures to spread and explain the message of Christ to all nations … and to give it better expression in liturgical

---

82   Rembert Weakland, OSB, *A Pilgrim in a Pilgrim Church* (Grand Rapids, Michigan: William Eerdmans Publishing Co., 2009) p. 203.

celebrations and in the life of the diversified community of the faithful.[83]

Also *Sacrosanctum Consilium* (Constitution on the Sacred Liturgy) was very strong in affirming that the liturgy of the Church does not require uniformity in the various regions and cultures of the world: "Even in the liturgy, the Church does not wish to impose a rigid uniformity in matters which do not affect the faith or the good of the total community."[84] Such affirmations by Vatican II opened the door to liturgical diversity within the Roman Rite after centuries of official uniformity.[85]

Nevertheless, in the almost fifty years since Vatican II, many obstacles were placed in the way of this enlightened norm for liturgical diversity throughout the Church. Here in the United States, the translations of liturgical books were often restricted. For example, Rome insisted that all the English-speaking countries of the world must accept the same translations, even though there were notable differences in the vernacular of these countries. More significantly, the Bishops' Conferences of the Oriental and African nations were not given freedom to introduce liturgical changes according to their diverse cultures—despite their own unique familiarity with their own traditions.

Concerning translations of liturgical books for all eleven English-speaking countries, the Vatican Council itself created an International Commission on English in the Liturgy (ICEL). It consisted of bishops as well as liturgical and scriptural experts from the various English-speaking countries. For over thirty years, the ICEL followed a widely consultative process for the translations of the sacred texts and prayers of worship. But Rome was unsatisfied with the direction of this commission

---

83   *AAS*, 1966, 234; *Gaudium et Spes*, 58.

84   *AAS*, 1964, 110; *Sacrosanctum Consilium*, 37.

85   See Mark Francis, CSV, *Liturgy in a Multicultural Community* (Collegeville, MN: The Liturgical Press, 1991), pp. 14-18, 47.

and essentially supplanted it by its own agency, the Vox Clara Committee, and gave it a mandate to advise the Congregation for Divine Worship on English translations. In January 2010, the Vox Clara Committee released a statement that its work on a new English translation of the Sacramentary (formerly called the Roman Missal) was nearly complete and will be the norm for all English-speaking countries in 2011.

Similarly, in the United Sates during the 1990s, the National Conference of U.S. Bishops convened a group of theologians and professional liturgists, who worked for six years on a new translation of the American Lectionary (including all the readings for the three-year cycle of Sunday Masses). After completing their extensive work on the new Lectionary, they sent their moderate translation to Rome for approval. After some time, Rome rejected their translation. Meanwhile, in 1997, without even consulting the American bishops, the Vatican hosted a secret meeting of eleven men, chosen by them, to overhaul the American lectionary. Within two weeks, these men undid the work accomplished by the American bishops over several years. They managed to sort-circuit the debate on inclusive language in the lectionary by retaining many of the controversial uses of masculine vocabulary and revamping the texts approved by the U.S. bishops. This rejection was particularly troublesome to many women in the United States, who had expected that a moderate inclusive-language text would finally be approved. Again, these women felt excluded— even by the language used in our liturgy.

In a similar rebuke to women in the Church, the National Conference of U.S. Bishops, in the 1990s, attempted to write a pastoral letter on women in the Church in order to show equality and inclusiveness of women in the Church. When they sent their draft to Rome, it was repeatedly rejected by Rome, so that they finally abandoned the whole effort of trying to encourage women in the U.S. Church by means of a positive-sounding pastoral letter.

Other matters of Church discipline are more problematic, for they seem to involve questions related to Scripture. Consider the question of women's ordination to the priesthood. In 1976, the Sacred Congregation for the Doctrine of the Faith issued a "Declaration on the Question of the Admission of Women to the Ministerial Priesthood," which declared that the ordination of women to the priesthood was not possible, and was not even to be discussed. Karl Rahner carefully critiqued this document in the article "Women in the Priesthood"[86] He concluded that the negative statement could not be regarded as definitive and could be reversed; in his mind the argument from Scripture was unconvincing. Coincidentally, the Pontifical Biblical Commission completed a two-year study of the Bible as to whether women could be ordained priests and reported (by a vote of 17-0) that the New Testament does not settle the question in a clear way.[87] Also, the Canon Law Society of America agreed that there is nothing in Scripture that positively excludes the ordination of women.[88] In other words, one cannot definitely exclude women from the ordained priesthood by appealing to Scripture. So, if we agree with St. Augustine that Scripture is "the soul of theology," and realize that Scripture does not answer this question definitively, then the Church could decide this issue regarding equality of women in the Church according to the norms of prudence and justice.

Regarding this issue, there are many weighty arguments relating to Scripture, Canon Law, and justice and equality for women in the Church. The issue, however, is eminently important to the future of the Church, and the solutions might be diverse and nuanced. There is no one answer that looks the best to me. But it seems that this issue deserves an honest and extensive discussion. Very cautiously, let me gently make this

---

86   See Karl Rahner, *Theological Investigations, XX* (London: Darton, Longman and Todd, 1981), pp. 35-47.

87   See this report, "Can Women be Priests" in *Origins*, 6/6, July 1, 1976, pp. 92-96.

88   See the "Consensus Statement from the Symposium on Women and Church Law," in James Coriden, ed., *Sexism and Church Law* (New York: Paulist Press, 1977), pp. 150-60.

suggestion: let Rome call a high-level commission of theological experts—representing all sides of the issue—similar to the commission that Pope Paul VI called regarding birth control. Such a commission might find one or more solutions that could renew our Church.

An allied question is that of ordination to the priesthood of married men. In the early Church, priests were not required to be celibate. From the time of Pope Leo the Great, in the fifth century, celibacy was recognized as fitting for priests. For the next six centuries, celibacy was required of priests in the Western Church sometimes and in some places—with only partial observance. From the eleventh century, celibacy was universally required of all priests in the Western Church. Throughout the last millennium, the vow or requirement of celibacy was generally observed in some countries, but poorly kept in others. In the Middle Ages, even some bishops and popes were not celibate; in one case, a pope was actually the son of the previous pope! However, in the Eastern Catholic Church, priests could always marry before they were ordained; but if they did, they could not become bishops. In recent times, Protestant ministers who were married and then became Catholic, were often permitted to become priests in the Catholic Church, even though they were married. Also, in November 2009, Pope Benedict XVI opened the door for Anglican priests or bishops who are married to be ordained Catholic priests and be welcome in our Church. Perhaps hundreds of married Anglican priests will soon join the Catholic Church. It must be concluded, then, that the requirement of celibacy for priests throughout our history has been a discipline of the Church that was imposed by the Church at certain times, with many, many exceptions tolerated by the Church, even in this century.

So the question might be asked: Would any change in the requirement of celibacy for priests truly benefit the Church? The answer could be found by weighing the relative value of two opposing goods. The image we might picture here is that of the old style scale with two opposing trays; a weight is put on one side of the scale, and an opposing weight is put on the other side, to determine which is the heavier. In our example here, one weight is celibacy, the other is the availability of the sacraments. **Celibacy** in the priesthood is a profound good in the Church, for it is a forceful symbol of our priests' commitment to Jesus and the People of God, and to their hope of everlasting life. Only the priest's faith in eternal life makes sense of such a commitment. The second and opposing good is the **availability of the sacraments.** Our Church is essentially a sacramental Church—more than any other church. And for the administration of most of the sacraments, we need priests. Above all, we need priests for the celebration of Mass and Eucharist. Without the Eucharist, our friendship with Jesus becomes problematic, because any human friendship demands regular, external contact among friends. For us Catholics, the primary, regular, and external contact with Jesus is in the Eucharist. Without the availability of the Mass and Eucharist (and the other sacraments), our friendship with Jesus loses its best source of regular, external union with Jesus.

The Church, then, must weigh the relative value of these two profound goods: celibacy for all priests versus the adequate availability of the sacraments for our people. In most countries today, there are fewer and fewer priests ordained each year, resulting in less access to the sacraments for our people. Especially in North and South America, we can see how this imbalance increases each year. And the more this imbalance increases, the more the requirement of celibacy seems counterproductive. For some places in the world, where priestly celibacy is not well observed by its priests, there is even less weight to the value of celibacy as a symbol for the Church.

One surprising event relative to this question is worth noting. As early as 1969, the Union of Superiors General of all the religious orders from around the world met in Rome for a synod. The question was raised about mandatory celibacy for the diocesan clergy. They agreed that celibacy was a great value for the Church. However, many religious superiors held the opinion that celibacy should remain obligatory for religious order priests, but that celibacy for diocesan priests should be optional. Their discussion seemed to include the notion of weighing the two values, celibacy vs. the availability of sacraments. When they finally prepared to vote on this issue, they were told that the ballots had to be signed by each member, so the pope (and the Curia?) would know how each member voted. As a result, the proposition failed.

Celibacy for priests is a **discipline** of the Church; it is certainly not a matter of **faith**. It has been a universal requirement for Latin priests only since the eleventh century. And throughout all of our history, the Church made exceptions for oriental priests and for priests who were converts from other Christian churches. Rather than aggressively debating the issue publicly (as sometimes has occurred), wouldn't it be more reasonable for the Church to call for a high-level commission to study this issue privately and thoroughly? One universal answer may not be the best solution. There may be several ways of deciding this issue that will permit the Church to provide the sacraments to our Church throughout the world.

There are many other disciplines of the Church found in canon law that have been reexamined by the Church over the past 100 years, and many that have been officially changed. The new Code of Canon Law, which was published in 1983, included numerous changes. Such reform of Church law is evidence that Rome believes in the notion of *ecclesia semper reformanda* (the Church is always in need of reform). Wisely, when the Church reflected on the more important changes in our modern culture, they saw the need to change some of these canonical rules. With lightning-like changes in our secular world, some prudent changes in canon law can also be expected. Whenever individual laws that are not based on

Scripture are being reconsidered, then this rule of prudence might guide the Roman decisions for possible change: Prudence demands that when a discipline causes more harm than good in the Church, it should be modified or removed.

REFLECTIONS

1. In 1983, the total number of canon laws was reduced by a quarter in the Church. Would you prefer even fewer laws?

2. In your experience, how do you feel about the discipline of celibacy for Catholic clergy? How do you see the pros and cons relating to this issue?

3. What is your opinion about liturgical practices, especially in the Mass, being the same throughout the world? How much diversity should be permitted in liturgical practices in order to accommodate the variety of cultures in our 21st century?

CHAPTER 9

A Very Human Church

In the next few chapters, let us talk about our human Church. Just as we must believe that Jesus, the Son of God, was truly human, with all the limitations of human living, so also God's kingdom on earth is a very human kingdom. The Catholic Church, which is a prominent form of God's kingdom, is a very human Church. It is made up of millions of poor, obscure, uneducated, unimportant people. Worse than that, it is made up of many scandalous, sinful, even repulsive people. For example, some Church leaders abuse their authority and make it a means of autocratic rule instead of servant leadership. Others in the Church take rigid moral positions and condemn other self-righteously. Others are proud of their racial standing and are quite prejudiced. Others are often selfish, mean, petty, thoughtless, or unkind. To many people, this human element in the Church of Christ is a "stumbling block." They protest that they cannot belong to such a faulty, sinful, proud, legalistic Church of Christ.

However, for many of us this Catholic Church, so very human and faulty, is also divine in the sense that it is the Body of Christ on earth and its soul is the Spirit of God. It teaches the message of Jesus, which can only perdure in a community of faith. It is the means of our relating to Jesus, which we cannot do alone. It is the source of grace and salvation in keeping with the mind of Jesus. It is our spiritual home, in which all the ultimate questions about human life are adequately answered for all ages. It is the supporting group that moves us to a love of God and our neighbor, after the model of Jesus, our Savior. It is the enduring source of hope in Jesus, who conquered the world and rose from the dead.

After I was a priest for a few years and took off the rose-colored glasses that newly ordained priests commonly wear, I began to see how human this Church of Christ really is. I had been teaching mathematics and religion at Quigley Preparatory Seminary in Chicago in the 1960s. At that time, we happened to have a U.S. president, a Chicago cardinal, and many Chicago politicians who were at least poor leaders, or at worst corrupt. One day I was talking to Fr. Michael Hartnett, a professor of history at Quigley. I complained to Mike that so many of our political and church leaders were inadequate, shady, or corrupt. Mike listened to me for a while and then answered, "So what's new about that? Throughout all of history, there have been leaders who do more harm to their people than good, because they only revel in positions of authority and power." I knew that Mike was not a pessimist or cynic; he was just a fine and very realistic historian. The older I get, the more I realize that there will always be people in authority who are ineffective in their work, or lovers of power, and they will exist in all walks of life. So there are bound to be people in the Church also who restrict good people or do great harm. That historical perspective can serve us well, now, in the Church. We can even be assured that there will always be leaders in the Church who are more concerned with their position than with service, who are afraid of all forms of democracy, and so restrict collaboration and shared responsibility on all levels; they mistrust change in the Church and are negative towards any kind of reform.

I spent ten years teaching at Quigley Seminary in Chicago. The faculty consisted of about twenty priests and four lay people (who were the first laity on the faculty). I grew to appreciate them all as the most intelligent, educated, mature, and spiritual group of people I would ever know. We often discussed politics and religion in our free time. During those years of the 1960s, there were many leaders to be proud of; Pope John XXIII and President John F. Kennedy were outstanding examples. But we also saw another president who was impeached, a cardinal who was authoritarian, governors of Illinois who eventually went to prison, a contentious Chicago

City Council, and politicians caught up in scandals. When we were particularly discouraged with such ineffective leaders, someone on the faculty brought us up short by recalling an observation by Sir Winston Churchill. He first agreed that democracy often had inadequate, corrupt leaders, and ineffective, unjust laws, and therefore was a defective form of government. But, he wisely added, "Democracy is an ineffective form of government—until we consider all the alternatives." Something similar could be said of our human institutional Church: It does not have the best form of government or consistently fine leaders, but there is no ideal alternative.

We have all noticed over the years how politicians and church leaders are very reluctant to admit faults, and will only offer an apology when some grave moral failure has been made public. And even worse, leaders of nations almost never apologize for the sins of their government. When was the last time you heard a national leader apologize to his people or to the world about a major injustice his country perpetrated on former generations or on some other country? However, one Sunday in Rome in the millennium year of 2000, Pope John Paul II did something no pope had ever done. In the spirit of the millennium jubilee year, he asked forgiveness for the Church's major failures throughout history. He solemnly asked God's mercy for past sins committed by the leaders and members of the Catholic Church. His inspiration for doing this is found in Scripture. Like the people of Israel in the Psalms, he and the Church acknowledged a history of rebellion, of sin, and of failures (Ps 78:40-56).

Pope John Paul II agreed that the "scandals of the past can become an obstacle to the Church's witness today," for such actions are a betrayal of the gospel. Then he humbly asked forgiveness of God and people throughout the world for the grave harm and injustice done by the Church throughout 2,000 years. The following is his humble apology; however, the last four items are my own additions. The Church seeks forgiveness for:

- Persecution and oppression of Jews throughout history, especially the horror of the Holocaust
- Intolerance of Islam and condemnation of Muslims, both during the crusades and in our day
- Contributing to Christian divisions by corrupt leadership and antagonism to other faiths throughout the second millennium
- Using violence and torture in the service of truth, especially during the Inquisition
- Tolerance of slavery and a perduring sense of superiority over African Americans and Native Americans
- Humiliation and marginalization of women in the Church
- Condemnation of homosexuals and offenses against gay members
- Causing grave suffering to communities and victims because of sexual abuse by priests and mismanagement of this by bishops
- Condemning theologians and Catholics without due process

For all these grave injustices by leaders or members of the Church, forgiveness was humbly asked. In the words of Pope John Paul II, the Church "takes upon herself the weight of past faults in order to purify memory and to live the renewal of the heart and life according to the will of the Lord." He hoped that acknowledging the sins of the past "can foster renewal and reconciliation in the present." Such actions can also awaken our consciences to the faults of the present. All of us who are followers of the compassionate Jesus are in need of constant purification. Our repeated prayer is that God may purify us and renew our Church.

In the following chapters, I want to inquire about some aspects of the human Church in the spirit expressed by Vatican II for free expression in the Church: "[L]et it be acknowledged that all the faithful, clerical and lay, possess a lawful freedom of inquiry…and the freedom to express their minds humbly and courageously about those matters in which they enjoy competence."[89] Then, seven years after the council concluded, Rome published a "Pastoral Instruction on the Means of Social Communication," in which it commented positively on the value of public opinion in the Church: "Catholics should be fully aware of the real freedom to speak their minds …. Those who exercise authority in the Church will take care to insure that there is responsible exchange of freely held and expressed opinion among the People of God …."[90]

However, when we talk about needed reform in the institutional Church, we want to do it in a proper attitude of Christian criticism. St. Thomas Aquinas, in his premier work, *Summa Theologica,* asks whether one can and should criticize his ecclesiastical superior. He then answers:

> Fraternal criticism, which is an act of love, is a matter for everyone in regard to anyone whomsoever he is meant to love [but] in criticism of an ecclesiastical superior by a subordinate, an appropriate manner of criticism must be used; it must not be imprudent and harsh but mild and respectful. [Then he quotes 1 Tm 5:1:] "Do not rebuke an older man, but appeal to him as a father."[91]

In addition, Thomas refers to the example of Paul correcting Peter (cf. Gal 2:11-14). He even cites Augustine to the effect that, in that instance, Peter left an example to those in authority; that should they stray from the right path, they

---

89   *AAS,* 1966, 1084; *Gaudium et Spes,* 62.

90   "Pastoral Instruction on the Means of Social Communication" nos. 115-119, found in *Vatican Council II,* ed Austin Flannery, OP, (Northport, NY: Costello, 1975), pp. 330-31.

91   Thomas Aquinas, *Summa Theologica,* II-II, q. 33, art. 4.

should not resist being corrected by others. In the next couple chapters, I want to take a realistic look at some of the things that happened in the Church since Vatican Council II, and then gently and respectfully criticize some elements of the institutional Church.

In the early years following the council, there were more notable changes throughout the Church than at any other time in its history, with the exception of its first 100 years, and the time of the Reformation. The liturgical changes were most impressive, the synods of bishops were promising, the gathering of national conferences of bishops seemed to offer hope for regional changes, the reform of parishes in terms of councils and boards introduced representative structures, and the formation of many new organizations of the laity indicated the emergence of new life. For many in the Church in those years, there seemed to be an enthusiastic march, a great forward progression of a church with a shared vision and purpose. But little by little, there was a growing reaction from the Roman Curia, which had opposed much of what happened during the council. As Monica Hellwig observed:

> The reaction [of the curia] was one of new efforts to centralize and control everything. We have seen efforts to control language in the liturgy, in Bible translations, in instruction …. We have seen efforts to curtail the freedom of bishops and bishops' conferences to teach and to speak according to their own pastoral discernment. We have seen efforts to assert canonical control over freestanding institutions such as hospitals and universities and colleges.[92]

My favorite rabbinical story, told to me by a Jewish lady in 1969, is appropriate here. In order for us to understand the significance of this story for our discussion, we need to describe what happened in the Church in the twentieth century. Before the council, some people felt **badly** about things they

---

92   Monica Hellwig, "A Note on Vatican II", p. 126.

experienced in the Church. The Mass was in Latin, with the priest facing away from the people and acting as the sole celebrant; canon law was in need of reform; theologians had to seek an *imprimatur* (permission to print) for anything they wrote; and the new guidelines for Scripture study were not yet well known. Then came Vatican II, and many of the same people began to feel **good** about the Church again. The liturgy and Mass were transformed in a short time, with English and lay participation in many forms; Catholic Scripture scholars were just beginning to catch up with others in the new norms of interpreting Scripture; the bold statements of the council about freedom of religion, collegiality, and ecumenism warmed their hearts. They witnessed the Church being reformed! The people even began to speak up in the Church and even to **sing out** that the restrictive days were now over. But many of those in authority in the institutional Church were convinced that all this change and freedom would destroy the Church's authority as they perceived it. So they began to pull back the reins on reform and succeeded in reversing many of the changes. They couldn't destroy the reform, but they certainly wanted to restrain it.

Now, this classic story told by the rabbis can be a wonderful metaphor for what happened in the Church in those years. It takes place in Russia, many years ago, on one of the coldest days of the winter. An elderly Russian was walking along the road and noticed a sparrow on the side of the road that seemed almost frozen, with ice on his wings. The old gentleman went over to the motionless sparrow and picked him up. He held it against his chest, and tried to warm it up with his gloves. But the air was so bitterly cold, he was not able to really help the sparrow. Then he saw a horse-drawn carriage pass by on the road, and as he watched, the horse dropped some manure on the road. He noticed steam coming up from the manure and thought maybe that would restore the bird, so he went over and made a donut of the manure and put the bird in it. He stood there for a while and watched the little bird begin to shake itself and then slowly get rid of the ice on its wings. In a few moments, the sparrow felt much better and then began to chirp and sing. The old man felt good about all this and walked away. But nearby, in some bushes, there was a fox that noticed the sparrow; he ran out on the road, grabbed the bird and ate him! There are three morals to this story. The first moral: Not everyone who puts you into the manure is your enemy. The second: Not everyone who takes you out of it is your friend. And the third is: When you're in it, don't sing!

REFLECTIONS

1. In your relationships with pastors you have known, think of someone whom you considered a poor leader. What qualities made him a poor leader? Would you be less offended by him after considering this chapter?

2. Reflect on Pope John Paul II's apology for the grave harm and injustice done by the Catholic Church throughout its 2,000 years. Would you agree with the individual points he made?

3. What is your reaction to the classic rabbinical story at the end of this chapter?

CHAPTER 10

Ways of Being Pope

On May 25, 1995, Pope John Paul II published his encyclical, *Ut unum sint* (That They May be One).[93] The entire encyclical was a notable contribution to ecumenism, but one section of it can only be called revolutionary. In it, the pope admits that the papacy itself constitutes a difficulty for most other Christians.[94] And he personally wants to respond to this problem for ecumenism regarding the other Christian churches:

> I am convinced that I have a particular responsibility … above all in acknowledging the ecumenical aspirations of the majority of the Christian Communities and in heeding the request made of me to find a way of exercising the primacy which, while in no way renouncing what is essential to its mission, is nonetheless open to a new situation.[95]

This call for the reform of the papacy itself was entirely unique in modern history. The radical and precedent-setting character of the encyclical has not been fully appreciated by Catholics in general, but within three years of its publication it elicited serious and thoughtful responses from Olivier Clement, an Orthodox theologian,[96] as well as from the Church of England,[97] and from Herrmann Pottmeyer.[98] Also, in 1996, the Congregation for the Doctrine of the Faith sponsored a

---

93 Pope John Paul II, *Ut unum sint* (Vatican City: Libreria Editrice Vaticana, 1995).

94 Ibid. par. 88. As John Quinn notes below, Pope Paul V, himself, sought ways of reforming the papacy because he saw it as an obstacle to Christian unity.

95 Ibid. par.95.

96 Olivier Clement, *Rome autrement* (Paris: Desclee de Brouwer, 1997).

97 A formal response from the Church of England was entitled *That They All May Be One* (London: Church House Publishing, 1997).

98 Hermann Pottmeyer, *Toward a Reform of the Papacy* (NY: Crossroad, 1998). This was a carefully reasoned discussion on the reform of the papacy.

symposium on the primacy of the pope in Rome.[99]

A very cautious and prudent response came from Archbishop John Quinn, to whom I am indebted for much of what follows in chapters 10, 11, and 12. He first indicates how unique this formal request of the pope really is:

> For the first time it is the Pope himself who raises and legitimizes the question of **reform and change in the papal office of the church.** Pope John Paul II calls for a widespread discussion of how this reform could be brought about and what shape it could take.[100]

In his encyclical, *Ut unum sint,* the pope acknowledged that such reform is critical and basic for his entire ecumenical stand toward fostering unity among the Christian churches. Our Holy Father agrees with Pope Paul VI: "In accordance with the hope expressed by Pope Paul VI, our declared purpose is to re-establish together **full unity in legitimate diversity."**[101] His stated attitude toward diversity in the Church is not grudging tolerance, but positive acceptance: "… [L]egitimate diversity is in no way opposed to the Church's unity, but rather … contributes greatly to the fulfillment of her mission."[102]

Though the pope does not spell out in detail what legitimate diversity is, he does offer an overriding principle of imposing nothing beyond what is necessary: "In this process, one must not impose any burden beyond that which is strictly necessary."[103] And he is aware that diversity was a quality of the early Church, for the New Testament itself, and the history of the first 200 years of the Church, manifest considerable differences both in structure and practice in the one Church

---

99   Published in *Il primato del successore di Pietro* (Vatican City: Libreria Editrice Vaticana, 1997).

100 John R. Quinn, *The Reform of the Papacy* (NY: Crossroad, 1999), p. 14 (emphasis added).

101 Pope John Paul II in *Ut unum sint, par. 57.*

102 Ibid. par. 50.

103 Ibid. par. 78.

of Christ. But he does add a practical model for a new way of practicing the primacy of Peter:

For a whole millennium Christians were united in a "brotherly fraternal communion of faith and sacramental life …. If disagreements in belief and discipline arose among them, the Roman See acted by common consent as moderator."[104]

The pope then explains that the Church in the first millennium could be a model in terms of both structures and practices:

… [T]he unity, which … was experienced in the first millennium … in a certain sense   serves as a model …. The structures of the Church in the East and in the West evolved in reference to that apostolic heritage. … If today at the end of the second millennium we are seeking to restore full communion, it is to that unity, thus structured, which we must look.[105]

What were the structures of the first millennium that should serve as a model? First, in the early Church, even though the Bishop of Rome was an indispensable norm of ecclesial community and had a unique role of primacy, he did not intervene in the affairs of the other Christian communities on a routine basis or in normal times. Rather, he generally intervened **only in periods of crisis,** especially those having to do with matters of faith that could be definitely resolved only in union with Rome; even the Eastern Church recognized this norm.[106] Therefore, if the first millennium is to serve as a model in this way, it would not include a **routine** role for the bishop of Rome in the affairs of regional churches throughout the world.

To conclude this study of the encyclical *Ut unum sint,* we can summarize it by paraphrasing the conclusion of Archbishop John Quinn in *The Reform of the Papacy:* It was

---

104   Ibid. par. 95.

105   Ibid. par. 55.

106   See Klaus Schatz, *Papal Primacy* (Collegeville MN: Liturgical Press, 1996), pp. 59-60.

clearly precedent setting, even revolutionary, because the pope himself encouraged a discussion of the papacy by all Christians, with the goal of finding a new way of exercising that primacy, modeled after the Church of the first millennium. This meant that the papacy would continue to have a unique role of primacy, but would not regularly interfere in the affairs of the other regional churches, except in serious crises.[107]

Archbishop Quinn wrote his book as a response to an encouraging suggestion of Pope John Paul II himself. Shortly after he published his book, he came to the retreat house at St. Mary of the Lake Seminary in Mundelein, IL. I attended the retreat that he directed. One evening, in a discussion session, I asked him what kind of reception his book received in Rome. He told us that he went to Rome and personally gave a copy of his book to Pope John Paul II and to others in the Curia. The pope received it without comment, and the curial members never had a negative comment about his book. He then added that many other Catholic and Christian leaders were almost unanimous in their appreciation of his work. He also explained that while he was writing the book he sought the suggestions and criticisms of countless Christian leaders and scholars. When we asked him how many revisions he made of the book before the final version, he answered simply, "About 20!"

REFLECTIONS

1. In the encyclical, *Ut Unum Sint,* Pope John Paul II admits that the papacy itself constitutes a difficulty for most other Christians. Recall personal experiences when someone questioned or criticized the authority of the pope. How did you react?

2. What do you think about the pope's suggestion that the structures and procedures of the first millennium of the Church might be a model for our modern Church? Do you

---

107 See John Quinn, p. 34.

think the Church would remain secure, if the pope only intervened in matters of crisis?

3. Given the diverse history of papal authority in the Church, do you think it necessary that the pope reserve to himself all important decisions? Would you prefer that some decisions be made by national conferences of bishops?

CHAPTER 11

Problems with the Roman Curia

The Roman Curia consists of all the leading members of the various formal congregations of the Vatican. Individual congregations (or "dicasteries," the word comes from the Greek word for court) deal with specific ministries of the universal Church: doctrine of the faith, ecumenism, bishops, clergy and religious, lay organizations, sacraments, Scripture, and marriage tribunals. Historically, from the earliest times there were always advisors to the pope. Gradually, over a period of centuries, the structure of advisors became more elaborate. In the eleventh century, the advisors were first called the "Roman Curia." Then in the sixteenth century, Pope Sixtus V established multiple congregations and tribunals along the lines of the Curia today. The modern Curia is a large bureaucracy of more than 1,700 people. Few people understand its complex structure, overlapping jurisdictions, and Byzantine procedures. The structures of the Curia have been copied from secular governments such as the ancient Roman senate and the Byzantine imperial court. In the twentieth century, three popes—Pius X, Paul VI and John Paul II—have introduced changes into the Curia.

Let us begin our discussion about the Roman Curia with the time immediately **before** Vatican Council II. During those years (1959-1962), there was a strong cry for decentralization and reform of the Curia.[108] Many bishops throughout the world had a decidedly negative attitude toward the Curia. For some, the Curia was a barrier between the episcopate and the Pope; others regarded the Curia as high-handed and autocratic,

---

108 See Kevin Smyth, "Curia Reform and Present Structure," in *Sacramentum Mundi,* vol. 2, p. 52. Also, Thomas Reese, SJ, *Inside the Vatican* (Cambridge, MS: Harvard University Press, 1996). John O'Malley claims that "few would have wagered that an overwhelming majority of bishops, hovering between 85 and 90 percent, would so early on, so consistently and so insistently side with "the Transalpines;" see John O'Malley, p. 290.

superior to the bishops. Edward Schillebeeckx noted that, "Many bishops did not want so much a new approach in theology as to break the power of the Curia where it set itself above the bishops."[109]

During the council, Pope Paul VI was aware of the strong feelings of the bishops about the Curia and personally invited the council to discuss the issue. The results of the discussions on the reform of the Curia are found in the Vatican Council decree, *Christus Dominus* (Decree on the Pastoral Office of Bishops in the Church). The decree calls for a reorganization of the Curia:

> The Fathers of the Sacred Council [very much desire] … that these departments should be reorganized in a manner more appropriate to the needs of our time and of the different regions and rites, especially in regard to their number, their titles, [and] their procedures …."[110]

Specifically, Vatican II called for three changes in the Curia: 1) internationalization of the members of the congregations; 2) better communication among the departments; and 3) participation by diocesan bishops and laity.

Admittedly, there has been significant internationalization of the members of the congregations since 1965. At least two-thirds of the heads of Vatican congregations now come from countries other than Italy. However, an unexpected problem soon arose in that many of these new curial members often became Romanized; that is, after a short time they tended to lose their national identity and their real contact with their own countries.

Also, communication among the departments of the Curia is still a problem, causing some embarrassment and confusion at times. The purpose of assigning more bishops and laity to

---

109 Edward Schillebeeckx, *Je suis un theologien heureux* (Paris: Edition du Cerf, 1995), p. 46.
110 *AAS*, 1966, 676; *Christus Dominus*, 9.

the Curia was so that they could represent to the pope and the Curia the mind, aspirations, and needs of all the churches. Though many international bishops have been appointed to the Curia, even when other Roman congregations were dealing with the bishops' own native countries, they did not adequately consult the native bishops. And regarding the participation of laity on the congregations, thirty-five years after the council half the Roman congregations still had no lay members.

During the **first days** of Vatican II, there were two major turning points that emphasized the negative attitude of the council fathers, as we saw above (pp. 8-9). On the very first day of the council, the bishops of the council rejected the list of committee chairmen suggested by the Curia, and a few days later they voted against the draft of the important document on Scripture and Tradition drawn up by the curial theologians. In such a dramatic way, the institutional power of Roman Catholicism had swung from the Curia to the Council of Bishops, at least for much of the council.

Later in the council, the bishops appealed to Pope Paul VI about the continuing autocratic ways of the Curia. Wisely, the pope invited the council fathers to discuss the problems regarding the way that the Curia dominated the early stages of the council. With his positive input, some of the bishops' suggestions for the reform of the Curia were eventually included in the *Decree on the Pastoral Office of Bishops in the Church (Christus Dominus).* As the bishops discussed collegiality in the council, they expressed intense feelings regarding the power of the pope and the Curia over the conferences of bishops. The issue of the Roman Curia controlling and dominating the bishops' conferences became a hot issue for the great majority of bishops. Yet when the *Decree on the Pastoral Office of Bishops (Christus Dominus)* finally was published, there was only a short passage reflecting the bishops' strong objections, and the tenor of that passage was placid and weak. As a result, the bishops achieved a somewhat satisfying council **document,** but failed to gain the substantial and effective **reforms** they so intensely sought.

After the council, Paul VI continued to try to reform the Curia. He himself was not conservative, but he was not willing to endure constant turmoil among the Curia fathers. His approach was moderate and conciliatory. He seemed to be convinced that he should continue to reach out to the more conservative members of the Curia, while gradually appointing more moderate members. The goal may have been gradually to let the greater diversity of members and the eventual influence of the council lead to positive reform. In 1967, Pope Paul VI finally made an effort to restructure the Curia; he instituted new councils and placed them under the authority of two secretaries of state. He appointed Archbishop Giovanni Benelli secretary of state for internal affairs and Archbishop Agostino Casaroli secretary of state for external affairs. And he had the curial officials report to these two trusted men more and more; but some curial officials were not happy with that arrangement, because they no longer reported directly to the pope himself.

As Pope Paul VI grew older, he realized the Curia was not willing to change; so he shifted course and more often supported the conservative members of the Curia. Near the end of his papacy, the constant turmoil made him feel more isolated and unwilling to force further reform; as a result, the leading conservative members gradually regained control of the process and found ways to obstruct reforms. And the progressive block of bishops, who earlier had been delighted with Paul's part in the council, found themselves somewhat alienated from the pope.[111]

Meanwhile, between the years 1966-1970, the National Pastoral Council of the Netherlands was held, followed by synods in Germany and Austria. At these councils, every imaginable topic was discussed and voted upon. These

---

111 See Rembert Weakland, *A Pilgrim in a Pilgrim Church,* pp. 219-20.

national councils seemed to project a model of church that was local, congregational, and democratic, as an alternative to the traditional, hierarchical model. The Curia saw the Dutch National Council—and to a lesser degree, the synods of Germany and Austria—as splitting the Church and setting one faction against the other. Pope Paul became alarmed, and throughout the 1970s again and again appointed very conservative bishops in Holland. The reaction in the Church of Holland was deep bitterness and division, resulting in many priests leaving the priesthood and the laity feeling confused and betrayed. The previously vibrant Dutch Church became weak and in disarray.

Finally, just a few words about the long and influential pontificate of Pope John Paul II. Much of chapter 10, above, was taken up with the pope's own call for the reform of the way the papacy operated. And chapter 12 will cover his dealings with the national conference of bishops. Here, let me make just one general comment related to the pope's approach to reform in the Church and in the Curia. As we will see in chapter 12, his pontificate was marked by a centralizing tendency in terms of the Holy See and an emphasis on papal teaching to the exclusion of other ideas.

Where is the Church **today** in terms of the Curia? Many bishops today would consider that some members of the Curia seem to have a proprietary sense over the Church, avoiding any reform of the Curia itself, resisting new liturgical reforms, censoring theologians, appointing new bishops with little or no consultation of the local episcopate, and restricting the power of the bishops. In the next chapter we will consider the national conferences of bishops, in terms of the pope and the Curia.

REFLECTIONS

1. Briefly describe the responsibility of the Roman Curia, as you see it. Explain how the institutional power of Roman Catholicism had swung from the Roman Curia to the

councils of bishops in the first days after Vatican Council II.

2. "The popes come and go throughout the years, but the Curia remains!" That is the cynical comment about the difficulty any pope has in trying to reform the Curia. Would it take another Ecumenical Council to bring about curial reform?

3. Describe how Pope Paul VI moved from being a moderate and conciliatory leader to a more conservative one after the close of Vatican Council II.

CHAPTER 12

Limitations on Bishops

At Vatican Council II, the bishops made two surprising early moves to change the agenda and tenor of the council (as above, pp. 8-9). They managed to overcome the strong hand of the Curia, who had tried to direct the whole process. These two epoch-making moves were the turning point for the rest of the council. The resulting documents of Vatican II were truly an *aggiornamento* for the whole Church, because of the continuous efforts of the attending bishops, along with their personally chosen expert theologians (*periti*).

One primary concern of the bishops was to finish the work of Vatican I, which proclaimed the primacy of the Petrine office, but was not able to clearly delineate the doctrine of the collegiality of the bishops of the world and their relationship to the pope. Now in Vatican II, they needed to articulate the doctrine of the collegiality of the bishops at the same time as they affirmed the true primacy of the pope. During the third session of Vatican II, from Oct. 20 to Nov. 10, 1964, the new draft of the Pastoral Constitution of the Church in the Modern World was discussed. After much discussion, the council wanted to get an expression of the bishops on two propositions regarding collegiality. The first proposition read:

> The Body or College of Bishops succeeds to the college of the apostles in its function of evangelizing, sanctifying and pastoring. And this Body, in union with its head, the Roman Pontiff, and never without its head ..., enjoys full and sovereign power over the universal Church.[112]

And the second asserted: "This power belongs to the College of Bishops, united to its head, **by divine right**."[113] When the

---

112 J. Grootaers, *Primaute et Collegialite* (Leuven: Leuven University Press, 1986), p. 29.

113 Ibid. (emphasis added).

vote was taken, the great majority of bishops approved both propositions. These both became the solemn teaching of the council's constitution on the Church, *Lumen Gentium.* That meant that the collegiality of the bishops is clearly essential to the Church by divine right. Therefore, the college of bishops must be enabled to function effectively in the Church.

Shortly after the end of the council, Pope Paul VI convened an International Synod of Bishops from around the world. Such **international** synods were proposed by the pope in order to promote closer cooperation between the pope and the college of bishops. But within a few years, the synods had become more and more closely orchestrated and controlled by Rome. These international synods were usually held in Rome, and the prefects of the Roman Curia were members of the conferences. The topics for discussion and the *instrumenta laboris* (division of work) were controlled by Vatican officials. The synod did not have a deliberative vote; its deliberations were secret, and the pope wrote and issued the final document after the bishops had returned home. Because of all these tight restrictions, within a short time these international synods lost much of their potential for free discussion, sharing information, or choice of pastoral options.

But during the 1970s and 1980s, there were several **national conferences of bishops** that were quite effective; they were held in France, England and Wales, Canada, the U.S., and other nations. Some of the documents published by these conferences were excellent; as for example, the two letters by the U.S. Bishops on the economy and on peace. These two documents were so well received that they were considered to be models for other bishops' conferences.

During these twenty years after the council, the proper theological basis for these episcopal conferences was often discussed. The position of Vatican II seemed to be that these conferences were not just an administrative convenience but rather a providential development; they appeared to be a valuable new intermediary between the pope and the bishops. As early as 1964, Joseph Ratzinger affirmed the value of these national episcopal conferences and **rejected the opinion** that these national conferences lacked any theological basis; he called such an opinion distorted and one sided: "The collegiality of bishops signifies that there should be in the Church … an ordered plurality. The bishops' conferences are, then, one of the possible forms of collegiality that is here **partially realized** but with a view to the totality."[114] That is, he affirmed that the bishops' conferences **did have theological basis** even if they were only a partial expression of the total Church.

But then, in 1984, Ratzinger **drastically changed** his point of view: "We must not forget that the episcopal conferences have **no theological basis ….**"[115] What led him to make such a drastic change? The cautious answer is, it was a fear that the conferences were becoming a threat to papal authority, reminiscent of the council-versus-pope controversy of the Middle Ages. Strangely, Cardinal Ratzinger's position seems opposed to the new Code of Canon Law, which came out in 1983. Canon 753 expressly states: "Bishops … gathered in conferences of bishops … are **authentic doctors** and teachers … of the faith."

In 1985, an Extraordinary Synod of Bishops was convened and a resolution was approved asking for a further study of the teaching authority of the episcopal conferences. But it was not until thirteen years later, in 1998, that Pope John Paul II responded to that request of the bishops through an apostolic letter (*motu proprio*),"On the Theological and Juridical Nature of Episcopal Conferences." In this formal letter, the pope clearly limited the ability of these conferences to declare any doctrinal

---

114 Joseph Ratzinger, "The Pastoral Implications of Episcopal Collegiality," in *Consilium* (Glen Rock, NJ:Paulist Press, 1964) (emphasis added).

115 Joseph Cardinal Ratzinger with Vittorio Messori, *The Ratzinger Report* (San Francisco: Ignatius Press, 1985), pp. 59-60 (emphasis added).

teachings. In particular, he determined that any **doctrinal** declaration of an episcopal conference must be approved **unanimously** by all the bishops or, alternately, if approved by a two-thirds majority, they needed the approval of the Holy See before they could be published. Such a stringent criterion is greater than that required in any other form of ecclesiastical teaching. Since such unanimity is not likely to be achieved, this requirement in effect rules out a doctrinal role for any episcopal conference and reduces the vitality of the national conferences of bishops.

Two other conclusions also should be mentioned: First, the very promising proposal of Pope Paul VI and Vatican II about how the collaboration of the bishops with the pope as a part of the ordinary magisterium (teaching authority) of the Church had been gradually undermined over a period of thirty-five years. The conciliar documents that spoke of a more active engagement on the part of bishops' conferences in the decisions that affected the life of the national Church were now diluted and ineffectual. The papal and curial control of the bishops' conferences was now total. Second, the practical result of this Roman policy that diminished the doctrinal authority of the bishops' conferences is that Catholics tended not to pay attention to the national conferences of their own country.

One other issue concerning bishops is very important for the Church today: the selection and appointment of bishops. We might start with the way ordinaries (i.e., bishops who head dioceses) were chosen in the U.S. Some neighboring bishops were usually consulted, and some priests in the diocese itself were asked to recommend names. The names of three priests would be suggested as likely candidates. Each episcopal candidate was then asked to answer a lengthy questionnaire. (If any of his answers indicated that he was in favor of married priests, women priests, or birth control, he would not be recommended to the apostolic delegate in Washington, D.C.) The apostolic delegate, then, sent his candidate-choices to

Rome. Finally, the pope made his choice. In this process, the apostolic delegate is the important intermediary with the pope.

In the period 1974-1981, our apostolic delegate was Archbishop Jean Jadot. Jadot was most conscientious about recommending episcopal candidates. He would analyze what the particular diocese needed, consult with bishops and priests of that diocese, and then send his three choices to Rome. The choices he customarily made were more often pastoral-minded men rather than administrative-minded. They tended to be open-minded and independent thinkers. So, most of the bishops appointed in the U.S. in those years were popular and open-minded priests, not men who were looking for Rome to validate everything they did. However, once Archbishop Pio Laghi succeeded Jadot as apostolic delegate in 1980, episcopal appointments changed in the U.S. His first two major choices were Cardinal John O'Connor of New York and Archbishop Bernard Law of Boston. After them, other conservative bishops were chosen quite regularly. During Pio Laghi's five years as apostolic delegate, he named almost 100 new bishops.

Another strange occurrence happened in Austria in 1986. Cardinal Koenig, one of the leading bishops of Vatican II, was not even consulted about his own successor. Such a lack of consultation with leading national bishops was repeated in various countries throughout the world. That is, archbishops were sometimes not consulted about Rome's choices for local diocesan bishops, nor were religious order superiors consulted about members of their own orders who were being considered for appointments as diocesan bishops. The situation in Holland became a prime example. After the bishops and laity held their very open and democratic national council, Rome felt threatened by a very diverse and independent Church there. So Rome independently chose archconservative bishops in several dioceses, in order to control the situation in Holland. As a result, Rome managed to centralize the Church there, but it lost many of Holland's priests and people, who felt betrayed by the Church.

We might summarize the effect of Roman influence in the national and international conferences of bishops and in the appointment of individual new bishops this way:

> … [T]he increasingly close supervision and scrutiny by the pope, working through the Roman curial offices, … have resulted in the selection of bishops … who are reluctant to take prophetic stances that could be interpreted as lack of loyalty to the Holy See. Never before in the history of the Catholic Church … has the papacy held such a controlling command over the church universal. … Closely connected with that phenomenon … has been a diminishment in the teaching office of bishops, specifically through episcopal conferences.[116]

REFLECTIONS

1. Bishops, as leaders of dioceses, have been selected in innumerable ways throughout history. If you had your "druthers," how would you like to see them selected?

2. In your view, can a local bishop ever dissent from the pope's teaching in non-dogmatic matters? Why or why not?

3. Reflect on the mission of the bishops as leading teachers of the faith in their own diocese. What would you consider some of the prerogatives and limits of their mission?

---

116 Michael A. Fahey, "Some Trends in American Catholic Theology Since 1965," in Dermot A. Lane, ed., *Catholic Theology Facing the Future*, p. 64.

CHAPTER 13

Censures of Theologians

In our study of Vatican Council II (above, pp.10-11), we noted the influence of Yves Congar on Pope John XXIII's decision to convoke Vatican II. Yet, only a few years before the beginning of the council, Congar had been removed from his teaching position. Also, outstanding theologians Edward Schillebeeckx and Karl Rahner, as well as other theologians whose writings had been criticized by Rome or who had been removed from teaching posts, became the theological force behind the entire work of the council. Schillebeeckx was not even permitted to be a *peritus* (a bishop's personally chosen expert theologian) at the council. Despite that, it was the theology of such men, who had been condemned in some way, which triumphed at the council.[117]

One transforming development changed the way many theologians studied our faith, particularly the central teachings of Christology. Shortly after the council, Catholic theologians realized that decades of historical research by Scripture scholars needed to be incorporated into Christology and other teachings. That is, Christology should not begin from the doctrines of the Incarnation, as Thomas Aquinas did; nor should the methods of Scholasticism be its primary focus. Rather, it should begin from the New Testament narratives, the story of how the man Jesus is discovered as Lord; for the origins of our faith are the New Testament account of the life, death, and resurrection of Jesus Christ. Therefore, those gospel narratives need to be scrutinized in the light of the best modern scriptural exegesis.[118]

During most of the twentieth century, Scripture scholars created an upheaval in the Christian churches regarding

---

117   See Fergus Kerr, *Twentieth Century Catholic Theologians*, p. 65.

118   Ibid. p. 59.

the question of how much of the New Testament is strictly historical and what part is not. That argument regarding the historicity of the New Testament took most of the century to be solved satisfactorily. Finally, Schillebeeckx believed that the New Testament, properly studied with the tools of modern critical research, delivers substantial, verifiable information about Jesus of Nazareth. He was convinced that such critical scriptural history "… can then show us what exactly it was that very early Christianity understood by the affirmation: he is the Christ, the son of man, the Son of God, the Lord."[119] He reasoned that if Christianity is neither to become "an historical relic" nor to appeal to "supernatural hocus-pocus," its message must be reconstructed historically. Quite simply, by re-creating the scriptural history of how faith in Jesus of Nazareth arose, it becomes possible to arouse faith in Christ in people who had not been Christian believers and who would not find ready access to him through the doctrines of the Church.[120]

In the years since Schillebeeckx' book, *Jesus,* more and more theologians are considering anew the doctrines of our faith, as defined by the early councils and expounded in classical theology, and reworking them in the light of modern scriptural exegesis. Particularly in Christology (Who is Christ?) and soteriology (How did he save us?), we need to begin with Jesus as he is known in Scripture, and only then move on to the classical definitions of the early councils. Karl Rahner, probably our greatest twentieth century theologian, would agree, because for him Christianity is simply Jesus of Nazareth, and our Christian faith is embedded in the historical existence of Jesus as known first of all in Scripture. So our theology should be founded above all on the experience of Jesus Christ as Lord and Messiah as attested in Scripture.

Now let us look at what **personnel changes** have happened in the field of theology in the years after the council. In the

---

119   Edward Schillebeeckx, *Jesus,* pp. 437, 440.

120   See Fergus Kerr, pp. 60-62.

1940s and 1950s, most of our Catholic theologians were priests who taught in seminaries. Their purpose was not scholarship, for few seminary professors published scholarly articles. Rather, their purpose was to train future priests for the ministry, by teaching the classical doctrines of the Church, so that they knew enough theology to preach and teach the mysteries of faith. In the 1960s, the understanding of theology as an academic discipline began to change dramatically. The changes brought about in the field of theology, as a result of Vatican II, made theology a very appealing field of study for many Catholics. Also, as students reflected on the role of the Church in the modern world, they required academic scholarship and professionalization. The ethos of theology courses in Catholic universities moved from a simple explanation of the teachings of our faith to a more academic one, even with degree programs for ordinary students. As this trend in theology from seminaries to universities continued, many Catholic universities responded with academic courses in theology and religious education; thus, early academic departments were established at Catholic University of America, Marquette University, Notre Dame, and Fordham. The academic aspect of Catholic theology continued to intensify, and professors of theology, like all university professors, were expected to publish as well as teach. The number of books and articles published in Catholic universities soon far exceeded the number before Vatican II. The very positive result of such renewed interest in theology by Catholics in higher education was that the number and quality of theologians in the U.S. increased dramatically. Today, scholarly publishing in theology in general, and in moral theology in particular, has increased a hundredfold since the days before Vatican II. Now the number of Catholic theologians in the U.S. is far greater than in any other country of the world.[121]

And today's theologians are no longer all white males, mostly from Europe and the U.S.; rather, they are much more

---

121 Cf. Charles E. Curran, *Loyal Dissent*, (Washington, DC: Georgetown University Press, 2006), pp. 219-26.

diverse. Today we have theologians from all over the world, including Africa, Asia, and South America, whose theologies grow out of their different cultures. More significantly, many of them are women—married, single, and religious. And today, because our theology is much more complex and demanding, most theologians specialize in only one particular area of study, like Christology.

This great expansion of the number and diversity of theologians has resulted in **significant changes** in how doctrinal theology and moral theology are taught throughout the world. First, our modern Catholic theology is no longer exclusively Euro-centric. As our Church becomes increasingly a world-Church, it can no longer be dominated exclusively by European thinking; it quite rightly reflects the immense diversity of cultures and philosophies of the world.

Second, our Catholic theology seeks academic freedom and rejects authoritarian statements about non-dogmatic teachings that do not seem rationally proved. Thus Catholic **moral law** is based on "natural law" reasoning; that is, on universal truths rooted in human nature, which in principle anyone can recognize. That assumes that right and wrong, truth and falsehood, are real qualities that exist in nature, which human beings can discover using their consciences, aided by faith. Therefore, the ultimate validity for saying "x is wrong" rests on an absolute truth about human nature. If Catholic moral judgments rested ultimately not on reason but on a legislative act of the Church, we would be reduced to **positivism**, a system of morality resting principally, not on natural law, but on the authority of the Church. Similarly, **doctrinal theology** needs to be founded on rational theological arguments, not only on authoritative decisions. Certainly, the dogmas that we believe are based on Scripture and informed by our faith. And many other theological doctrines taught by the Church are certain and worthy of our belief, because they are rationally derived from Scripture. But there are many theological questions that are still conscientiously debated by theologians, without entirely convincing answers. These should remain open to discussion, without a decision from Rome that tries to close off all discussion.

The Church has reacted to the increased number and diversity of theologians by attempting to control this expansion of theological teaching and questioning in three ways. First, the Vatican now requires that anyone teaching Catholic theology in a Catholic university must have a **mandate** from the Church. That means that Rome could remove the mandate from anyone it judges to be teaching erroneous doctrines. Many theologians are most reluctant to agree to this requirement of a mandate, because they claim it violates their academic freedom, especially in terms of disputed questions.

The second means of control is by investigating or censuring individual theologians. This censuring of theologians has greatly increased in the twentieth century. In **moral and pastoral theology**, two of the greatest moralists, Bernard Haring and Joseph Fuchs, were condemned. Others were condemned or removed from teaching: Anthony Kosnik, John McNeill, Andre Guindon, Rene Simon, Sean Fagan, Charles Curran, and Tom Dailey. For moral theologians, especially, "… because the authoritative atmosphere of Rome has made it impossible for [moral] theologians to … publicly dissent from hierarchical church teaching. … [Therefore,] the development of Catholic moral theology has shifted from Rome to other parts of the globe."[122]

In **doctrinal theology**, even outstanding theologians such as Schillebeeckx and Rahner were investigated, sometimes censured, or silenced. Others in the last century were either forbidden to teach in Catholic universities or to publish: Henri de Lubac, Yves Congar, Marie-Dominique Chenu, Hans Küng, John Courtney Murray, Pierre Teilhard Chardin, Jacques

---

122   Ibid. p. 226.

Maritain, Leonardo Boff, Gustavo Guttierez, Tissa Belasuriya, Anthony de Mello, Jacques Dupuis, and Roger Haight,[123] and several others.

The final means of control is simply the privacy and injustice of the Roman procedures regarding investigations of theologians. Rome never seemed to be able to create fair and **just processes** for investigations of individual theologians. Nor did they create tribunals and courts in Rome that were examples for the rest of the Church. Cases dragged on for years; due process was not followed, and proper defenses were not regularly permitted. As a result, many theologians were confused by the processes and lived in fear of them for years.

REFLECTIONS

1. The number of theologians is increasing greatly throughout the Catholic Church. Why did this happen? Would you consider this mostly a positive development?

2. According to Edward Schillebeeckx: "If Christianity is neither to become 'an historical relic' nor to appeal to 'supernatural hocus pocus,' its message must be reconstructed historically." He means that our Christology and theology in general should begin with the historical life of Jesus: his life, ministry, teaching, death, and resurrection. What difference would that make in our understanding of church dogma?

---

123 Jacques Dupuis, SJ, and Roger Haight, SJ, have been quoted a few times in this book. They both were investigated by the Congregation for the Defense of the Faith. They both tried to answer Rome's objections to some of their writings, but were never able to completely satisfy their critics. Some of the terminology they used was quite different than the traditional language of the past, which made mutual understanding difficult. Dupuis' book was required to include a copy of the CDF "Notification," indicating some hesitation with parts of his work. However, in 2001 Pope John Paul II acknowledged Dupuis' "pioneering" work on the meaning of other religions in "God's plan of salvation of mankind." Regarding all the theologians mentioned above, it should be noted that Roman censure does not mean that all their work is suspect. Many early Christian writers were also censured by the Church, yet they are still highly regarded for their work in general. Two early Church writers, Origin and Tertullian, were censured by the Church, yet their writings are still quoted in our Breviary.

3. Regarding moral theology, if even expert theologians are not rationally convinced of some moral decisions from Rome, might that affect the integrity of their teaching?

CHAPTER 14

Vatican II, Fifty Years Later

The title of this chapter, Fifty Years after Vatican II, is a condensed way of describing an evaluation of Vatican II from the perspective of almost fifty years after the council. Chapters 10-13 dealt with the institutional Church shortly after the Vatican Council. Now we are in position to evaluate how effective the council was, especially in terms of changing the way the institutional Church and the central Roman authorities dealt with the rest of the Church. Let us start with the conclusions of John O'Malley in his careful historical study of Vatican II.[124] At the beginning of his study, he mentions three underlying issues that scholars rightly consider as hallmarks of the council: 1) When **change** is appropriate in the Church and the arguments with which it can be justified; 2) How **authority** is distributed between the papacy and Curia and the rest of the Church; 3) The **style** or model according to which that authority should be exercised.

The first issue of **change** deals with "development of doctrine," which is a particular problem for an institution that draws its lifeblood from a belief in the transcendent validity of the message it received and that is duty-bound to proclaim it unadulterated. Change cannot contradict an earlier doctrine, but it can indicate a better way to describe it in modern terminology. The second issue deals with **authority** and concerns the relationship of the Roman center to the rest of the Church. The primary question is whether the Church had sidelined the authority of bishops and had become too centralized for its own good. Since the Middle Ages, the role of the papacy was formulated in a monarchical framework. After Vatican Council I, which declared the primacy of the pope, the sharing of the pope's authority with the world's bishops was still

---

124   John W. O'Malley, *What Happened at Vatican II*.

unresolved. This issue also entails the relationship between the Roman curia and the bishops. The bishops sometimes felt the Curia dealt with them in a high-handed fashion and trampled on their prerogatives as the primary cooperators with the pope. The third issue deals with the **style** of the Church and of the council; that is, with a change from an authoritarian style and language to a more reciprocal and responsive style. The model of Vatican II was based largely on persuasion and invitation; it spoke in pastoral language, using words like charism, dialogue, partnership, cooperation, and collegiality.

At the end of his careful historical study of Vatican II, O'Malley returns to these three underlying issues of the council. Regarding the first issue, **change** in terms of development of doctrine, he notes that *aggiornamento* (updating) was not a problem for either the majority of the bishops (those who were primarily responsible for transforming the council) or the minority (Romans and others who were resistant to much change). Both groups **generally** recognized that development was a legitimate and necessary category. Still, it became a problem, again and again, in terms of limits (How far could it legitimately go?) and its pastoral appropriateness (Would it accomplish what it promised?). Nonetheless, the council frequently employed change-implied words and did so to such a degree that they became part of its most characteristic vocabulary.

The second underlying issue that became prominent throughout the council was that of the **authority** of Rome and the Curia with respect to the collegiality of the bishops. This was central to the drama of the council: the relationship between the center and the periphery. In the nineteenth century, the papal dominance developed incrementally; then after Vatican Council I declared the primacy of the papacy, it accelerated at almost breathtaking speed. At Vatican II, the conservative, minority group of council fathers believed that the collegiality of the bishops was unworkable, unacceptable, and even dangerous. The majority of council fathers fought passionately to redress the imbalance between the authority exercised by the Roman congregations and the bishops' authority as heads of local churches. The decree on The Pastoral Office of Bishops (*Christus Dominus*) was a significant success for the bishops, because it affirmed their collegiality with the pope and provided for regular synods of bishops after the council. But their success was only verbal and documental; it never actually succeeded in modifying the Church's central operating system. O'Malley very accurately summarizes how "the minority" (i.e. the Roman congregations) emerged even stronger in the years after the council:

> On the center-periphery issue the minority never lost control. It was in that regard so successful that with the aid of Paul VI the center not only held firm and steady but, as the decades subsequent to the council have irrefutably demonstrated, emerged even stronger ....[125]

The third underlying issue is that of **style**. The style of the documents of Vatican II sets it apart from all other councils of the Church. The style changed notably from that of earlier councils; it was not authoritative but pastoral; it was consistently biblical and patristic, not just repeating defined dogmas. Its style indicated the kind of institution the Church was to be, the identity it wanted to project to the world. It spoke in rhetorical forms, not judicial or legalistic terms. It favored dialogue over negative judgments. Instead of declaring canons, anathemas, and guilty verdicts—it did not issue a single canon—it was more intent on winning inner assent to truths and values.

John O'Malley concludes his description of the new style of the council by contrasting what might be considered two

---

125 Ibid. p. 311.

different visions of Catholicism:[126]

FROM	TO
Commands	Invitations
Hostility	Friendship
Laws	Ideals
Rivalry	Partnership
Threats	Persuasion
Suspicion	Trust
Coercion	Conscience
Fault-finding	Appreciation
Monologue	Dialogue
Autocratic	Collaborative
Ruling	Serving
Prescriptive	Principled
Vertical	Horizontal
Withdrawn	Integrated
Exclusion	Inclusion
Passive acceptance	Active engagement

His final word is that on the center-periphery issue, the central Roman group never lost control. As the years went on, the center emerged even stronger. Collegiality won a verbal but empty victory in some documents, but it ended up as an ideal that was no match for the deeply entrenched system.[127]

* * * * *

David Gibson,[128] in 2003, looks at what has happened since the end of Vatican II and expresses the opinion of some modern Catholics this way:

> Others would like to convene a third Vatican Council to magically resolve the current problems, or at least

---

126 Ibid. p. 307.

127 Ibid p. 311.

128 David Gibson, *The Coming Catholic Church*. p. 15.

implement what they see as the lost dream of the Second Vatican Council. … The Catholic world has always pitched a big tent, but today it is more African, more Asian, and more Latino than ever. … [I]t encompasses … also the one billion *other* Catholics in the world who happen to call Rome home and who have other, much different priorities. … The process is already underway, and while it will be a difficult road ahead, it promises also to be inspiring and invigorating.[129]

Finally, Hans Küng,[130] also in 2003, speaks of the "betrayal of the council" in the last fifty years. But he also mentions several "… signs of hope that the renewal of the Catholic Church is continuing … ."[131] My own estimate would add to the comments of Gibson and Kung. The Catholic Church is no longer Euro-centric and, in fact, the majority of its members are in other continents. Also, I am convinced that the women of the Church will increasingly demand greater equality and representation in the Church. Before this century is over, those forces will help to continue the renewal begun at Vatican II.

REFLECTIONS

1. The style of language used by Vatican II was strikingly different from other Ecumenical Councils, as indicated above. Do you approve of this style? Would you add any cautions to such an approach?

2. If the Catholic Church is no longer Euro-centric but truly universal, what accommodation do you believe would be appropriate regarding the diverse cultures of the Catholic world?

3. What do you personally believe would be the result of Rome treating the national episcopal conferences with

---

129 Ibid.
130 Hans Kung, *The Catholic Church*, pp. 187-95.
131 Ibid. p. 198; he describes those signs on pages 199-201.

as much freedom as possible in keeping with *Christus Dominus* of the Vatican Council? Would such freedom be unworkable and dangerous or mostly positive?

CHAPTER 15

One Church, Diverse Cultures

"[For the followers of Christ] Nothing that is genuinely human fails to find an echo in their hearts …. That is why [the Church] realizes that it is truly and intimately linked with the human race and its history …. So this council … now addresses itself without hesitation … to the whole of humanity … and it wishes to set down how it understands the presence and the functions of the Church in the world of today."[132]

With these words from the *Pastoral Constitution on the Church in the Modern World*, the Catholic Church, for the first time, clearly indicated that it would be entirely open to our modern culture. It proclaimed an evident **openness** to the fundamental elements of our twentieth century world culture. That new attitude toward our modern culture is one of the most characteristic notes of this pastoral council. Instead of envisioning itself **above** the world or **against** the world, it realistically proclaimed that it is **of** the world, and it pledged to collaborate with this actual culture. That means that it would be willing to learn from the world, to be open to all the theories of modern science, and to "scrutinize the signs of the times." The Church, too, is struck with the wonders of the discoveries and scientific advancements of our day, and wants to join in the conversation about the role of humankind in the universe as well as its material and human progress. The most distinctive note sounded in this text is that the Church puts herself at the **service** of the human family.

Admittedly, these are only words, but the kind of words we hardly ever heard before. Such words also recognize that all the human arts and sciences deserve legitimate autonomy

---

132 *AAS*, 1966, 163; *Gaudium et Spes*, 1-2 (emphasis added).

and freedom in using their own methods and principles. They exhibit an optimism about our culture and encourage all Christians to work with all people to construct a more human world in keeping with God's plan for creation. Even though the Church is one throughout the world, she "is not tied exclusively and indissolubly to any race or nation, to any one particular way of life, or to any set of customs ancient or modern" but affirms "she can enter into communion with various cultural modes ...."[133]

At the beginning of this constitution, it describes some of the dramatic characteristics of our modern world:

> Today, the human race is passing through a new stage of its history. Profound and rapid changes are spreading by degrees around the whole world. Triggered by the intelligence and creative energies of man, these changes recoil upon him, upon his decisions and desires ... and upon his manner of thinking and acting .... Hence, we can already speak of a true social and cultural transformation which also affects the spiritual life.[134]

In view of such "profound and rapid changes," it suggests that the world and the Church must cooperate more than ever. Accordingly, it then describes the **mutual relationship** between the Church and the world and provides the basis for dialogue between them. First, it mentions the **Church's value to the cultures of the world**:

> [T]he Church ... believes that ... [it] can help to make the human family and its history more human ... [This it does, first] by the way ... it elevates the dignity of the human person .... There is no human law so well fitted to safeguard the personal dignity and human freedom as is the Gospel of Christ.... [Second,] the Church proclaims human rights. It

---

133 Ibid. 58.
134 Ibid. 4.

... greatly esteems the dynamic movements of today, which are fostering these rights all over the world. [Third, the Church fosters] an evolution toward unity .... By her very universality, it can be a very close bond between the various communities of peoples and nations ....[135]

Second, it affirms the **world's value to the Church**:

[The main purpose of every social organism and nation is to provide for the common good,] making available to all its members everything necessary for leading a life truly human, such as food, clothing, and shelter ... the right to education, to employment ... to respect ... [and] to protection of privacy.[136]

Gaudium et Spes recognizes the amazing advances that our secular world has achieved in the twentieth century and the goals it has yet to achieve:

- "[R]ecent studies of science, history, and philosophy raise new questions which influence life and demand new theological investigations."[137]

- "[P]rogress in the production of agriculture and industrial goods ... is rightly aimed at making provision for ... meeting the rising expectations of the human race."[138]

- "It is the duty of society ... to help its citizens find opportunities for adequate employment [and] the right of freely founding labor unions ...."[139]

- "[T]he right to have a share of earthly goods sufficient for oneself and one's family belongs to everyone."[140]

- "[T]he rights of free assembly, of common action, of

---

135 Ibid 40-42.
136 Ibid. 26.
137 Ibid. 62.
138 Ibid. 64.
139 Ibid. 67-68.
140 Ibid. 69.

expressing personal opinions, and of professing a religion, both privately and publicly."[141]

- [Peace among nations and among peoples] "cannot be obtained on earth unless personal values are safeguarded...[with] a firm determination to respect other men and peoples and their dignity ...."[142]

All this adds up to an overwhelming need for mutual cooperation between the Church and the cultures of the world. *Gaudium et Spes* rightly concludes: "Today the bonds of mutual dependence become increasingly close between all citizens and all the peoples of the world. The universal common good needs to be intelligently pursued and more effectively achieved."[143]

Such is the idealism expressed in *Gaudium et Spes*. But the actual situation throughout the world shows the stark differences between the ideal and the real, regarding any claim that such cooperation among governments, cultures, and religious groups works smoothly and effectively for the common good. Many governments throughout the world are ineffective or corrupt, many cultures are too turbulent or impoverished, and the hierarchical nature of the Catholic Church restricts free participation. Yet, in some cultures there is much to be praised in the way that culture and the Church cooperate.

Let us concentrate now on the interplay between culture and religion in the United States. First, we will consider the unique history of our **American culture and government** with respect to religion. Then, we will look at present-day tensions between American culture and our Church.

It is no exaggeration to assert that the history of the interplay of culture and religion in the United States, when compared to that of other countries, is simply **unique and**

---

141   Ibid. 73.
142   Ibid. 78.
143   Ibid. 84.

remarkable. The dialogue between faith and culture is persuasively advanced by the experiment in democracy worked out in the United States of America. The very first settlers in our country were Puritans, who sought a land where they could practice their religion without government interference. In the years that followed, various Protestant groups migrated to America seeking freedom of religion. And Catholics fled from European countries to Massachusetts and the east coast.

Then in 1776, the prologue to the Declaration of Independence proclaimed: "We hold these truths to be self-evident: that all men are created equal, that they are endowed by their Creator with certain inalienable rights, among these are life, liberty and the pursuit of happiness." So, this declaration already indicated that the United States did not accept a secularist ideology that would drive religion from the public sphere. In 1789, the Bill of Rights added that "the civil rights of none shall be abridged on account of religious belief or worship, nor shall any national religion be established;" and the First Amendment of the Constitution required that "Congress shall make no law respecting an establishment of religion." That meant that the framers of our constitution guaranteed freedom of religion, inasmuch as the state would remain separate from religion, neither sanctioning nor prohibiting its exercise. This very ideological **neutrality** regarding religion is what is unique and remarkable about our constitution. As a result, our American culture remains appealing to people of various religious persuasions, because our American culture leaves them free to practice their faith without restraint.

This guarantee of "life, liberty, and the pursuit of happiness," was echoed in the cry of the French Revolution, "*liberte, equalite y fraternite,*" and soon became part of the rhetoric of the American revolutionary period. Americans sensed that they were a part of a land of fresh beginnings and a new **life;** they rejoiced in their **liberty**—as no longer dependent on England, no longer restrained in the practice of their religion; and they began to sense the hope and opportunity of this new nation for their own **pursuit of happiness.** Such ideals worked their way quickly and deeply into the national consciousness, so that Americans felt they were a people with a mission, a divinely sanctioned democracy. Throughout the succeeding centuries, Americans continued to develop their national sense of democracy and equal rights for all. They learned from the writers and activists of the revolutionary period that they were no longer victims of history and foreign rule. They discovered that their new nation was almost unlimited in land and opportunity, as evidenced by the western movement of the pioneer generations. Through the crucible of a devastating Civil War, they finally agreed that all citizens are to be forever free and equal. In the nineteenth and twentieth centuries, many Americans were immigrants themselves, filled with hope and eventually welcomed as equal citizens. From their own experience and that of others who followed after them, they recognized that all these waves of immigrants from other countries eventually were welcomed, found work, and made a life for their families. They were all part of the melting pot of diverse peoples who were united into one great nation. They understood the great motto of the United States: *e pluribus unum* (from many people, one nation).

When Pope John Paul II visited the United States in 1979, he found much to praise about the culture of America. When he came to Chicago, he preached at the lakefront to about a million people on the theme of the U.S. motto, *e pluribus unum.* He reminded us all that we had come from a great variety of cultural, ethnic, and religious backgrounds. He exulted in the fact that from this great diversity we had created something new:

> You brought with you a different culture and you contributed your own richness to the whole; you had different skills and you put them to work, complementing each other, to create industry, agriculture and business;

each group carried with it different human values and shared them with others for the enrichment of your nation. *E pluribus unum:* you became a new entity, a new people ….[144]

This was how the pope praised the wonderful sense of our national unity that had developed over the centuries. He highlighted the *praxis* of **America,** the amazing achievement of painfully but effectively forging unity out of diversity. Then he described the transnational communion of the Church over the centuries. And he drew a parallel to the *praxis* of the **Church,** the joining the diverse people throughout the world into the universal communion of the People of God. He hoped that the idea and practice of *e pluribus unum,* which forged such a strong secular union, would make Catholics even more receptive to their sacred union in the Body of Christ: "The Body of Christ is a unity that transcends the diversity of our origin, culture, education, and personality." When he returned to the United States in 1987 and spoke at Dodger Stadium, he continued on the theme of unity in Christ in a dramatic way; looking out at an audience of striking diversity, the pope affirmed: "Christ is Anglo and Hispanic, Christ is Chinese and Black, Christ is Vietnamese and Irish, Christ is Korean and Italian, Christ is Japanese and Filipino … and many other ethnic groups."[145]

The pope's point is appealing and should be effective for American Catholics who are proud of their country's motto, "*e pluribus unum.*" For our secular unity in this great American culture is parallel to our Catholic unity in the Body of Christ.[146] And the Pope reminds us that our unity in the Body of Christ is profound and eternal.

---

144 Pope John Paul II, Oct. 5, 1979, in *U.S.A.: Message of Justice, Peace, and Love* (Boston: St. Paul Editions, 1979), p. 198.

145 John Paul II, Homily in Dodger Stadium, Sept. 16, 1987.

146 Cf. Francis Cardinal George, OMI, *The Difference God Makes* (NY: Crossroad Publishing Co, 2009), pp. 150-154. The cardinal quotes the pope and expands on his positive approach to our American culture.

Second, consider how **other aspects** of our American culture negatively affect our faith and the practice of our Catholic religion. For, though our culture contains many positive values and is admired for its leadership in the world, we cannot ignore our consumerism, our materialism, our criminal violence, and our history of oppression of minority groups. These negative aspects of our culture have a powerful influence on the practice of our faith. As sociologists observe, we are first Americans and second Catholics; that is, we are a part of this secular culture and cannot avoid being strongly affected by it. All of us must learn to balance the strong influences of our American culture and our commitment to the way of Christ.

However, for some Catholics, the influence of the American way is so strong and dominant in their lives that the institutional Church seems more of a **hindrance** to their American way of living. That is, the tensions between American culture and the Church create difficulties for them. Here are four tensions that some Catholics see between their American culture and their Catholic existence:

- The American way is very practical and realistic; it concentrates on careers and achievements. For some Catholics, however, the Church seems to teach and insist on things that are more intellectual or theoretical, such as teachings of the Church and moral laws.

- The American way is often criticized for its materialism and consumerism. But pre-Vatican II style Catholic spirituality deals with rites, devotions, and prayers, which are added to ordinary daily living.

- The American way is one of freedom and reliance on individual conscience. Yet many Catholics see the institutional Church as quite centralized and restrictive.

- The American way is famously the most democratic of societies, while the institutional Church is not collegial, but authoritarian and hierarchical.

Some of these contrasts between American culture and the Church are quite notable. Let us take a realistic view of each one.

First, what the Church preaches usually does begin with the traditional teachings of the Creed, and such doctrines are basically intellectual. However, in recent years, there is a new focus to the development of its teaching. Because theology today is focused on Scripture, rather than on teachings of the ancient councils, the starting point for our faith and life is the human person of Jesus as proclaimed in Scripture. Christianity is founded on Christ, who is the human revelation of God, the model for our Christian living, and on the Messiah who promises eternal life. Our faith begins with the real, historical Jesus, not with abstract doctrines.

Second, Christian spirituality does include rites, sacraments, prayers, and spiritual activities. For a thousand years, the Christian ideal centered on the "way of perfection" of the monastic way of life—including the vows of poverty, celibacy, and obedience. Ordinary Catholics, who were not monks, could follow only a watered down "way of perfection" by being poor in spirit, chaste in their marriage, and obedient to the laws of the Church—along with other spiritual activities that they added to their lifestyle, such as the rosary, the stations of the cross, and novenas. But since Vatican II, there is a new lay spirituality that focuses on the ordinary lives of Christians. There are two elements to this new spirituality. The first element is the work that we do all day long. That work is not just something we "offer up to God;" rather, the work itself is valuable as service to God's people and so is essential to our following of Christ. And the second element is our relationships to the people we meet and deal with all day long. Our life is hardly ever without people, and how we react to them, serve them, care for them, is our way of following our model for living, Jesus Christ. His only command to us in Scripture is: "This is my commandment: love one another as I love you" (Jn

15:12). So our Catholic spirituality is concerned most of all with our daily work and our constant relationships with others.

Third, the institutional Church is definitely centralized and restrictive. Vatican Council II opened the windows of the Church and began a reform of the institutional Church, including the Roman Curia. The council succeeded in introducing many collaborative elements in parishes, dioceses, and even conferences of bishops. Parish councils, finance councils, school boards, parish staffs, liturgy teams, and other new forms of parish life developed quickly in the years after the council. But, as we saw above (in chapters 9-12) the pope—and especially the Curia—have managed to regain central control of the Church and of the conferences of bishops throughout the world; they have managed to diminish open dialogue and to quiet appeals for change. Nevertheless, we have not seen the final chapter of the effects of Vatican II.

Fourth, the Church we know in Scripture was not uniform. It had many elements of shared decision-making, as well as various approaches to the traditional Jewish laws and practices, and there were diverse forms of authority in Rome, Antioch, Corinth, and Jerusalem. Nevertheless, we must admit that the Church in the New Testament was not a democracy. Today, however, the Church we experience in the United States can only be described as hierarchical. Yet on the parish level, elements of collaboration are constantly increasing: parish councils, finance councils, liturgy committees, and various lay leaders in our schools and parish activities. Clearly, we have a long way to go; but, ultimately, only one point is important for us Catholics to keep in mind: As true believers, our faith is not centered on laws or disciplines or the hierarchy, but only on our authentic following of Jesus, who alone proclaims: "I am the way and the truth and the life" (Jn 14:6).

Part II, starting with chapter 18, will offer some insights into these contrasts between the American culture and the institutional Church. Still, the **focus** in part II will not be on contrasts between the American way and our Catholic faith, or even between the institutional Church and our personal faith; instead, our focus will be entirely on our **personal life in Christ** in this twenty-first century.

REFLECTIONS

1. Can the dignity of the human person and the inalienable right to "life, liberty and the pursuit of happiness" be adequately grounded in anything less than a belief in God?

2. "All of us must learn to balance the strong influences of our American culture and our commitment to the way of Christ." Apply that claim to your own personal experiences as a Catholic in the U.S.

3. In a strongly democratic nation, with a great diversity of religious groups, what might be a prudent stance for people of any religion regarding the passage of civil laws?

CHAPTER 16

Evolution and Faith

For more than a century, the theory of evolution has grown more and more prominent as a way of understanding our amazing universe. During the last few decades, there has been an ongoing **debate** about the relationship between evolution and faith. Creationism and intelligent design both see evolution and faith in some kind of conflict. Creationism believes that the Bible is literally true and, therefore, the universe is no more than 10,000 years old. Intelligent design rejects the need for an evolutionary mechanism because the intelligent designer (God) can create **anything** without relying on any natural intermediary or mechanism; therefore, all the order we see in nature in terms of the development of species, as well as all the discontinuity of species, comes directly from the intelligent designer.

Both creationism and intelligent design are contrary to the theory of evolution, yet the scientific evidence for evolution is beyond any reasonable doubt. In 1998, the National Academy of Sciences proclaimed:

> Compelling lines of evidence demonstrate beyond any reasonable doubt that evolution occurred as a historical process and continues today .... It is no longer possible to sustain scientifically the view that living things did not evolve from earlier forms or that the human species was not produced by the same evolutionary mechanisms that apply to the rest of the living world.[147]

If evolution, is "beyond any reasonable doubt" according to science, then we need to ask two questions: 1) Exactly what

---

147 National Academy of Sciences, *Teaching about Evolution and the Nature of Science,* (Washington, DC: National Academy Press, 1998), p. 16.

does evolution teach? 2) How do we reconcile evolution and our Catholic faith?

A. WHAT DOES EVOLUTION TEACH?

Cosmology teaches that our earth is a minor planet about 4.5 billion years old, revolving around the sun in our Milky Way Galaxy.[148] This galaxy is relatively small, far from the center of the cosmos, containing perhaps a billion stars. Cosmology also claims that the entire known universe began some 13.7 billion years ago, with the "Big Bang," the explosion of an inconceivable amount of mass and energy concentrated in a single point. Over billions of years, the resulting matter cooled down to form the stars and planets that make up our existing cosmos. Today, our universe contains perhaps 100 billion galaxies and is continually expanding. The **age** of our universe was determined by geophysicists according to radioactive disintegration of certain elements such as 235U. The **size** of our cosmos was determined by astronomers, such as Edwin Hubble, based on the unchanging speed of light that takes billions of years to reach us from the distant galaxies.

Physicists have also determined that the **infinitesimally small** units all around us are similarly astounding. Scientists used to consider the atom as the smallest building block of nature. Now they have identified more than fifteen other physical constants that constitute or influence atoms.[149] There are several minute components of atoms: protons, neutrons, electrons, quarks, neutrinos, and muons. And there are forces such as gravity, strong and weak nuclear forces, and electromagnetism. All these microscopic elements and forces constitute all inanimate elements, as well as all plants, animals, and humans.[150]

---

148 See Francis Collins, *The Language of God* (New York: Free Press, a division of Simon and Schuster, Inc., 2006), pp. 57-84 and Kenneth Miller, *Finding Darwin's God* (NY: Harper, 1999), pp. 38 and 223-26.

149 See *Finding Darwin's God*, pp. 227-28.

150 See *The Language of God*, pp. 59-62 and *Finding Darwin's God*, pp. 227-28.

Even more amazing are their findings regarding the **interplay** of all these forces and components. That is, each of these elements that constitute our universe, as well as everything that exists on earth, could only begin, continue, and survive if they had the precise values that permit them to subsist and not destroy each other. The smallest variations in these elements would not permit any biological life on earth to exist and develop, or any stars and celestial bodies to continue to exist. In fact, the more scientists learn about our universe, the more amazed they are that it ever came into existence.

Let us first limit our question about the status of these scientific discoveries to the evolution of **biological life** on earth. That is, does evolution explain how the great variety of present-day species can be traced back to similar but different ancestors? Do the natural processes we observe today in nature explain the biological connections between the present and the past? Scientists answer that such evolution of biological life is an **absolutely accurate** description of what we know about life on our planet; that is, evolution explains accurately this amazing process from single cell organisms to the most complex forms of biological life on our planet. That is the sense of the statement by the National Academy of Sciences at the beginning of this chapter.

Second, let us consider evolution on the **cosmological level,** as the explanation of the origin of our cosmos, from the Big Bang to our present immense universe. That is, does evolution accurately describe the cosmological beginning and development of our entire universe up to our present day? During the last century, cosmologists have observed and amassed vast amounts of knowledge about the constitution and changing elements in space, and the orbits and mutations of stars. To the degree that all this scientific knowledge can be tested and verified, it fits together in a **consistent and**

well-defined theory. In fact, there is **no other** consistent cosmological theory that has any scientific credence.[151]

Two important conclusions can be drawn about the science of evolution. First, the process of evolution does not describe a static world, but a world of **amazing and constant change.** All the natural sciences describe evolution as a process of constant change: 1) Astronomy presents a universe that began in a Big Bang of unimaginable, explosive productivity from the minute to the immense; 2) Physics shows that all of past history, and the future (as long as the laws of physics remain constant), are both entirely open and unpredictable; 3) Geology and paleontology teach that our earth itself continually changes and transforms itself over time; 4) Biology testifies to continuous, complex wonders of biochemical and molecular selection and mutation; 5) Cosmology observes endless variations of planetary movement and reconfiguration.[152]

And second, such amazing transformations throughout almost fourteen billion years prove that not only has our universe evolved in a wondrous fashion, but also that these sciences are able to **identify, test, and verify** such continuous change. Therefore, scientists maintain that, from the Big Bang until today, all of evolution has a natural autonomy, self-sufficiency, and internal consistency. It does not require any other direct physical intervention; it is dynamic, flexible, and logically complete.[153]

B. HOW DO WE RECONCILE EVOLUTION AND FAITH?

What is the connection between evolution and faith? In the last several years there has been an ongoing debate about the relationship of evolution and faith. Creationism and intelligent

---

151 See Brien Greene, *The elegant Universe* (NY: Vintage Books, a division of Random House, Inc., 2000), pp. 124-26.

152 See Kenneth Miller, *Finding Darwin's God,* p. 290.

153 Ibid. p. 289.

design both see evolution and faith in some kind of conflict. Thus, creationism holds that the Bible is literally true and the universe is no older than 10,000 years old; and intelligent design teaches that God does not need the mechanism of evolution, but rather creates everything directly, without the need for natural selection and mutation over billions of years. The National Academy of Science admits that such religious teachings present an "apparent conflict" between evolution and religion:

> At the root of the apparent conflict between some religions and evolution is a misunderstanding of the critical difference between religious and scientific ways of knowing. Religions and science answer **different questions** about the world. Whether there is a purpose to the universe or a purpose for human existence are not questions for science.[154]

Just because science and religions answer different questions about our world, most **mainline Christians** are confident that science and religion are not in conflict. And the National Academy of Sciences certainly agrees:

> Science and religion are not in conflict, for their teachings occupy distinctly **different domains ...** science in the empirical constitution of the universe, and religion in the search for proper ethical values and the spiritual meaning of our lives. The attainment of wisdom in a full life requires extensive attention to both domains.[155]

That is, science is the only legitimate intellectual way to investigate the universe and our natural world, and the scientific method is the only reliable way to seek out the physical causes of natural events. Nevertheless, science alone does not answer many important questions about the universe and the meaning of human life. For example: 1) How can something come from

---

154 Ibid. p. 169 (emphasis added).
155 Ibid. p. 170 (emphasis added).

nothing? 2) Is there a purpose to the universe? 3) What is the meaning of human existence? 4) What is the source of our sense of absolute truth and universal moral law? 5) Is there life after death? Such questions require the wisdom of both science and religion. Even Albert Einstein claimed, "Science without religion is lame, religion without science is blind."

The most common way of affirming the compatibility of science and faith is one that affirms creation by God in an evolutionary form. Some people call this union of evolution and creation by God **theistic evolution**: Theistic because it affirms the God of creation; evolution because it accepts all the findings of natural evolution. Theistic evolution rests on the following premises: 1) The universe came into being out of nothingness, with a Big Bang approximately fourteen billion years ago; 2) Throughout several billion years, billions of galaxies developed, each containing many millions of stars and planets; 3) Despite impossible odds, the elements of all matter gradually came together with great precision and order; 4) Biological life arose in single organisms and, over billions of years, the process of evolution and natural selection developed an endless diversity of species; 5) The continuing process of evolution is self-sufficient, without intervention required by any outside force; 6) Humans are a part of this evolutionary process, sharing a common ancestor with the great apes; 7) Humans are also unique because of their spiritual nature of intellect and will, because of their sense of absolute norms of truth and morality, and because of their search for God, found in every human culture.

These seven premises lead to an entirely plausible, intellectually satisfying, and **logically consistent synthesis** based on the existence of God, who created this universe and established natural laws that govern it. God chose this elegant mechanism of evolution as a means of developing billions of galaxies along with an endless variety of microbes, plants, and animals. This mechanism also gave rise to intelligent creatures with a sense of absolute truth, and right and wrong, and a desire to seek fellowship with God.

This theistic evolution (whatever name we give it) is **compatible with the great monotheistic religions** of the world. In general, this is the view espoused by most Hindus, Muslims, Jews, and Christians. Catholics can refer to the encyclical *Humanae Generis* of Pope Pius XII in 1950, in which he gave freedom to Scripture scholars to discuss the theory of evolution. More positively, Pope John Paul II, in 1996, speaking to the Pontifical Academy of Sciences, offered this defense of theistic evolution: "[N]ew findings lead us to the recognition of evolution as more than a hypothesis."

Science alone cannot prove or disprove God, because it is limited to testing and verifying only material things. Religion alone cannot grasp the amazing evolution of our natural world. But science and faith together, as theistic evolution, are the **key to understanding evolution as well as our relationship to God.** By it, we know that all the events of nature follow the evolutionary and biological laws, including the endless changes, mutations, and natural selection that are a part of our universe; and we understand that this evolutionary process is self-sufficient, so that God's intervention in this process, and in our human life, is not direct. Because evolution is not static and rigidly determined, human beings also have real freedom in a world of authentic moral and spiritual choices. Because of our faith, we can be assured of God's care and love, despite all the tragedies of life; we can be inspired by his written word; we have a human model for integral human living; and we have an amazing hope of final life with God. Francis Collins, the scientist, concludes very strongly:

> I find theistic evolution … to be by far the most scientifically consistent and spiritually satisfying …. This position will not go out of style or be disproven by future scientific discoveries. It is intellectually rigorous, it provides answers to many otherwise puzzling questions, and it allows

science and faith to fortify each other like two unshakable pillars, holding up a building called Truth.[156]

REFLECTIONS

1. In the past, did you consider the claims of evolution questionable or somewhat reliable or solidly reliable?

2. While reading the above explanation of evolution, what were your personal reactions?

3. Karl Rahner explains: "Natural science investigates … individual phenomena which human beings (ultimately through the experience of their senses) encounter in their world, and the relationship of these phenomena to one another. Theology has to do with the totality of reality as such, and with the ground of this reality …. Consequently, there need be no fear of a conflict of competence between natural science and theology …."[157] Do you see this as an adequate distinction of boundaries? Would you add any caution about possible conflicts?

---

156 See Francis Collins, *The Language of God,* p. 210.

157 Karl Rahner, *Theological Investigations, Vol. XXI,* p. 19.

CHAPTER 17

Upside-down Church in 2050

Sociology, the study of society and social institutions, is critical for an understanding of our Church and our world in this twenty-first century. In this chapter, I will first describe what sociology tells us about the dramatic changes that are likely to occur in this century, in the world in general, and in our Church. Then I will propose the likely implications of these changes for our Church, along with some tentative suggestions for the future.

John Allen recently published *The Future Church*,[158] which is a sociological study of the world, the Catholic Church, and the United States Church in the twenty-first century. The validity of any sociological predictions and evaluations comes from the **trends** observed in our present world; if those trends continue in the near future, then we can predict what our different societies will look like in the future. With the help of John Allen's scientific observations, we can get a fair idea of the demographic changes for the next fifty years or more in a) our world, b) our Church, and c) the Church in the United States.

A. WORLD DEMOGRAPHICS

It is no exaggeration to say that the "mother of all mega-trends in this century is globalization:"

> In its literal sense, globalization refers to the transformation of local and regional realities into global ones, uniting the peoples of the world in a single global market and society. Globalization is the "mother of all mega-trends," in the sense that it has become a catchall designation for the accelerating global integration of economics, politics, culture, communications, spirituality and

---

158 John Allen, *The Future Church* (NY: Doubleday, 2009).

virtually everything else that matters. Analysts assert that globalization is the historical equal of the agricultural and industrial revolutions in terms of transforming social impact.[159]

That is, what the agricultural revolution was to the eighteenth and nineteenth centuries, and the industrial revolution was to the twentieth century, so globalization will be to the twenty-first century. Some of the characteristics of globalization are: the rise of transnational organizations and movements; the worldwide dimensions of business, trade, finance, technology, and information; increasing cultural homogenization of free markets, limited government, and the rule of law; the gradual elimination of political and economic barriers, such as tariffs.

Let us concentrate, first, on the trends that will result in immense demographic changes in this century:

> In the first half of the twenty-first century, population will grow across most of the global South [the southern hemisphere]... and will fall in most of the North [especially Europe]. More than 95 percent of the world's population increase will happen in developing countries .... After leveling out at 9 billion sometime around 2050, the population of the planet will begin to fall, and will do so with increasing momentum throughout the rest of the century.[160]

The single cause of this dramatic shift in world population is that the declining fertility rate is almost a universal phenomenon. For any population to remain steady, the fertility rate needs to be about 2.1 per family. If there are less than 2.1 births per woman in any country, the population will fall below replacement rate and begin to decline.

In very general terms, the fertility rates in the **northern**

---

159 Ibid. p. 260.
160 Ibid. p. 144.

hemisphere are already at or below replacement rate. Back in 1957, when the European Union was founded, every one of the twenty-seven nations that are now EU members had fertility rates above 2.1. Today not one of them does! As a result, between now and 2050, Europe's population is estimated to drop from 728 million to 590 million. In China and Japan, the fertility rates have imploded in recent years. Japan now has a fertility rate of 1.3 per woman. By 2050, Japan could lose one-quarter of its population. China has seen the most dramatic fertility declines on the planet. In 1960, China's fertility rater was 6.1, which it realized was unsustainable. So they instituted the oppressive "one child per family" policy; now their rate is 1.8 (or even lower, according to some demographers). In the second half of this century, their population losses could become massive. Fertility rates in Russia, South Korea, and Singapore are also extremely low.[161] Although the Middle East has a high fertility rate now, and will have major growth in the short term, their fertility rates are beginning to fall faster than anywhere else in the world.[162]

The United States is a unique situation. Our population should grow to 400 million by 2050 and may overtake the total population of Western Europe by that time! But much of this population growth is due to immigration; the United States accepts by far the largest number of legal immigrants in the world (in the 1990s, the number was over nine million) and it also receives millions of illegal immigrants. Another reason why our population continues to grow in the U.S. is the fertility rate of Hispanics in the U.S.; it was almost three in 1990, though now is about 2.3. By contrast, the fertility rate for white (non Hispanic) Americans is 1.8, well below replacement rate.

---

161   The population for Russia alone should drop by 30 million. The fertility rate in South Korea is 1.23 and in Singapore is 1.35. See ibid. pp. 151 and 170.

162   For example, Iran in 1950 had a fertility rate around 6, but now it stands at 2; so, it has fallen by two-thirds. Turkey's rate is now about 2.3 and dropping; in Egypt, the number of children will begin dropping by 2017. Similar population declines are expected for Iraq, Algeria, Saudi Arabia, Syria, Lebanon and Jordan. See ibid. p. 153.

In the **southern hemisphere**, there will probably be a decline in fertility rate as well. Nevertheless, the South will still increase substantially in numbers, because their fertility rates are well above replacement rate now. For example, the United Nations Population Division predicts that Latin America and the Caribbean will rise from 561 million in 2005 to 782 million in 2050.[163] Most of South America had high birth rates and some, such as Argentina and Colombia, are still relatively high. The largest Catholic nation in the world, Brazil, had a fertility rate of 6.1 in 1960, but its rate has fallen precipitously to 2.1 now.

The demographics of Africa are even more remarkable. Of the ten nations with the highest fertility rates in the world, eight are in Africa. The fertility rate for sub-Saharan Africa is now 5.6, easily the highest of any zone on the planet. Nigeria, for example, should increase in population by almost 50% by 2050. All of sub-Saharan Africa, by 2050, will grow by a remarkable 132%, from about 700 million to 1.6 billion!

All these statistics add up to surprising conclusions for our world and our Catholic Church. First, they indicate that this twenty-first century will result in an **upside-down** world. That is, population will grow across most of the Southern Hemisphere (dramatically in sub-Saharan Africa) and will fall in most of the Northern Hemisphere (dramatically in Europe, Japan, and China). Second, 95% of the population increase of the world will happen in **developing countries**, mostly in rapidly expanding urban areas.[164] Third, the general population of the North will become older, while the general population of the South will become younger. Thus, while half of the world's population today is under the age of 24, 90% of those under 24 live in the South.[165] Fourth, according to the fertility trends around the world, the total world population will probably

---

163 Ibid. p. 151.
164 See ibid. p. 144.
165 Ibid.

grow from almost seven billion today to about nine billion by 2050; then it will likely begin to fall and do so with increasing momentum throughout the rest of the century.[166]

B. CATHOLIC CHURCH DEMOGRAPHICS

All of these world demographics have great significance for our view of the Church today, for not only is our planet in general becoming an upside-down world, but our Church is also becoming an **upside-down Church**. Here are some of the ways that our Church is being turned on its head by a series of new forces in this twenty-first century.[167]

First, during the twentieth century, our Church was dominated by the global North; most of the Church's leadership came from Europe and North America. Today, two-thirds of its members live in Africa, Asia, and Latin America; and its leadership will increasingly come from all over the world to a degree never before experienced. Second, a large proportion of our Catholic population had been in countries that were growing in population and had many young people; now, especially in the North, that population is aging rapidly. Third, a church that always relied on clergy to deliver pastoral care and leadership now must depend increasingly on lay leadership in a great variety of ways. Fourth, the watchword of our Church after Vatican II was *aggiornamento,* including a willingness to reach out to the modern world; but the increasing centralizing tendencies of the Church seems to erode rather than foster such outreach. Fifth, for centuries, our primary interreligious relationships had been with other Christian churches and with Judaism; now our Church must come to terms with newly assertive Islam, not just in the Middle East and Africa, but even in Europe and the U.S. Sixth, in diplomatic matters, in the past, our Church could rely on great Catholic ruling powers;

---

166 Ibid.
167 Ibid. pp. 2-3.

now it is moving into an ever more multipolar world, in which many of the poles are not even Christian.

Another way of looking at this upside-down Catholicism is in the demographic **religious changes** of our world. Early in the twentieth century, there was a tight identification between the Western World and Christianity, but that unique situation disintegrated throughout the century. At the beginning of the twentieth century, only 25% of the Catholic Church population lived outside Europe and North America. By the century's end, 65% of the Catholic population of the world was found in Africa, Asia, and Latin America.[168] Certainly, the South will not completely replace the North in influence in the near future, but rather ideas, movements, and controversies will become increasingly global.

In order to analyze the previous paragraph, consider our changing Church demographics in the past century. **In 1900,** there were roughly 266 million Catholics in the world, of whom over 200 million were in Europe and North America, with 53 million in Latin America, and only 13 million scattered throughout the rest of the planet. By contrast, **in 2000,** there were almost 1.1 billion Roman Catholics throughout the world, of whom just 350 million were European and North Americans. The overwhelming majority of Catholics, 720 million people, lived in Latin America, Africa, and Asia. John Allen concludes: "Projecting forward to the year 2025, **only one Catholic in five** in the world will be a non-Hispanic Caucasian. This is the most rapid, and most sweeping, demographic transformation of Roman Catholicism in its two-thousand-year history."[169] And by the year 2050, United Nations Population Division predicts that, for the first time, three African nations—the Democratic Republic of the Congo, Uganda, and Nigeria—will take their place among the largest Catholic nations of the world (they will probably rate fifth, sixth and ninth in Catholic population).

---

168 Ibid. p. 15.
169 Ibid. p. 17.

And seven of the ten largest Catholic nations in the world, including Brazil, Mexico, Argentina, and the Philippines, will be south of the U.S.

We can be even more exact about this amazing growth of Catholic population in the twentieth century. In terms of all sub-Saharan Africa, the Catholic population in the twentieth century went from about 2 million to more than 130 million! Even Asia expanded from 1.2 percent Catholic to three percent by the end of the century. And India's Catholic population grew from under two million to over 17 million; by 2050, it should grow to at least 26 million. Also, South Korea more than doubled its Catholic population in the last 20 years to over 11% of the country. And in the year 2000, the Philippines, a very Catholic nation, has had more Catholic baptisms than most of Europe combined. Finally, in terms of Christianity as a whole, in 2007 there were 350 million Christians in Asia compared to 372 million Buddhists; and by 2010, there might be more Christians in Asia than Buddhists![170] These statistics give quite a different impression of the story of global Catholicism than we generally hear in Europe or the U.S. The actual statistics show not a decline, but a decided growth. Notice also that, while the total global population went from 2.5 billion people in 1950 to 6.5 billion in 2005, the Catholic population grew, during the same time, from 460 million to 1.1 billion. That means that both the total world population and the total Catholic population grew by a factor of roughly 2.5; thus, the overall expansion of the Catholic Church kept pace with the global population.

Surely Europe and the U.S. will continue to be important to world Catholicism, but the global south will provide a steadily growing share of leadership and vision. Karl Rahner described this process as the emergence of a "World Church":

---

170   Ibid. p. 19.

Rahner believed that the Second Vatican Council (1962-1965) launched a "qualitative leap" toward a new stage in Church history, in which the Church would no longer be dominated exclusively be European or Western cultural forms, functioning in other parts of the world like an "export firm." As a theological matter, Rahner said, Catholicism had always been a "World Church" in principle, but now that identity is being realized as a sociological fact.[171]

C. THE CHURCH IN THE UNITED STATES

To understand the Church in the United States sociologically, we might focus on two realities that constitute the American Church. First, we need to be aware in a general way of the progressive and conservative elements that so influence Catholic life. According to Richard Gaillardetz of the University of Toledo, **progressive Catholicism** in the twenty-first century is less of an ideology than a pastoral phenomenon. That is, the moderate-to-liberal camp represents a disproportionate share of the Church's work force in the parishes of the U.S.; that includes priests, deacons, religious, laity and professional teachers, and theologians. They exist in so many parishes that have a flourishing catechumenate, vibrant liturgies, thoughtful preaching, multiple lay ministries, and many groups that are determined to keep alive the vision of Vatican II.[172]

Today, many priests, deacons, and members of religious orders of men and women belong in this moderate-to-

---

171 Ibid. p. 16. Cf. also, Rahner's own words in his *Concern for the Church (Theologiocal Investigations XX)*, pp. 110-11: "As far as the Church as a whole is concerned, it will turn to an increasing extent and **increasingly rapidly** from a European church with Christian exports to all the world into a world-Church, in which the churches of Africa, South America and even Asia, will be really autonomous elements with their own specific character and their own importance in the whole Church.... Such a world-Church... cannot simply import and imitate the life-style, law, liturgy and theology of the European church" (emphasis added).

172 See Ibid. p. 73.

liberal group, but, with the dramatic decline of priests and men and women religious, the overall numbers will decline. Many progressive groups have grown up in the U.S. in the years since Vatican II, hoping to further the agenda of the council: such groups as Call to Action, We Are Church, and Voice of the Faithful. Numerous other groups also exist in conservative circles. Rather than describe these groups as liberal or conservative, it might be more accurate to refer to such movements as a form of "tribalism," because they form a definite subculture that focuses on one issue or general theme. Still they would not characterize themselves by that one issue, but consider themselves more generally as simply traditional or faithful Catholics.

Conservative Catholicism also contains many movements that foster evangelical or conservative commitments. It's also apparently true that conservative dioceses in the U.S. tend to generate larger numbers of vocations to the priesthood. Similarly, conservative orders of nuns seem to be the only orders that continue to generate numerous vocations. Finally, those lay Catholics who are more conservative are more acceptable to recent American bishops, so they are more often chosen for diocesan positions.

The other significant element in our American Church today is the encouraging and even surprising story of **lay ministry,** that has expanded at a dizzying pace since Vatican II. Lay ecclesial ministry refers to laity who perform ministries such as being parish coordinators, administering parish finances, preaching, teaching the faith, consoling the sick, and coordinating parish liturgy. The characteristics that define lay ecclesial ministers include authorization by the hierarchy, leadership in a particular area of ministry, and proper formation for their role. The National Pastoral Life Center in the U.S. found that the percentage of American parishes employing lay ministers at least 20 hours a week went from 54% in 1990 to 66% in 2005. This amounts to a "virtual revolution in parish ministry." All told, in 1990, there were some 22,000 lay ministers in the U.S.; today, there are an estimated 31,000 lay ecclesial ministers working in Catholic parishes. In less than twenty years, the number of Catholic priests in the U.S. dropped from 49,000 to 43,000, while the number of lay ministers rose by 9,000.

John Allen makes an even wider **temporal** comparison:

… fewer than one percent of ministerial positions in the Catholic Church [in the U.S.] were held by laity before the Second Vatican Council. The jobs lay ecclesial ministers are doing today either didn't exist 40 years ago, or they were held almost exclusively by priests or nuns. There are [now] somewhere between 500 and 600 parishes in the United States that are without a resident priest and are administered by a layperson.[173]

It should be noted that Vatican II endorsed the expanded lay ecclesial roles long before the priest shortage became apparent in Europe and the U.S. Still, there is no doubt that the persistent shortage of priests in the U.S. (and in various parts of the world) has contributed to the explosion of lay leadership. Catholic leaders recognize that the gaps in parish and diocesan pastoral care can only be filled by laypeople stepping into roles once held only by priests and religious. Presently, there are more than 20,000 lay people in the U.S. in programs of formation to become ecclesial lay ministers. And when we take a closer look at the 31,000 lay ecclesial ministers who are already working in Catholic parishes, we find that roughly 80% of them are women! That is, 64% of them are laywomen, 16% of them are religious women, and 20% are laymen. One conclusion from all this is that higher level positions in the Church may be held by males, but the new lay professional roles are very disproportionately held by women.

---

173 Ibid. p. 193.

All of these lay positions mentioned so far are in parish ministry. There are several categories of lay ministers that are not included in the above statistics. Laypersons who minister in the name of the Church in hospitals and health care systems or on college campuses add to these totals. Also, there are 8,500 pastoral musicians and 5,500 lay principals of elementary and secondary Catholic schools, and there are probably more than 100,000 teachers in our Catholic schools. All of these statistics, showing the increase in professional lay ministers, are evidence of a vital Church ministry in the U.S. that is continuing to grow in numbers and in professionalism.

D. WHAT IT ALL MEANS

What does all this sociology mean for our Church? What are some of the practical implications of all these statistics? What might be the results of such an upside-down Church in the twenty-first century? The **first** result for our future Church will be major **differences** between the Church in the northern hemisphere and the Church in the southern hemisphere. That is, the practical issues, needs, and concerns are quite different in the North and the South. In Europe and the U.S., most of the **issues** are *ad intra,* referring to the internal life of the Church: abortion, sexual morality, papal authority, Roman Curia, Episcopal collegiality, celibacy of the priesthood, ordination of women, and institutional reform. Whereas, in the southern hemisphere, most of the issues are *ad extra,* referring to engagement of the Church with broader religious and social questions outside the Church: the alleviation of poverty, human rights, liberation theology, relations of the Church to Islam, Hinduism, and Buddhism, and freedom of the Church in restrictive societies. A major **concern** for the South will be to deal with the swelling urban centers that are replacing the predominantly rural and agricultural communities of the last century. Instead of the traditional rural social networks of the past, new forms of Church ministry will need to evolve, staffed by lay volunteers. Also, in the South, the problem of inculturation will be greater; that is, the faith will need to be expressed differently according to the diverse cultures and customs. And as the number of cultures in which the Church lives increases, its own internal diversity will increase. Finally, in Europe and the U.S. the great challenge and concern for the Church is secularism, while in the South the real challenge comes from the great diversity of religions and the aggressive competition it represents for the Church.

The **second** result flows naturally from the first. That is, just because the issues, needs, and concerns of the South are very different from the North, the Church will be **pulled in different directions**. And as the Church in the South becomes more dominant, Rome will have to listen to its issues and concerns more and more. By the end of this century, almost two-thirds of the Catholic population will be found in Africa, Asia, and South America. There will be a greater diversity of cultures, theological ideas, and moral positions that the universal Church must deal with. Christianity cannot effectively progress in the East and the South if it insists on imposing Western culture there. In order to flower, it must respond to the yearnings and expectations of cultures that are shaped by non-western traditions. Cardinal Gracias of Mumbai expressed a new urgency for such inculturation, especially in terms of China and India:

> In Asian societies, religion is seen as a necessary part of the culture. I believe the West has got to learn to respond to the signs of the times. Change and adaptation is necessary, and maybe the churches of the South, especially in Asia, can offer an example. Today, we try to be open to the Spirit with self-confidence, believing that inculturation is not going to take the church to the ruins.[174]

There is a long and troubling history concerning this problem of conflict between a dominant Western (European

---

174 Ibid. p. 366.

and especially Roman) Church and other strong native cultures. In the sixteenth century, Fr. Robert de Nobili and his fellow Jesuits went to India and attempted to balance the universal faith, expressed in western terms, and the local culture of India. Then, in the seventeenth century, Fr. Matteo Ricci tried to convert people of China to the Catholic faith. In both cases, their efforts were not successful, because of the clash of Roman Church ideas and the sacred local traditions. Whether the Church authorities addressed those questions adequately 500 years ago is not entirely clear, but certainly such a balance needs to be found in this twenty-first century, if our faith is to be presented in a way that is appealing to the people of India, China, Japan, and the Arab countries.

There is some evidence of a more enlightened approach to this problem by the Church. As early as the year 1659, the Roman Congregation for the Propagation of the Faith wisely taught:

> What could be more absurd than to transport France, Spain or Italy … to China? Do not introduce all that to [the people of China], but only the faith. It is the nature of men to love and treasure above everything else their own country …. In consequence, there is no stronger cause for alienation … than an attack on local customs, especially when these go back to a venerable antiquity.[175]

The **third** point is only intended as a question for the whole Church. This question flows directly from the first two points above: If the Catholic Church is increasing rapidly in this century from a European Church to a world Church, in which the churches of Africa, Asia, and South America are to have some of their own character and culture, then how can they not have their own life-style, law, liturgy, theology, and regional decision-making? If the dialogue between the Church and the people of very different cultures and traditions is to

---

175   Ibid. p. 444.

continue, then does not the European-style Church need to treat these cultures as worthy of respect and equal standing? As theologians multiply in numbers and mature in ability, with their necessary application of Scripture to their major problems, will not this undeniable diversity make its mark on theology as a whole? If national conferences of bishops in these countries know their indigenous cultures better than anyone else, should they not have more authority to decide important issues for their regions? Finally, how can the Catholic Church become truly a world Church without Rome giving as much authority as possible to the various national conferences of Bishops? If the national or continental conferences of bishops had as much authority as possible, they would be more likely to find solutions to their indigenous problems and to certain disciplines of the Church in their region. For example:

- The Church in South America might reform liberation theology as a driving force for the alleviation of the scourge of poverty throughout their region.

- The Church of Asia might be more effective in the competitive marketplace of diverse religions by presenting the faith in more appealing terms.

- The Church of Africa might be more effective in dealing with polygamy and other marriage problems.

- The churches of India and Japan might effectively incorporate some of their sacred traditions into their liturgy.

- The churches that are growing rapidly in the South, without adequate priests, might expand their various base communities, led by laity, to teach the faith and spread it.

- Churches of one nation or groups of nations that speak one language would have authority to translate their liturgical books into their indigenous language.

- National churches would be able to incorporate inclusive language for women into their liturgical books.

- Churches where vocations to the priesthood have dropped off dramatically might carefully consider some alternatives to the celibate, male priesthood.

If the Church were to give the national conferences of bishops such authority, then it would go a long way toward becoming a truly world Church. According to Karl Rahner:

> [T]he Second Vatican Council is the beginning of a tentative approach by the Church to the … realization of itself as *world-Church* …. [T]he council seems to me to be the first act in a history in which the world-Church first began to exist as such. [T]he responsibility for this council … was in the hands of an episcopate from the whole world …. [T]he actualization of the Church's nature was manifested at the Council only in a very rudimentary way ….[176]

REFLECTIONS

1. If the world population growth will be much greater in the southern hemisphere than in the northern hemisphere, what one positive result would you see because of such a change? Also, what one negative result would you expect?

2. If the Catholic Church also becomes upside-down in the sense of the Church in the southern hemisphere becoming more populous than that of the northern hemisphere, what positive results would you expect to see by 2050? What possible changes cause you some concern?

3. What particular trends related to Church growth are likely to greatly influence the way the Church guides her people in the twenty-first century?

---

176 Karl Rahner, *Concern for the Church*, pp. 78, 91 and 79 (emphasis in original). This point is the main topic of his chapter 7, pp. 90-102.

CHAPTER 18

Division in the Church

In this chapter we want to focus specifically on the Church in the United States. Our situation now is undeniably a time of sharp tensions, a time of polarization of leadership, a time of division for the laity. Some conservative writers suggest that progressives are preaching heresy and promoting moral laxity; they criticize progressives for picking and choosing the teachings they will follow and for rejecting those practices that don't suit them. On the other hand, progressives accuse conservatives of betraying the spirit of the gospels and rebuffing the Holy Spirit; they are discouraged by the efforts of the Church leaders who try to centralize and control everything.

In 1996, Cardinal Bernardin of Chicago was convinced that the Church of the United States was seriously threatened by the acrimony and polarization among Catholics in general, which resulted in a paralysis of leadership throughout the country. With the backing of twenty-five prominent Catholics, including seven bishops, he announced a **Common Ground Initiative** to restore constructive discussion between conservative and progressive factions in the Church of the United States. He released a three-thousand word statement, "Called to be Catholic in a Time of Peril," which generated wide attention in the press and stirred both enthusiasm and opposition in the Church. The main question of the statement was: "Will the Catholic Church in the United States enter a new millennium as a church of promise ... able to be a leavening force in our culture .... Or will it become a church on the defensive, torn by dissension and weakened in its core structures?" He believed the outcome would depend on whether the Church can reverse the polarization and overcome the ideological walls that inhibit candid discussion. Some of the problems mentioned that required reasonable discussion were: 1) the changing roles of women, 2) the effectiveness of religious education, 3) the meaning of human sexuality, along with related moral problems, 4) the declining number of priests and women religious, 5) the succession of laypeople to positions of leadership and their adequate formation, 6) the survival of Catholic school systems and of health care facilities, 7) the manner of decision making and consultation in the Church, 8) the capacity of the Church to minister to African-American, Latino, and Asian populations, 9) the responsibility of the Church to the poor and defenseless, and 10) the responsibility of theologians to authoritative church teachings. This list includes items typically of concern to both conservatives and progressives.

Two weeks later, Cardinal Bernardin learned that he had pancreatic cancer. His last public address—some three weeks before he died—dealt with this Common Ground Initiative. The initiative is still active today, but without its inspired leader.

Certainly, much of this division in the American Church is a result of the decrees of the Second Vatican Council and the changes that followed. The council itself introduced progressive changes in Catholic policy and practice, which required everyone to adopt a new faith paradigm. Conservative Catholics felt that the Church went too far too fast in accommodating itself to the spirit of the times, thereby undermining the way the Church has been acting for centuries. At the same time, many church leaders in Rome were opposed to the efforts to implement the decrees of the council. Progressive Catholics felt the Church had not moved fast enough and had failed to carry out the reforms that were called for by the council documents. They feared that a reaction had set in, which tried to restore the closed and centralized Catholicism of the previous century. This mounting division and opposition led to ever-increasing distrust and criticism by both groups.

So our discussion about the division in the U.S. Church will cover three topics: 1) a description of the conservative and progressive elements, along with the issues involved; 2) a clarification of the different degrees of assent that are required by the various church teachings and practices; and 3) some positive solutions for this divisive polarization.

A. DESCRIPTIONS

Some Catholics become annoyed when terms like conservative, rightwing, liberal, or progressive are used to describe individuals or groups within the Church. They are understandably troubled when such categories are used with the implication that one side is bad—especially when it refers to their outlook—and the other side is good. In addition, they often feel that such wide labels are used indiscriminately for a great variety of positions.

Let me begin by offering a general, working definition for conservatives: They are people who "**conserve**" the good that we have achieved and now enjoy in the Church; they are happy with the way things are and they generally oppose change. They want to hold fast to what is abidingly true and of enduring value in their faith life. They maintain that many of the reforms and renewal inspired by the Vatican Council are leading to a breakdown of discipline and an increase of uncertainty in matters of faith. Progressives, on the other hand, are those who want to "**progress**" toward greater freedom from some restrictions of church law; they often favor change over stability and freedom over regulations. They believe that there is room for pluralism in many aspects of our church life, especially in devotional matters, in liturgy, and in church discipline. They agree that dogmas are indeed unchangeable, but the words we use to express those dogmas can change; especially with regard to the diverse languages and the lightening-like changes existing in our modern world.

Two objections are frequently raised against the progressive outlook. First, it is argued that progressive attitudes more often lead to dissent, confusion, and disorder in the Church. But Avery Dulles, SJ, who is not a progressive theologian, disagrees:

> Historically, rigorists and anarchists have caused as much trouble for the Church As ... progressives. The Montanist and Novatian heresies, Jansenism and more recent disturbances connected with Fr. Leonard Feeney are cases in point. The Church today abounds in right-wing Catholics who dissent from the social teaching of the popes and bishops or reject the liturgical forms of Vatican II ....[177]

Second, progressive Catholics are often accused of practicing a kind of "cafeteria Catholicism," because they seem to be picking and choosing among the Church's doctrines and morals, deciding according to their own personal tastes what teachings they will accept and what rules they will observe. Conservatives feel justified in criticizing them for that, for they sincerely believe that rejection of any papal teaching or moral law is inconsistent with Catholic faith itself. They insist that Catholic faith must be taken as a whole, so that loyal believers must accept everything the pope declares. In particular, they insist that when the pope restates the traditional teaching on birth control, the ordination of women, clerical celibacy, or certain liturgical practices—such as norms for inclusive language—all Catholics should obey him entirely, without picking and choosing what they will follow.

But if this norm is truly invariable, namely that the rejection of any papal teaching is inconsistent with the Catholic faith, it would also mean that when the pope restates the Church's traditional teaching on social justice and human rights, there is no way anyone should reject such teaching either. So conservatives should also heed the pope's many social encyclicals, which demand the rights of workers for a just wage

---

177 Avery Dulles, SJ, in *New Oxford Review,* Jan.-Feb. issue, 1979.

and for forming unions, and which require that the superfluous wealth of rich nations be placed at the service of poor and starving nations, and which seek absolute equality for all people regardless of sex, color, ethnic race, or sexual orientation. Pope Paul VI was even more explicit in 1979 at Yankee Stadium, in speaking of the responsibility of all to come to the aid of the destitute poor of the world: "Christ demands an openness that is more than benign attention, more than token actions of half-hearted efforts that leave the poor as destitute as before or even more so."[178] I suspect very few conservatives (or any other Catholics) would honestly claim that they accept all those social teachings of the papal encyclicals or act upon them. In addition, they can hardly claim ignorance of such papal teachings about human rights, because the popes have written more encyclicals about the rights of labor, the poor, and the equal rights of all people than they have regarding sexual ethics or any other topic. The conclusion is that such conservatives are doing the same thing that many progressives are accused of doing in other matters: They are picking and choosing which teachings and rules of the Church they care to follow.

B. LIMITS OF CHURCH AUTHORITY

For hundreds of years before Vatican II, theologians indicated different degrees of assent that were required concerning various teachings and rules of the Church. Recall what a great variety of teachings and laws have been promulgated throughout these 2,000 years: dogmas, less solemn teachings in encyclicals and formal documents by Roman congregations, simple clarifications of previous teachings and pastoral letters by national conferences of Catholic bishops, as well as all the rules of canon law. Throughout history, theologians have attached "notes" to many doctrines in order to indicate how closely they are related to the essence of our faith:

---

178   Pope Paul VI, in Encyclical, *Populorum Progressio,* 1967.

de fide definita, de fide ex juge ministerio, proxima fidei, certa et communis, communis, probabilior. They often did not agree on the exact "note" to be attached to a teaching, nor did they always agree on the penalty attached to denying such teaching or acting against rules of canon law.

What is clear is that there are at least three levels of doctrines, which require various degrees of assent: 1) teachings solemnly defined (dogmas based on Scripture); 2) teachings that are "authoritative" (because they are declared "definitively"); and 3) everything else (including minor laws, incidental teachings in various responses from Roman congregations, explanatory additions to papal documents, and papal instructions and homilies.) All agree that dogmas must be believed, because they are founded on Scripture and solemnly declared by popes and ecumenical councils of the Church; they are the core of our faith. The dogma itself cannot be changed, but the **words** used to explain the truth are not irreformable because, throughout time, the meaning of words does change and the philosophical terms—defined according to one particular philosophy—might no longer have the same meaning. For example, the dogma about Christ—that there are two natures in the one person of Jesus—and the dogma about the Trinity—that there are three persons in one nature—were proclaimed by the early ecumenical councils and so must be believed by all. But the **terminology** used to express these dogmas in the fourth century included terms, such as nature and person, substance and *hypostasis*, from early Greek philosophy. But theologians today maintain that those early Greek terms do not mean the same thing in modern philosophy, so they need to find other terminology that better expresses that ancient and true dogma.

The second level of doctrines—"authoritative" teachings—needs careful consideration. Pope John Paul II wrote an important *Motu Proprio* in 1998, entitled *Ad Tuendam Fidem.*[179]

---

179   Pope John Paul II, in *AAS,* 90 (1998), pp. 457-61.

This document entitled this second category of teachings as **"definitive,"** and explained that it was not infallible but still irreformable. To clarify what that category required, he added a second paragraph to Canon 750 of the official Code of Canon Law:

> Each and every thing which is proposed **definitively** by the magisterium of the Church concerning the doctrine of faith or morals, that is, each and everything that is required to safeguard reverently and to expound faithfully the same deposit of faith, is also to be firmly **embraced and retained;** therefore, one who refuses these propositions which are to be held definitively is opposed to the doctrine of the Catholic Church.[180]

That means that every doctrine, which is required to safeguard the defined deposit of faith, can be the object of a "definitive" statement by the magisterium (teaching authority of the Church). Once it is declared "definitive," it becomes part of "the doctrine of the Church" and must be embraced and held as irreformable. To enforce the observance of this new provision, the *Motu Proprio* added a clause to Canon 371 that institutes a "just penalty" for anyone who "obstinately rejects the doctrine mentioned in Canon 752 ¶ 2…." In addition, all those who refuse to affirm these "definitive" doctrines would not be allowed to hold any of those leadership or teaching positions in the Church that are mentioned in Canon 833.[181]

The notion of a "definitive" doctrine has clearly entered the realm of theology; *Ad Tuendam Fidem* has added the idea of non-infallible but unchangeable teachings. The opening paragraph of this *Motu Proprio* explains why it found it necessary to add such a new "norm": "To protect the Catholic faith against errors arising on the part of some [theologians]…

---

180 Ibid. (emphasis added).
181 Ibid.

it appeared highly necessary…to add new norms."[182] This new
legislation attributes unchangeable permanence to doctrines
to which the universal Church has not committed itself
infallibly. This category of "definitive" doctrines includes all
those teachings which are "necessarily connected with divine
revelation" as a logical consequence. Neither Vatican I nor
Vatican II proposed such a category of doctrines. Nor was there
any sustained consultation on this issue among the bishops of
the universal Church.[183]

As a follow-up to that *Motu Proprio,* the Congregation for
the Doctrine of the Faith promulgated a new formula of the
"profession of faith."[184] This profession of faith included not
only the Nicene-Constantinopolitan Creed (the creed recited
at Sunday Mass), but also **three additional paragraphs:** one
saying, in substance, that "I believe all that is divinely revealed
even if not in the Creed," another stating that "I embrace and
hold all that the Church has definitively taught," and the third
affirming that "I adhere with religious respect or submission
(*obsequium*) to official proclamations, even if they are not
intended to be definitive." Thus, the official profession of faith
now includes in one integral structure both the **"profession
of faith"** and the added three paragraphs, called the **"oath of
fidelity."**[185]

The fundamental problem with this new profession of faith
is that it includes not only the Creed, with all its articles of
faith but also doctrines that are **not defined,** and therefore are
not strictly matters of faith, yet the whole complex is called the
"profession of faith." The traditional purpose of the *symbolum
fidei* (profession of faith) has always been to distinguish the
articles of faith from all other knowledge. However, this new

---

182 Ibid.

183 See Ladilas Orsy, SJ, *Receiving the Council* (Collegeville, MN: Liturgical Press, 2009), p.
     112.

184 See *AAS,* 81 (1989).

185 See *AAS,* 81 (1989).

symbolum fidei confuses the issue of the heart of our faith by including articles that are not defined dogmas. One critical result of this conflation of dogmas and "definitive" teachings is that it weakens the permanent, living bond among separated Christians (such as Anglican, Orthodox, Lutherans, and others) who have traditionally professed this central Creed. A reasonable solution might be found in the very terminology used by Rome itself in distinguishing the proper "profession of faith" (the Creed) from the "oath of fidelity." That would avoid any confusion of joining dogmas to "definitive" teachings.

What are some examples of definitive teachings that are included in this new category? The very Roman commentary added to the *Motu Proprio* offers these examples: 1) the reservation of priestly ordination to men only, 2) the legitimacy of the election of the pope, 3) the canonization of saints, 4) the invalidity of Anglican orders. But theologians have grave reservations about some of these examples and about other teachings that Rome would likely consider "definitive." For example: regarding 1) the Pontifical Biblical Commission, after a two-year study, reported by a vote of 17-0 that the New Testament does not settle the question of women's ordination in a clear way (see above, pp. 80-81). Regarding 2) several times throughout history, the election of a pope has been declared illegitimate by Rome itself. Could it not happen again? Regarding 3) several saints who had been canonized have been removed from the list of saints by Pope John Paul II. Regarding 4) some theologians have serious doubts that the declaration of the invalidity of Anglican orders was a defined doctrine or even "definitive."

Regarding former doctrines of the Church, such as religious freedom for all, the historicity of events in Scripture, and the centuries-old slogan, "outside the Church there is no salvation," all were considered "definitive" doctrines before Vatican II, but have been reformed by Vatican II. Finally, regarding the 1968 encyclical, *Humanae Vitae,* the declaration against birth control was not intended to be an infallible statement, but would be considered a "definitive" doctrine; yet it seems the great majority of moral theologians privately disagree with it (though they are cautioned not to speak publicly against it).

Notice, also, what a confusing and unjust situation results from joining the "oath of fidelity" with the "profession of faith" (the Creed), as if they are both a matter of irreformable doctrine of the Church to be affirmed by all. This joint profession is now required for all those Catholic leaders who are mentioned in Canon 833: cardinals and bishops, priests and deacons, teachers of philosophy or theology, pastors of parishes, and religious superiors. If they refuse, they are simply **excluded** from such important positions in the Church; and many of these leaders of the Church can hardly be condemned for refusing, because they find some of the "definitive" doctrines as less than certain and unchangeable. If they were perfectly honest with their conscience (without any mental reservation), they would have to refuse such an oath, and then would be excluded from any teaching position in the Church. The resulting loss of such capable leaders would be quite devastating for the worldwide Church.

To conclude this discussion regarding "definitive" teachings, we need to indicate what kind of response should be given them. Theologians do not respond in exactly the same way, but generally they maintain that "definitive" teachings ordinarily deserve our assent and we should not publicly disagree with them. But once we have serious doubts about any teaching, because of careful study of the matter or because theologians doubt the biblical or rational foundation of it, we can privately disagree, And if the matter is critical for the life of the Church, or relates to establishing equality for certain groups in the Church, then we can feel free to speak out publicly.

The third level of teachings includes everything that is not a dogma or a "definitive" teaching, such as incidental teachings included in papal or Roman documents, or simple informal talks by the pope or other leaders. All such expressions are clearly not intended as "definitive" and are clearly not matters of faith. We can thoughtfully disagree with them and express our own views. Also, minor disciplinary rules for religious orders or decisions for the faithful regarding fast and abstinence—all of these can be changed and many of them have been changed in our lifetime.

C. POSITIVE SOLUTIONS

This chapter began with a description of Cardinal Bernardin's Common Ground Initiative. That is the most concerted high-level effort to respond in a practical way to the severe polarization in our American Church. But there are other signs that offer some hope. One sign comes from a survey conducted several years ago by the National Opinion Resource Center at the University of Chicago, led by Fr. Andrew Greeley. The object of the survey was to study the one-third of the respondents who considered themselves "traditional" Catholics. Without using terms like "conservative" or "progressive," the survey described this group of Catholics by their own responses in the survey.

First, traditional Catholics are **devout.** Two-thirds of them attend Mass regularly. They pray daily in some form and often meditate. Second, they are **faithful.** Ninety-six percent of them believe in God; over three-quarters of them believe in eternal life. Over half of them think it is very important to follow church teachings in making moral decisions, but they also listen to their own consciences, especially regarding sexual morality. About two-thirds of them feel God's love for them and consider themselves strong Catholics. Third, they are quite **generous** to the Church. They contribute more than twice as much to the Church as other Catholics, and they willingly volunteer for work in the Church, as well as for other charities. Finally, they are **loyal.** About half of them have confidence in religious leaders and consider themselves "active" Catholics. Who are these traditional Catholics? They are generally not at either extreme of the theological spectrum: Labels such as archconservative or radical do not fit them. For the most part, they make up a large proportion of our faithful—devout, committed Catholics. They sometimes make their own decisions about moral matters, and they also tend to be tolerant of other groups in the Church. They generally belong to the "common ground" of committed Christians. In my fifty-four years as a priest, these are the kind of people I find most often in parishes. Such faithful and active Christians are a positive sign and hope for our Church in America.

Another positive motivation for conflicting groups to find common ground is the situation we find ourselves in, now in the twenty-first century. John Allen, in his book *Future Church,* claims that the dominant movement affecting almost every human field—finance, manufacturing, politics, trade, and technology—is **globalization.** And he is convinced that this universal movement will also be a dominant influence in the Catholic Church: "In a sense, there's really only one trend here, globalization, which is producing reactions inside the Catholic Church as well as creating a whole new series of challenges outside."[186] Because globalization will dominate this twenty-first century, the Church must respond to it actively, along with every other facet of our world society:

> "The twenty-first century will call forth another type of courage, one that will challenge all Catholics .... [It] will demand ... the courage to be *globally* Catholic, moving out of the parochialism of a given language, ethnicity, geographical region, or ideology, and embracing membership in a truly "catholic" Church .... It means no longer defining one's Catholicity primarily in terms of allegiance to a faction or to a fixed set of views on issues

---

186 John Allen, p. 10.

in the Church …. This undertaking is perhaps especially urgent for Catholics in the United States.[187]

He explains further by referring to the polarization within the Church consisting of the two poles of conservative and progressive. But he refines these categories somewhat:

> … the situation is more akin to **tribalism,** with a whole series of camps attending their own meetings, reading their own publications, and following their own heroes, generally viewing the other tribes with a mixture of disinterest and suspicion. Liturgical traditionalists, peace and justice Catholics, charismatics, reformers, pro-lifers, and neo-conservatives are a few of the tribes an ethnographer would … identify.[188]

His point is that tribalism in this twenty-first century would not only be unfortunate, but utterly unsustainable. Also, he believes that Catholicism has the opportunity to pioneer what a form of globalization might look like that prizes both the universal and the local. This is another way of describing the "ecclesiology of communion" that so many recent popes and theologians, such as Rahner and Schillebeeckx, have urged the Church to exhibit; that is, thinking beyond the interests of one's own Catholic tribe and conceiving the future Church as a bold synthesis of the best of each of the Church's constituencies.

For me, the best motivation for overcoming the polarization that so divides our Church is found in Scripture, in chapter fifteen of the Acts of the Apostles. It is a critical reading for our Catholic Church today. The situation in the early Church was very divisive. The question they had to answer was: Do gentile converts have to be circumcised, to eat only certain meats, and to observe the 613 prescriptions of the Mosaic Law? This was important enough. But implied in this practical problem was a

---

187 Ibid. p. 453
188 Ibid. p. 454.

more crucial question: Is this new Christian way just a new sect of Judaism or is it a new "church"? The apostles felt they had to establish some norm, some uniformity. The so-called "Council of Jerusalem" was called to do just that. According to Raymond Brown, the scripture scholar, this Council of Jerusalem "may be judged the most important meeting ever held in the history of Christianity ... [because it] decided that the following of Jesus would soon move beyond Judaism and become a separate religion reaching to the ends of the earth."[189]

The Acts describes that, after a prolonged discussion by the apostolic leaders, a solution was offered by Peter and finally announced by James. James was the leader of the Jerusalem Church and a most conscientious observer of the Mosaic Law. In James' words, "we ought to stop troubling the Gentiles" (Acts 15:19). His argument was that the Holy Spirit had been given to the Gentiles as well as the Jews at Pentecost. The external evidence of that were the charisms of the Spirit and baptism. That meant they were all one in Christ and were all justified by faith, not by observance of the Mosaic Law. He concluded: "It is the decision of the holy Spirit and of us not to place on you any burden beyond these necessities, namely, to abstain from meat sacrificed to idols ... and from unlawful marriage" (Acts 15:28-29). He thus decided the practical question, which so divided them: that Gentiles were not required to follow all the Jewish laws, but need only do what even the Book of Leviticus asked of them. In general, the council did not decide how exactly the Christian Church was related to the Hebrew Law; it did not solve the critical theological issue (what kind of "church" they all were a part of). Rather, it only gave a practical Jewish solution, which amounted to this: Jewish Christians should "stop troubling the Gentiles;" they should not force them to follow their ways, not condemn them. The council did not decide what was absolutely true or false, or uniformly right

---

189 Raymond Brown, SS, *An Introduction to the New Testament (Anchor Bible Reference Library)* (NY: Doubleday, 1997) 306.

or wrong, or what had to be done uniformly by everyone. They wanted both groups to exist side by side in mutual acceptance and peace.

Our situation in the Church today is also critical. There are a multitude of questions facing the universal Church, especially after the great changes resulting from the reforms of Vatican II. On one side, people are troubled over sacramental changes regarding Mass and the Eucharist, about recent findings of Scripture studies of the last 60 years, and about the use of inclusive language in the liturgy. On the other side, some are distressed over recent disciplining of several theologians, or strict regulations from Rome that tend to centralize all authority, or the exclusion of women from many facets of the Church. In the face of all this, some say it is imperative that the Church establish some norms, some clear direction: They should insist on uniformity. But the solution today could well follow the same lines as in the early Church. Both sides in the deep division need to remember that the essence of our faith is not at issue; almost all these problems deal with secondary issues, not essential truths of our faith. Conservative Catholics should not quickly condemn progressives or try to force them to follow their way; nor should progressives ridicule or dismiss conservatives. In the majority of cases, it is simply not necessary to decide what is absolutely true or false, what is uniformly right or wrong. Both sides can exist side by side in peace and mutual acceptance. In a word, there can be a lot of common ground in our Church; we only need a tolerance of ambiguity in non-essentials. After all, we follow Jesus our Savior, who earnestly prayed for **unity but not uniformity** (Jn 17:20-23) among his followers. All groups need this spirit of Jesus and of the early Church: "It is the decision of the holy Spirit and of us not to place on you any burden beyond these necessities." This worked in the early Church; it can work for our global Church today.

REFLECTIONS

1. What is your reaction to Cardinal Bernardin's critical question: "Will the Catholic Church in the United States enter a new millennium as a church of promise ... able to be a leavening force in our culture ...? Or will it become a church on the defensive, torn by dissension and weakened in its core structures?"

2. The Congregation for the Doctrine of the Faith promulgated a new profession of faith, which includes in one integral structure both the "profession of faith" (the Nicene Creed) and the "oath of fidelity." Does this new profession of faith confuse the issue by including beth defined dogmas and doctrines that are not defined and therefore not strictly matters of faith?

3. The so-called Council of Jerusalem (Act 15) solved the primary question that threatened to divide the early Church into separate groups of Jews and Gentiles following very different moral codes (Mosaic Law vs. freedom from Mosaic Law). The solution was a definite compromise. How could that kind of solution serve as a model for our Church in the twenty-first century?

PART II: CATHOLICS

CHAPTER 19

Personal Faith

From all that we have considered above, it is very clear that our Catholic Church is a very human body of Christians. Its members are often poor, obscure, uneducated, unimportant people. Worse than that, it is made up of scandalous, sinful, even repulsive people. Its leaders sometimes abuse their authority and make it a means of autocratic rule, instead of the effective service that Vatican II called for. Some of its priests, sadly, are pedophiles. Certain members often take rigid moral positions and condemn others self-righteously. Others are proud of their racial standing and are quite prejudiced. Others are often selfish, mean, petty, thoughtless, and unkind. This human element is most obvious in our Church. For many people, this human element in the Church of Christ is a "stumbling block:" they protest that they cannot belong to such a faulty, sinful, proud, legalistic Church of Christ.

Most of us, in this same, very human and faulty Church, believe it is also part of the Kingdom of God; it is the Body of Christ on earth; its soul is the Spirit of God. It teaches the message of Jesus, which can only perdure in a community of faith. Its sacraments are the external, individual means of our relating to Jesus our friend. It is the source of grace and salvation in keeping with the work and intention of Christ. It is our spiritual home, in which the ultimate questions about human life are answered for us. It is the supporting group that encourages us to love God and our neighbor, after the model of Jesus. It is the enduring source of hope in Jesus, who conquered the world, rose from the dead, and opened the way to eternal life.

All the Christian churches are made up of similar faulty, sinful, selfish, mean and offensive people; all the established churches, as well as the communities of Jews, Muslims, Hindus, and Buddhists, have only human and imperfect members. But they are also important religious communities, because of their prophets and teachers, sacred writings, moral laws, and traditional ways of worship. That spiritual element makes them valuable means of following God's ways and coming to the salvation that God offers to all human beings.

Yet none of the leaders of these faiths proposes himself as the perfect model for living that faith; no one human individual claims to be the complete ideal, the perfect example for all the members. What distinguishes Christians from the disciples of all other faiths and religious leaders is that true Christians follow a **person,** not a teaching. For us, Jesus himself is "the way…and the life" (Jn 14:6). For us Christians, the very person of Jesus is the **living embodiment** of his cause, the **supreme model** for our view of life and way of living. That is, the person of Jesus is inseparably united with his teaching as our way of living. And as our human model, Jesus does not command us, force us, or demand our obedience. Rather, he draws us, calls us, and encourages us to live as he lived. His influence is not the force of commandments or the pressure of abstract principles or ideals; Jesus' influence is the appeal of a **person,** the power of a lover. Only a living person—not a principle—can call, invite, challenge, and summon us. Only a concrete, historical person— not an abstract ideal—can encourage us to attainable ideals, to realistic norms and values. The human Jesus himself is the model for our human life. His teaching, his life, his person, are the way to human wholeness.

Karl Rahner expresses that another way: Christianity is Jesus of Nazareth; it is radically embedded in the historical existence of Jesus Christ; God's Word has become incarnate in

Jesus Christ.[190] Hans Kung adds that the criterion of what is Christian "is … the original figure of Christianity: the concrete, historical Jesus of Nazareth, who for Christians is the Messiah, that Jesus Christ from whom any Christian church derives its existence."[191]

If the concrete, historical Jesus is the criterion for what is Christian, then the primary source of our understanding Christianity is the testimony of Scripture. That is why leading theologians today, such as Schillebeeckx, Rahner, Küng, Elizabeth Johnson, Lisa Sowle Cahill, and Monika Hellwig, insist that this original faith-testimony found in Scripture forms the basis of Christian theology:

> This Jesus Christ is neither an unhistorical myth nor a superhistorical idea, doctrine or world view. He is rather the historical Jesus of Nazareth, who according to the testimonies in the New Testament is the standard for believers of all times …. [A] Christian theologian … has no other testimony to faith than those originally written down in the Old and New Testament, which was transmitted through the ages … and always has to be retranslated for contemporary men and women.[192]

For modern theologians, then, our Christian faith depends only on the **person of Jesus Christ,** who is the only criterion for our commitment to his way of salvation, He, himself, chose disciples who were so clearly human and imperfect. Throughout 2,000 years of Christianity, his disciples—both leaders and ordinary members—were often terribly inadequate, abusive, and even scandalous, but they made up his very human Church on earth. However, Christ knew the failures of his first disciples and knows us too. He loves that Church and promises, "…

---

190   See Karl Rahner, *Hearer of the Word: Laying the Foundation for a Philosophy of Religion* , trans. by Joseph Donceel (NY: Continuum, 1994).

191   Hans Kung, *The Catholic Church,* p. xxiii.

192   Hans Kung, *Theology for the Third Millennium,* p. 156.

I am with you always, until the end of the age" (Mt 28:20). Hopefully the conclusion for us, who are often troubled by this human Church, is that we know and **expect** this Church of Christ to be always imperfect. But that obvious fact should not diminish this profound faith of ours: Jesus Christ is the sole criterion of our personal faith, the model for our Christian living, and the absolute foundation for our unfailing hope. In the rest of this book, I hope to show that even though our imperfect, institutional Church will always trouble us, nevertheless, our own faith, our emerging spirituality, our friendship with Jesus our Lord in prayer and the Eucharist, and our confident assurance that Jesus is "the way and the truth and the life" are wonderfully inspiring for us as Catholics in the twenty-first century.

REFLECTIONS

1. Have you ever met persons who argue that they have no need of religion? They claim that they have a personal relationship with God and do not need a religious community such as a Christian Church or any established religion? How would you answer such persons?

2. Clearly, the Catholic Church has many imperfect leaders and members. How do you explain this defect to a non-believer or to someone who has left the Church in anger?

3. Reflect on the following idea: "True Christians follow not a teaching but a person, Jesus Christ." Reflect how this can apply to your ordinary Christian life.

CHAPTER 20

Distinctive Lay Spirituality

Richard McBrien in his book, *Catholicism,*[193] accurately describes the history of spirituality throughout the 2,000 years of Christianity. From the earliest times, many forms of spirituality were seen as ways of following Christ's invitation: "Whoever wishes to come after me must deny himself, take up his cross, and follow me" (Mt 16:24). The first century focused on the Kingdom of God, which was thought to be coming soon in final form, so that Christians felt urged to preach the Gospel in word, sacrament, and witness in order to prepare for the end time. During the times of persecution, that witness to Christ sometimes took the ideal form of martyrdom ("martyr" means witness). After the persecutions ended for the most part, early Church Fathers, such as Origin, suggested that a life of complete self-sacrifice was a kind of unbloody martyrdom. In the fourth century, Anthony of Egypt started the hermitical way (living separate from the world and remaining poor), possibly as his understanding of Jesus' invitation to the rich young man: "If you wish to be perfect, go, sell what you have and give to [the] poor …. Then come, follow me" (Mt 19:21). In the following centuries, many hermits gathered in community in monasteries. In the tenth and eleventh centuries, various monasteries joined together and formed religious orders, such as the contemplative order of Cistercians and the begging orders of Franciscans and Dominicans. In the sixteenth century, Carmelites, such as Teresa of Avila and John of the Cross, taught the way of contemplation, the mystical way. Especially in the twelfth and thirteenth centuries, many books were written about the "way of perfection," referring to the vows of poverty, celibacy, and obedience taken by religious monks. These books developed the monastic attitude, "*de contemptu mundi*" (on the contempt

---

193   Richard McBrien, *Catholicism* (San Francisco: Harper and Row Publishers, 1981), pp. 1058-84.

of the world). For several hundred years, then, the "way of perfection" was centered on the three vows of religious life-style. As a result, lay men and women, who could not take the three vows, could only try to imitate the "way of perfection" in a lesser way, by being poor in spirit, chaste in their marriage, and obedient to the laws of the Church. In recent centuries, some spiritual writers, especially St. Francis de Sales, tried to develop an authentic lay spirituality. However, lay spirituality continued to be seen as inferior to the esteemed "way of perfection" of the religious orders; the best that lay people could do was to "offer up" their work, along with some pious practices and devotions. There was not much change in this evaluation of the "way of perfection" of the religious life as being superior to lay life in the last thousand years.

Around the time of Vatican II, another form of spirituality was beginning to develop. Theologians began to distinguish two different ways of looking at the world. Both of them are based on Scripture, and both of them are somewhat valid, but whichever view of the world we choose tends to determine our form of Christian living and spirituality. Let me delineate these two ways clearly.

The first catholic view of the world is that the world is **suspect.** It is based on these words in John's First Letter: "Do not love the world …. For all that is in the world [is] sensual lust, enticement for the eyes, and a pretentious life…" (1 Jn 2:15-16). The old translation is more familiar to some of us: "[T]he lust of the flesh, the lust of the eyes, and the pride of life." So the best thing for the Christian to do was to **flee** the world as much as possible. Such was the theme of countless books in the Middle ages, *De Contemptu Mundi*. In these books, not only excessive love of the world but also all love of pleasure, riches, and self was suspect. That was how the monkish "way of perfection" became the superior way of following Jesus. Such a spirituality stressed human sinfulness and the **evils of this**

world. It was an **eschatological spirituality**; that is, looking toward eternal life. The problem with such a spirituality was that it was only possible for about 1% of Christians—for monks and nuns. For everyone else, it was an impossible ideal that could only be practiced in a **marginal** or inferior way. Yet this was the spirituality many of us grew up with in the pre-Vatican II Church.

Since the council, there is a very different view of the world that is developing in today's Church. This view is based on the words of Jesus in John's Gospel: "For God so loved the world that he gave his only Son … not … to condemn the world, but that the world might be saved through him" (Jn 3:16-17). That is, God's purpose in creating and redeeming the world in Christ was to love the world and sinful humanity, not to condemn it. So the best thing a Christian can do is to **love** the world. In the words of Pope Paul VI, shortly after the Vatican Council: "We will love our time, our community, our technical skills, our art, our sport, our world." What is pleasing to God, then, is for us to grow and become mature human beings after the model of Jesus. We are to feel responsible for our world, seek to direct it, give meaning to it, and work to develop it. What this means, then, is that our family, home, job, free time, spiritual activities, sexual life, relationships to others, are all a part of our holiness. Such spirituality stresses the need to **love** sinful humanity and to try to form this imperfect world in the spirit of Christ. It is an **incarnational spirituality,** concerned with forming this world; it is life affirming, aware of God's grace and presence in our world. It is a spirituality at the **center** of our life, involving every moment of it.

According to this spirituality, we do not try to abandon the world, but try to live our life in the world according to the model of Jesus. We do that by accepting the reality of our life just as it comes to us. We do that by having the same attitude toward the world that God himself has: "For God so loved the world that he gave his only Son … not … to condemn the world, but that the world might be saved through him" (Jn 3:16-17).

Developing this same attitude toward the world is critical to this new spirituality. If we concentrate on two elements that mainly constitute our lives, this spirituality will become simplified and practical. First, our lives consist of constant **relationships with people**. All day long we have contacts with people on various levels: incidental contact, business relationships, regular acquaintances, real friends, and family. We are never without people. We Christians are told by Jesus himself that all of these people are related to him: "[W]hatever you did for one of these least … you did for me" (Mt 25:40). We need to grow in our understanding that what we do to others, we do to Jesus himself. We can increase our sense that each one is a member of the body of Christ. Jesus even adds that it doesn't matter that we generally don't think about this relationship to him, because he, himself, considers it as done to himself.

Second, we can have a different view of our daily work, whatever it might be: homemaker, social worker, teacher, factory worker, businessman, scientist, service person, or whatever. We need to realize that all of our daily work is not just a way of secular living and supporting our families; rather, the **work itself** is valuable, because all of it is some kind of **service** to God's people. Whatever our job might be, it offers some service to others, even if our activity is far removed from the actual people helped by it. Even computer operators or accountants, who never see the people they are helping, or sanitary workers or demolition workers, whose jobs seem more negative than helpful—all of them are necessary for people to live well in our complicated modern world. We need to grow in this awareness of serving God's people by our work. These two elements, people and work, are with us always; they include all the joys, fears, sadness, troubles, sufferings, and challenges that make up our daily lives. God's will is that we accept them in the spirit of Jesus. We fulfill God's will for us by accepting all that happens to us naturally after the model of Jesus. There is one sentence in the Letter to the Colossians which nicely sums up all we have said about our modern spirituality: "[W]hatever you do, in word or in deed, do everything in the name of the Lord Jesus …" (Col 3:17). That counsel includes the people we meet and the work that we do each day.

This description of lay spirituality is very simple. Such a Christian life is very ordinary and common. It seems to leave a large hole in terms of the immense social needs of our world, the dire poverty of so many people, the ever-present suffering and persecution in so many countries. What can our common, ordinary lives ever accomplish in terms of relieving even the smallest amount of so much suffering? An adequate answer to this question would be almost endless, but consider this one example:

Francis was born into a wealthy family. As a teenager, he was a playboy and a spendthrift, as were his rowdy friends. When hostilities broke out between his town and a neighboring town, he joined the army and went off to fight. During the military conflict, he was taken prisoner and spent the next year of his life in chains in a dirty dungeon. After his release, it took him a full year to regain his health. That prison ordeal and year of recuperation changed his life forever.

As a result, he put aside his expensive clothes, renounced his family riches, and put on the garb of a poor workman. He left home and took up the life of a hermit. He made his home in an old, tumbledown church, where he spent days alone in prayer. Slowly, he developed a deep love and concern for the outcasts and rejects of society. This love grew in his heart as a result of his reading Jesus' words in Matthew's Gospel: "[W]hatever you did for one of these least brothers of mine, you did for me" (Mt 25:40). Francis was so moved by Jesus' instruction that he began to travel around preaching the gospel. He had no money and just depended on the alms of those he met and taught. He had an engaging personality and soon drew other young men to follow him. This group slept under the stars and ate whatever was given to them. They went about caring for the sick and helping the poor. By the time Francis was twenty-seven years old, his followers were so numerous that they eventually sought permission from the pope to form a religious community—of Franciscans.

This man, of course, was St. Francis of Assisi. He and his followers embraced poverty strictly for spiritual reasons, because it made them one with the poor and literally imitated the life-style of Jesus. Still, both then and now, people criticized Francis' approach to helping the poor. They say that his followers do not attack the roots of poverty; they do not mobilize public opinion and governmental action but attack poverty only superficially, putting band-aids on huge social wounds. It's true that people like Francis of Assisi, as well as Mother Teresa in the twentieth century, do not attack the root causes of poverty. But that does not minimize their great sacrifices and dedication in service to those who are poor and suffering. We must respect the different calls to service of such greathearted people, who do what they feel called to, in service to God's people.

That is the point I want to make here. Our lay spirituality is centered on the common and ordinary works of our lives, for that is what makes up our daily lives. But each of us can extend our care for people and our work of service in any ways that we personally feel called to. Not even the saints, like St. Francis and Mother Teresa, can cure the ills of our world. Nor can we. But at times we each feel called, alone or with others, to contribute what we can, simply or creatively, to the needs of those who are so needy and helpless.

I began this chapter by quoting Matthew 16:24: "Whoever wishes to come after me must deny himself, take up his cross, and follow me." This saying of Jesus (along with the parallel sayings) has been a constant source of meditation for Christians throughout history; any Christian spirituality must include some insight into the meaning of this invitation to be his disciple.

Edward Schillebeeckx has discovered that such sayings were common in the Greco-Roman world as early as 300 B. C.:

> Long before the time of Jesus, for both Jews and Greeks (see already Plato, *Republic II,* 361) the expression 'take up one's cross' meant to have the courage to die a violent death for a particular cause …. So what Matthew is saying in this story is that Christianity can result in a violent death …. [What] does this message mean for us … Christians who do not have to think of martyrdom and torture, and only know the miseries of any human being …? Briefly this. Within our own surroundings, however small-scale they may be, we must stand up for justice and love … even to our own disadvantage. This in itself will bring us persecution and suffering enough, which is what Matthew is ultimately concerned with.[194]

So when Jesus asks each Christian to carry one's cross, he is not referring to his crucifixion, which was not known then. Rather, he seems to refer to a common saying of the Greco-Roman world meaning to offer one's life for a cause. So Jesus suggests that following him means to surrender one's whole life to Jesus and his cause, to be so committed to Jesus as to be willing to die for him, or at least to live according to his example. Also, when Luke reports this saying of Jesus, he adds one word to his invitation: "[H]e must deny himself and take up his cross daily and follow me" (Lk 9:23). By adding the one word "**daily,**" Luke changes the meaning of this saying to include following Jesus and his way **every day.** Another way of expressing Jesus' invitation would be: If you are committed to

---

194   Edward Schillebeeckx, *God Among Us; The Gospel Proclaimed* (NY: Crossroad), pp. 202-03.

being my disciple, then you must accept all the sufferings that come to you naturally as a part of daily human living; follow my example all day, every day.

Every spirituality also has to come to terms with suffering in our lives. No matter what our spirituality is, we are bound to ask the insistent question about evil in our lives and the question of God's providence. Yet, throughout history our Catholic theology has never explained fully **how God's providence works** in human lives. As I write this, several great tragedies have occurred in our world lately: hurricanes, deadly floods, epidemics, earthquakes, and national food crises. Ordinary people and even the print media reflect on these natural disasters (as did the Chicago Tribune recently) and ask the question: "Where is God in the tsunami?" Or to put this another way: If God rules this world of ours, how could God permit the death of so many innocent people? We must admit that neither Scripture nor our Church gives a single, consistent answer to such questions. In the **Hebrew Scriptures** (Old Testament), God was seen as the cause of everything—all that was good and all that was bad. When rain came or a drought continued, it was God's doing; it was his punishment or reward for his people. When the Israelites won a victory in battle, God was praised; when they lost, it was because of God's anger with them. In a word, everything that happened was not simply natural or human; it was all attributed to God's direct action. In the latter books of the Hebrew Bible, such as in the Book of Job, the writers began to question this universal approach to God's action in the world; the Scripture writers agonized over this kind of question: "If God is all just, how can bad things happen to good people?" Like the mythical figure, Job, they never came close to solving this question.

But in the **Christian Scriptures** (New Testament), Jesus gives a much clearer answer. At one point, Jesus was walking with a crowd of people when he saw a man who had been blind since birth. His disciples asked him, "[W]ho sinned, this man or his parents, that he was born blind?' Jesus answered, 'Neither he nor his parents sinned; it is so that the works of God might be made visible through him'" (Jn 9:2-3). Twice in Luke, Jesus presents a similar question and answers it two times in a similar way: "Do you think that because these Galileans suffered in this way they were greater sinners than all other Galileans? By no means!" (Lk 13:2-5). That is, Jesus, in three cases, teaches that there is no causal connection between natural tragedies and God's punishment, between God's action and human guilt. We have to conclude that in this life there is no causal connection between natural tragedies and God's direct action.

In his own human life, Jesus lived out this sense of providence. There is no scriptural evidence that he envisioned any of his trials as directly caused by God. So much of his public life was filled with failures and suffering: His home town did not receive him; the Pharisees rejected him and then sought his death; many who heard him did not believe in him; Pilate and Herod refused to believe in his innocence; the apostles were slow to understand him, they deserted him in his passion; Judas betrayed him; he was unjustly condemned to death; he died an ignominious death; the entire end of his life was a failure and a fiasco. Jesus accepted all of these trials with patience and courage. He never considered that his murderers were God's secret coworkers or disguised instruments of the divine will. Rather he knew they were free human beings who acted in keeping with that freedom.

Certainly, his primary purpose in life was to fulfill the will of God: "My food is to do the will of the one who sent me …" (Jn 4:34; also: Jn 5:30; 6:38; 17:4). But he did not indicate that all these events were determined and sent to him directly by God, his Father; rather, he knew that whatever happened in his free human life was to be accepted with patience and courage and so fulfill God's will. That is, he found God's will not so much in **what** came to him, but rather in **how** he responded to all that happened to him humanly. That is exactly how he is the model for all of us, as St. Peter describes clearly: "... to this you have been called, because Christ also suffered for you, leaving you an example that you should follow in his footsteps .... When he was insulted, he returned no insult; when he suffered he did not threaten ..." (1 Pet 2:21-23). That is, his example consisted in how he accepted what happened to him. Similarly, when he cried out in Gethsemane, "[Not] my will but yours be done" (Lk 22:42), he did not mean that God directly ordered his passion, but that God's will was that Jesus **accept** his cross. So he did just that and became the **model** for all of us to follow.

What is our modern, Christian answer to why bad things happen to good people? We affirm that God is the "ground of all being" and the ultimate cause of all that exists. All of creation is eventually traced back to God's direct cause and continues to exist by his support. So the **ultimate cause** of everything is God, our creator. But all **natural** phenomena—such as floods, hurricanes, and earthquakes—are the result of nature acting according to the laws of nature and the defects of our natural world. The "why" of them is not to be sought in the predetermined will of God, but in the natural laws that cause them. And all **human evils** such as injustice, abuse, and violence—are the result of human selfishness and hatred. That is, because God made human beings to be really free, they can and will do senseless, dumb, foolish, and vicious things. The "why" has nothing to do with God's providence, but everything to do with human frailty and sinfulness. So the **immediate cause** of all human actions and of all natural occurrences is human or natural. God is simply not in the hurricane, earthquake, or human evil.

We can understand this better if we concentrate on human freedom. If we are really free human beings, then we are not marionettes on a string, manipulated by God. If we are really free, then we must be able to choose to disobey God's will and do senseless, harmful, and inhuman things. If we are really free, then things cannot always go our way, and life will not consistently be just and equitable. What all this implies is that God's providence **does not arrange things in our external world.** God does not make a farce of human freedom, does not interfere with the freedom he gave us; for without that freedom, we would no longer be really human. So when we talk about "doing the will of God," we are not referring so much to what happens to us, but rather how we accept what happens to us. For God does not determine **what** happens to us, but does show us **how** we are to accept the things that happen to us, after the model of Jesus. God is not the immediate cause of anything that happens to us, but God does want us to accept everything after the example of Jesus our Lord, with his courage, patience, and acceptance. In a word, we do God's will by accepting all that happens to us humanly according to the example of Jesus.

If all that is true about all the **external** events of life, then what do we mean by God's **providence** and care for us? Scripture and faith teach us that God's providence and care for us is **internal.** God's grace does act within our hearts and minds. That is, if we are faithful Christians, then God does have a **profound influence** on us without interfering with our freedom. Thus, because of our faith in God, we form our entire outlook on life. In God's calling us as Christians, we freely choose, day by day, a certain way of living. In God's word in Scripture, we are able to find our values for life. In Jesus, we have a model for our living. In Jesus, we have an adequate motive for loving all people. In God, we form our dreams and establish our hopes. In faith, our suffering can be meaningful, our struggles worthwhile, our acceptance of life's trials life-giving The more faithful we are as Christians, the more our hopes and dreams can be realized in Christ. This is **the way that God provides for us;** this is the way God's providence supports us freely and humanly. We remain entirely free; yet God instills within us—by the grace of the Holy Spirit—everything we need for mature, human living. God is then the God "in [whom] we live and move and have our being ..." (Acts 17:28).

An extraordinary example of someone who accepted the will of God for her with amazing determination, along with personal prayer, is the story of Wilma. In Nashville, Tennessee, Wilma was born prematurely and soon developed polio. As a result of her polio, one leg was badly crippled and her foot was turned inward. By the age of five, she could only hobble about on metal braces. When she was eleven, she often took off her braces and practiced walking without them, while her sister watched out for her parents who might stop her. For a whole year, she continued her secret walks. Then, one day, she mentioned what she was doing to her doctor; he was flabbergasted but let her continue. Besides constantly walking and practicing, she also prayed for God's help. Eventually she threw away her braces, and even began to run, more and more each day. By the time she was sixteen, incredibly, she qualified for the U.S. Olympic team. Then, in Melbourne, Australia she won a bronze medal. Four years later, 1960, in Rome, she became the first woman in history to win three gold medals in track and field. And the whole world came to know of this extraordinary achievement of **Wilma Rudolph.** She was also given the Sullivan Award as the nation's top amateur athlete. She is a living example of the power of perseverance despite extreme setbacks. With the help of prayer, she accepted what happened to her so tragically and overcame it so courageously.

REFLECTIONS

1. List some similarities and some differences between eschatological spirituality and incarnational spirituality. How does your own spirituality fit in here?

2. Throughout our 2,000-year history, Catholic spiritualities found different ways of responding to Jesus invitation, "Whoever wishes to come after me must deny himself, take up his cross, and follow me" (Mk 8:34). Was there anything wrong with their diverse responses? Was any one solution the only right way? What is your estimate of the modern lay spirituality proposed in this chapter?

3. The Church has never defined how the providence of God operates in our world. The common problem regarding belief in a provident God is: "How can so much tragedy, injustice, and evil exist in our world, if a compassionate and loving God rules the world?" Yet, if God created us to be really free human beings, what does that freedom necessarily imply about the existence of injustice, hate, prejudice, and human evil in this world of ours?

CHAPTER 21

Our Personal God

John's Gospel contains a profound spirituality of the Holy Spirit. Luke's Gospel and Acts of the Apostles also have an appealing spirituality of the Spirit (pneumatology). But let me concentrate on John's extraordinary teaching about the Holy Spirit in the individual lives of Christians.

In chapter 14, John's Jesus promises his disciples a "new Advocate" (14:16). That is, Jesus himself was their original Advocate: "[W]e have an Advocate with the Father, Jesus Christ ... (1 Jn 2:1), and now he promises the Spirit (a new Advocate) who would take his place and "be with [them] always" (Jn 14:16). Jesus even asserts that "... I tell you the truth, it is better for you that I go. For if I do not go, the Advocate will not come to you. But if I go, I will send him to you" (Jn 16:7). Jesus means that the disciples will somehow be "better off\'" after he has left them and sent them the Holy Spirit as their permanent Advocate! We can understand Jesus' amazing assertion here by considering the five Paraclete sayings in chapters 14 to 16.

1. "I will not leave you orphans ..." (14:18). "... I will ask the Father, and he will give you another Advocate to be with you always, the Spirit of truth, ...[who] remains with you, and will be in you" (14:16-17). Here Jesus establishes the foundation for the entire spiritual activity of the Paraclete in his followers. He asserts that the Paraclete will dwell with the disciples permanently as the new presence of Jesus in each one individually. The meaning of this immanence is that there is a permanent spiritual status for all who believe in Jesus, and he appropriates this divine immanence to the Spirit/Paraclete. Jesus goes on to explain this individual presence of the Spirit: "Whoever loves me will keep my word, and my Father will love him,

and we will come to him and make our dwelling with him" (14:23). He means that the Father and Jesus dwell in us in the **person** of the Holy Spirit.

2. "The Advocate, the holy Spirit, that the Father will send in my name—he will teach you everything and remind you of all that [I] told you" (14:26). First Jesus tells the disciples that the Advocate "will teach you everything." "To teach" in John is practically a verb of revelation. But the Spirit will not bring a **new** revelation: "He will not speak on his own, but he will speak what he hears .... [H]e will take from what is mine and declare it to you" (16:13-14). In John, the teaching of Jesus contains all that the disciples need to know, all the revelation of God. The proper function of the Spirit of Jesus, then, is to make them understand the teaching of Jesus clearly.

Second, Jesus promises that the Advocate "will remind you of all that I told you." Often in John's Gospel, Jesus promised that later—after the resurrection—the disciples would remember what he told them and come to understand it (see 2:22; 12:16; 13:7; 13:19; 14:19-20; 14:29; 15:20-21; 15:26; 16:4; 16:12-13). He meant that they could only understand the deep mystery of redemption by means of his suffering and death after they had experienced his passion and received the gift of the Holy Spirit.

These functions of the Spirit of Jesus, teaching and reminding, are also meant for us. Pope John Paul II affirms this: "The promise is not limited to the apostles and their immediate companions .... It extends to the future generations of disciples ... of Christ."[195]

John's entire Gospel stresses the necessity of letting Jesus' teaching enter into our hearts so that its teaching might attain its full effect. The Spirit is given to us precisely to make Jesus' way ever more personal and inspiring.

---

195   Pope John Paul II, *The Spirit, Giver of Life and Love* (Boston: Pauline Books, 1996), p. 22.

3. "When the Advocate comes … the Spirit of truth that proceeds from the Father, he will testify to me. And you also testify …" (Jn 15:26-27). Here Jesus asserts that the Spirit "will testify to [me]. And you also testify;" yet this will not be two sources of testimony but only one. That is, the Spirit will first convince the disciples internally of the reality of Jesus and God, and then encourage them to bear witness to Christ with great confidence. That is, when the disciples experience opposition from the world, the Spirit of Truth will work within their hearts to strengthen them in their own faith and provide them with unshakable confidence.

   In our contemporary society, some profess a scientific materialism that rejects anything spiritual or supernatural and accepts only material things as real. They tend to treat faith as fantasy and religion as myth. Jesus promises that the Spirit of truth "will testify" to God, to faith in Jesus, and to eternal life.

4. "[When the Advocate] comes he will convict the world in regard to sin and righteousness and condemnation: sin, because they do not believe in me; righteousness, because I am going to the Father and you will no longer see me; condemnation, because the ruler of this world has been condemned" (Jn 16:8-11). In John's Gospel, there is no mention of formal public trials and judges (as are mentioned in Mt 10:17-18 and Mk 13:9). Rather, Jesus here seems to refer to the same theological conflict that characterized the public life of Jesus in John's Gospel; namely the great opposition between Jesus and the world, the struggle for and against Jesus. Let me try to clarify this difficult passage by explaining five critical words. **Convict** (*"elenchein"*) can mean either "to convict" someone or "to expose" something as false or wrong. In the latter sense, Jesus means that the Paraclete will expose the world as wrong in refusing to believe in Jesus. **World** refers only to those Jews who reject Jesus and his teaching about God's

kingdom, especially some of the Scribes and Pharisees. It does not include those who are open to Jesus and come to believe in him; see 11:19, 31, 33, 36, 45; 12:9, 11. **Sin:** Others refuse to believe at all: "[T]his is the verdict, that the light came into the world, but people preferred darkness to light (Jn 3:19; see also 9:41; 12:37; 15:22-24). The disciples will continue in this contest against Jesus, and the Paraclete will be their "counsel for the defense" to prove the world guilty of disbelief in God and his Word. **Righteousness or justice**: The Paraclete will show that Jesus, whom the world judged guilty, was really innocent and just. **Condemnation:** That is, proof that in condemning Jesus the world itself was judged. For in the person of the Paraclete, Jesus is still present after his death; so if Jesus' passion represented the confrontation of Jesus and the Prince of this world (12:31; 14:30), then Jesus' victory over death is also his victory over the Prince of this world (see 1 Jn 4:3-4; 5:4-5).

Today, some people take different stances that threaten our witness to Jesus, our steadfastness in faith. Some reject God on the basis of the pervasiveness of human suffering; some attack the historical Jesus because not everything written about him is documented history; some criticize Scripture because of scientific or historical inaccuracies; some reject Christianity because of the grave faults of Christians. With such challenges to our faith in him, Jesus promises the witness of the Paraclete as our "counsel for defense" to strengthen us in our faith.

5. "The Spirit of truth … will guide you to all truth …. [H]e will speak what he hears, and will declare to you the things that are coming" (Jn 16:13). The functions of the Paraclete here are similar to those in 14:16: that is, to teach and to call to mind: but they are further developed here, especially by the addition of two phrases. First, the phrase "guide you to all truth" (or "guide you along the way of all truth," as in the Anchor Bible). This

phrase seems to include more than a deeper intellectual understanding; it also involves teaching a way of life in conformity with Jesus' teaching. The reason for saying this is bound up with the whole Johannine understanding of "way of truth." For John's Gospel thinks of truth, not as an abstract system of faith, but as a sphere of action similar to the Hebrew Scriptures' notion of "the way of truth;" as a way of life in conformity with the Mosaic law, and also similar to the notion of "the way" in the Acts of the Apostles.[196] The phrase "declare to you the things that are coming" does not involve any new revelation, for he adds, "he will speak what he hears" (16:13b). To paraphrase the meaning of "declare to you the things that are coming," the Holy spirit will **not predict what is coming,** but will help to **interpret what is coming.** As Raymond Brown rightly observes: "[This phrase] consists in interpreting, in relation to each coming generation, the contemporary significance of what Jesus has said and done. The best Christian preparation for what is coming to pass is not an exact foreknowledge of the future but a deeper understanding of what Jesus means for one's own time."[197]

Thus, the Paraclete will help each generation uncover the deep meaning of the person and mission of Jesus for their particular time and in their own historical context. And in our own period of history, the Spirit will offer new insights into the revelation taught by Jesus, so that we will find authentic responses to our modern, secular world.

Besides this explanation of these five Paraclete sayings of Jesus, I want to add one promise by Jesus about the Spirit's influence in our prayer that is very encouraging: "Amen, amen, I say to you, whatever you ask the Father in my name he will give you. Until now you have not asked anything in my name;

---

196 Raymond Brown, *The Gospel According to John, 13-21*, pp. 628-29.
197 Ibid. p. 716.

ask and you will receive …. The hour is coming when … you will ask in my name …" (Jn 16:23-26). This passage has a definite connection to John's treatment of the Paraclete in our lives. That is, after Jesus' resurrection, the disciples are promised the continued presence of the Spirit, and because of the new presence of the Spirit, they can have great confidence when they ask anything of the Father in Jesus' name. "Until now you have not asked anything in my name." That is, Jesus has not been their intercessor with the Father while he was with them. But after the resurrection and the sending of the Paraclete, the disciples will be so intimately united with the risen Jesus, by means of the Paraclete, they can then "ask anything in [Jesus'] name." In a parallel passage in chapter 14, Jesus promised that the prayers of the disciples would be heard: "[W]hatever you ask in my name, I will do" (Jn 14:13). Then he immediately mentions the gift of the Spirit (14:16-17), apparently so that they can have their prayers answered in Jesus' name (14:14). To paraphrase all this: Soon the disciples will have the new Advocate, the Paraclete, who dwells within them and unites them even more intimately with Jesus and the Father; therefore, anything the disciples (and we) ask the Father in Jesus' name will be granted.

Let me summarize John's theology of the Spirit now and draw some conclusions. In the first 13 chapters of his Gospel, John develops his Word Christology by showing that Jesus is the complete light, truth, and revelation about God; then, in chapters 14 to 16, he speaks in a parallel way about the work of the Spirit. He affirms that the Spirit of Jesus will perform many of the same functions as Jesus did for his disciples: to teach them, to be their advocate in trials, to intercede for them with God, to encourage them, to lead them to all truth, and to guide them in the things to come. Thus, as Jesus was the complete revelation of God, so the Spirit of Jesus will work in a parallel way for all believers to **understand all that Jesus revealed:** "The Advocate, the holy Spirit … will teach you everything and remind you of all that [I] told you" (14:26).

Second, John makes it clear that the Spirit of Jesus will be both a **permanent** presence and an **active** teacher and guide. The Spirit will dwell within all Jesus' disciples always: "… the Father…will give you another Advocate to be with you always, the Spirit of truth …" (Jn 14:16-17). And the Spirit will be an active teacher and guide: "… the Spirit of truth … will guide you to all truth" (Jn 16:13; see also 14:26). Third, once Jesus has departed, the Spirit of Jesus becomes the "new Advocate;" this constant presence and guidance of the Spirit of Jesus in all believers can reasonably be described as the **era of the Spirit**. For just as John presents Jesus in his public life as the Word of God, the complete revelation of God, so he presents the Spirit of Truth as Jesus' mirror image present to all Christians to the end of time.

Such a theology of the Spirit can be a powerful source of spirituality for us today. It reminds us that we live in the age of the Spirit; we are to be guided by the Spirit of Jesus. Therefore, the new Advocate, the Paraclete, will perform many of the same functions for us as Jesus did for his disciples; he will be Jesus' **new persona**: to teach us, to be our advocate in trials, to intercede for us with God, to encourage us, to lead us to all truth, and to guide us in the things to come. The Spirit dwelling within us can be especially powerful in our prayer life, because we now have the Holy Spirit dwelling within us, who will personally "remind" us of all Jesus taught, who will "teach [us] everything," who will lead us "to all truth," and who will guide us in "the things that are coming."

REFLECTIONS

1. To paraphrase Raymond Brown: The Paraclete will help each generation uncover the deep meaning of the person and mission of Jesus for their particular time and in their own historical context. Relate this idea to something that is in the daily news.

2. The apostles could hardly believe Jesus words, "[I]t is better

for you that I go. For if I do not go, the Advocate will not come to you" (Jn 16:7). He meant that the Holy Spirit would only become their new Advocate and guide once he went to the Father. Do you agree with his words at least as it relates to us: "[I]t is better for you that I go"?

3. In John's Gospel, as Jesus was about to leave the apostles, he promised, "I will not leave your orphans …(14:18). He meant that the Holy Spirit would be their new Advocate "to be with you always." After reflecting on the five quotes of Jesus regarding the Holy Spirit in John, chapters 14-16, what do they tell you about the Spirit as our personal Advocate?

CHAPTER 22

Prayer and Friendship with Jesus

Let us begin with the common experience of prayer—which may reflect your experience too. The most common experience of people who were serious about prayer and meditation at some time in their life was something like the following: As young people, most of our prayer was vocal prayer. As we grew older, some of us learned more personal kinds of prayer in prayer groups or parish retreats. Some of us learned about meditation if we spent time in the seminary or religious life, or in some prayerful Christian community. One very common form of meditation taught in the last fifty years included an introduction (preludes), a reflection on Scripture or the life of Jesus (points), a personal reaction (acts of faith and affections), and a conclusion (final prayer or resolution).

This form of prayer (or other forms taught by various spiritual directors) may have been practiced for some time with varying degrees of success. Little by little our prayer tended to become less intellectual or theological and more personal and affective. Sometimes we felt more devotional; our feelings became warmer and stronger; prayer was often a delight to us; Jesus was our personal friend and model; we were attracted to him more and more; we were in love with our gentle Savior.

In time our prayer slowed down and simplified. We didn't find many new ideas to occupy our intellect and our emotions quieted down. We felt no need to be "busy about many things," like Martha, but were content to sit at the feet of Jesus, like Mary. It seemed very natural that our prayer should grow more and more simple. Though we were not so active, we experienced a deeper intimacy with our Lord. We still felt we were making progress, and experienced a feeling of comfort and confidence, but then many of us experienced a crisis in our prayer life; in time our prayer became so simple that it almost disappeared.

Not only were we without engaging ideas to occupy us, or spontaneous affections to hearten us, there was not even a sense of sitting at the feet of Jesus in simple love. There was no clarity of thought, distinctness of image, nor sensible fervor. And so the crisis grew—with a heavy sense of weariness and distaste for mental prayer. We felt frustrated and confused because we seemed to be getting nowhere; our prayer life seemed to fade away; we began to sense that our interior life had reached a dead end.

Let me describe what I did at this point, as one example. I continued to pray anyway, even though my prayer got more dry and dark. I found various alternative forms of simple meditation: reflection on a Scripture passage or an enlightening section in a spiritual book, or even centering prayer. But nothing really improved the situation. It became so painful to pray that I would find excuses to avoid prayer, or I would continue to spend the time only because I thought empty prayer was better than no prayer at all, and because some kind of prayer was essential for union with Christ.

Others who were faithful to prayer had different experiences. Some tried every form of meditation they came in contact with, whether it was yoga, *lectio divina* (meditative reading), praying with music and incense, praying outdoors with so-called creation prayer, centering prayer, praying with a sacred word or mantra, or the prayer of presence. In general, these were more simple forms of prayer, which recently are quite popular and often very effective. Whatever seemed to give us some personal contact with Jesus was our prayer of choice.

Still others just gave up regular mental prayer for a time. We told ourselves that our ministry to God's people was a way to experience God each day. Or if we were priests, we thought that our life was so full with Masses, weddings, funerals, baptisms, and prayer services that there was no time or need for meditation.

Throughout our life, most of us made various adjustments to our form of prayer—either with great deliberation and care, or with just an imperceptible drifting into a certain way of life. It was not that we were quite irresponsible or foolish; rather, we just didn't realize that so much of this prayer of ours was developing naturally and positively. We needed someone to encourage us to go forward on this road of prayer despite our experience of more simple or less satisfying prayer.

For me, the best spiritual direction at that point came from John of the Cross. His writings made it clear to me that this experience, which so many of us went through, was entirely natural—following the usual way of simplification of prayer. The place we came to was an integral part of the development of prayer; our experience was a necessary stage of the usual progress of prayer. This teaching of John of the Cross can be a great help for all of us, wherever we are in our prayer life:

> Perhaps the greatest debt that Christianity owes to John of the Cross is for the clarity with which he showed that [simple and less satisfying prayer] was not a dead loss in the spiritual life...but was an **integral part** of the development of prayer.[198]

To understand John's point about prayer becoming naturally more simple, consider a parallel to learning the English language. Throughout elementary school, we learned the rules for spelling, punctuation, and grammar. Then in high school, we learned more about writing and speaking good English, such as constructing paragraphs with topic sentences and coherent development of an idea. Eventually, we developed more complicated and diverse forms of writing: stories, theme papers, poetry, and plays. After we learned how to speak correctly, we

---

198 Leonard Boase, S.J., *The Prayer of Faith* (Chicago: Loyola Press, 1985), p. 78 (emphasis added). In the original quote, Boase had the words "the Dark Night of the Soul;" this phrase is part of John of the Cross' famous description for various stages of prayer. But in the context here, we chose to substitute "simple and less satisfying prayer," because it seems to translate John's term into equivalent, non-technical language.

would only rarely consult the rules for good grammar; rather, we would just speak naturally. Whether our speech was entirely grammatically correct or not, our speech came quite easily. All the complications we went though earlier in order to learn how to speak English correctly were necessary in the beginning, but we seldom returned to those elementary rules of speech. Generally, when we speak we don't reflect on the structures of the English language; our speech is effortless and natural.

Something like that happened with our prayer. Some of us learned complicated forms of meditation in our youth; others learned whatever we could about prayer throughout our lifetime. Once we gained some ability to pray, we didn't need to begin all over again. And if we practiced some kind of discursive meditation, over a period of time we did not consistently follow the same patterns. Our prayer tended naturally to become less regulated and more simple.

If we continued to pray regularly over a period of time, our prayer became less intellectual or theological; we didn't find many new ideas to occupy our time. If we were fortunate, that was the opportune time for us to learn one of the modern forms of prayer. Today, there are many simple forms of prayer that seem quite appealing. Some of the popular kinds of prayer today are: 1) *lectio divina* or a simple reflection on a passage of Scripture; 2) centering prayer,[199] which consists of a simple attentiveness to God in a peaceful, quiet waiting; 3) praying with a sacred word or mantra, such as "Jesus" or "Spirit," which is often repeated in order to keep our mind open and receptive to God; or 4) the prayer of presence,[200] consisting mainly of two attitudes— watching and waiting— in God's presence, trusting that God will reveal himself in good time. All of these methods seem proper and effective ways of becoming more intimate with Jesus, more open to God.

---

199 Thomas Keating has several books describing this way of prayer. See, for example: Thomas Keating, *Open Mind, Open Heart* (Rockport, MA: Element, Inc., 1986).

200 See Adrian van Kaam and Susan Muto, *Practicing the Prayer of Presence* (Mineola, NY: Resurrection Press, 1993).

Finally, today we might want to learn something about
the classic form of Catholic prayer called contemplation.
Sadly, very few Catholics in our day have heard much about
contemplation. In fact, contemplative prayer has been kept
under a cloud in the Catholic Church for the last 350 years.
The reason why it has been neglected for so many years is kind
of a well-kept secret. In the seventeenth century, there were
some extreme forms of mysticism, called Quietism, which
emphasized complete passivity in prayer. Thomas Keating
describes the reason for this 350-year lacuna:

> Quietism…was condemned in 1687 as a species of false
> mysticism by [Pope] Innocent XII…. [T]he controversy
> brought traditional mysticism into disrepute. From then on, the
> reading about mysticism was frowned upon in seminaries and
> religious communities…. [As a result] the unexpurgated text of
> [John of the Cross'] writings appeared only in our own century,
> four hundred years after its writing.[201]

Sadly, then traditional mysticism was in disrepute as a false
form of mysticism. Throughout all that time, the Church was
suspicious of all forms of mysticism, so that seminaries and
religious orders taught only discursive meditation. No mystical
writing of significance was published in the eighteenth and
nineteenth centuries. Even certain passages of John of the Cross,
the Mystical Doctor, were **omitted** from publication out of fear
of condemnation. Only in the last sixty years were his complete
writings published. Gradually, then, contemplative prayer took
its rightful place again in Christian spirituality. Modern writers
such as Thomas Merton, Ruth Burrows, and Thomas Keating
have introduced a large audience to the writings of John of
the Cross and Teresa of Avila. Any of their writings would be
a fine introduction to this classic prayer tradition of ours. My
recent book on John of the Cross, *The Practice of Contemplation*

---

201 Thomas Keating, pp. 23-24. This whole chapter (pp. 19-31) is a succinct and clear
explanation of the history of the Church's suppression of contemplation for the last 350
years.

According to John of the Cross,[202] is written for those who are serious about their prayer and practice regular prayer.

Let me end with a simple word of encouragement. Prayer, any form of prayer, is the atmosphere of Jesus. Whatever form of prayer seems right for us, it can lead us to greater friendship and intimacy with Jesus and God, our Father.

REFLECTIONS

1. How would you answer someone who asked you, "Why doesn't God answer my prayer?"

2. Write a short description of your prayer life now or at some time in your life. How has your prayer life changed over the years?

3. Does the above description, about the way that prayer often develops over time, resonate with your experience? Does it make sense to you that our prayer should become more simple over time?

---

202 James Kinn. *The Practice of Contemplation According to John of the Cross* (Washington, DC: ICS Publications, 2009).

CHAPTER 23

Thoroughly Human Jesus

Before we consider other aspects of Jesus our Savior, concentrate on this one fact: Jesus Christ was truly a human being. He was as really human as you and I are. The New Testament takes for granted that he was entirely human; it assumes his humanity as an undisputed fact (see above, chapter 3). In Scripture, we see Jesus with the same human characteristics we know so well in our own lives: human needs, emotions, infirmities and limitations. His human needs are presented quite simply: He was born of a human mother; he was a helpless infant; he had to "grow in wisdom;" he sought companionship and needed friends; he experienced joy, wonder, and compassion with others. Even negative emotions are presented openly, especially in Mark's Gospel: He was angry enough to overturn the tables in the temple and drive people away; he was so fearful as to groan, cringe, sweat, and become desolate in the face of severe suffering; he was so disappointed as to weep and cry over people's rejection of his message; he was also sorrowful, impatient, and deeply hurt. The infirmities he suffered are not hidden: At times he was hungry, thirsty, tired, and physically drained; he needed to go off by himself to get away from people; most of all, he suffered pain, rejection, and agony at the end of his life. Finally, the limitations of his knowledge are pointed out: He made a grave mistake with the choice of one apostle; he seems to have miscalculated the time of the parousia (the end of the world); he was uncertain about the details of his death, which added to his dread. He is seen as one who bore "all that belongs to our nature, included in which is ignorance," as St. Cyril of Alexandria observed. Also, he was not "unable to sympathize with our weaknesses, but one who has similarly been tested in every way, yet without sin" (Heb 4:15). Notice, that the only human quality that Scripture denies about Jesus is sin.

Traditional theology has lost sight of the true humanity of Jesus. It has so emphasized the divinity of Jesus Christ, that it distorted him into a purely divine figure. It presented him as God walking on earth; God teaching us in a human context; God who only appeared to be human. It so idealized and divinized the person of Jesus for us, that we saw him as God walking on earth with the appearance of a human being, but not fully human. We didn't realize that such a belief in Jesus as not really human is just what the heresy of Docetism taught. In the words of Jerome Murphy-O'Connor:

> Ever since the time of Arius this has been the lot of the humanity of Jesus. There was never any outright denial, but his humanity was seen in the light of his divinity, and as a result was accorded a perfection that took it out of the orbit of mankind as we know it …. Only in this century has there been an effort to restore the balance by emphasizing the humanity of Jesus.[203]

Only if we affirm that Jesus is truly human can we really understand Christianity. For faith in a human Jesus means that the gospel is also the good news about **human life**, not just the revelation of secrets about God and his forgiveness. Faith in a human Jesus implies that the way of God's presence is incarnation: that we can find God in human life, that human life is the locus of he divine. Faith in a human Jesus means that his human life is really a model for our lives.

Only a human Jesus, who experienced our human needs, emotions, infirmities, and limitations, can be a real model for us. That is, a Jesus who is not dependent on others for growth, learning, and support can still be our ideal; but a Jesus who had to slowly learn and grow, who needed others, and profoundly reacted to them can be a wondrous teacher of human growth and relationships. And a Jesus whose negative emotions either

---

203 Jerome Murphy-O'Connor, *Becoming Human Together* (Wilmington, Delaware: Michael Glazier, Inc., 1970), pp. 38-39.

didn't exist or only existed in some spiritual way is still our Lord; but a Jesus who struggled day in and day out with all the turmoil of human emotions is a Jesus whom we can strive to imitate as a real human model. In particular, a Jesus who was only passive, meek, and mild in every instance can still be a distant ideal, but a Jesus who could also be angry at times and boldly excoriate the religious leaders is a Jesus we can honestly attempt to follow. Again, a Jesus who suffered in some kind of ethereal way is still our Redeemer; but a Jesus who agonized over his approaching suffering, and especially for three long hours before he could drag out the words, "… [N]ot as I will, but as you will" (Mt 26:39), is a Jesus who went through life's real trials. Finally, a Jesus who knew with perfect certainty that, three days later, God would raise him up is a Jesus who can arouse our admiration; but a Jesus for whom the future was a mystery, a dread, and a troubled hope, is a Jesus who laid down his life with all the agony with which we humans have to lay it down. This is the Jesus we follow: a real, human, struggling, mature Jesus. Only such a Jesus can be a human model for our struggling efforts at maturity and Christian living.

Also, only if we affirm that Jesus is truly human can we understand how Christianity is unique among all the philosophies and religions of the world, for only we Christians follow a **person** instead of a teaching. Only we Christians put our faith in one who both modeled human living and actually died and rose again. No other religious leader is adhered to in that way by his followers, nor did he claim that his own person was the actual, personal way to eternal life. Confucius, Buddha, Socrates, Mohammed, and all the other famous religious leaders are followed with devotion because of their teaching and doctrine. The commitment of their followers is to their works and their teachings, which are separable in principle from their persons. Their followers admire them greatly, but they do not see their persons as the embodiment of their teaching. Their followers accept their way of life, they believe in their profound teaching, but they do not identify that teaching and the person who teaches it.

With Jesus it is different, for Christians understand the teaching of Jesus only in the light of his life, death, and resurrection; Christians find their plan of life in the mystery of the entire historical life of Jesus; Christians follow a way of life that is identified with the person, life-style, and way of life of Jesus. This constitutes the uniqueness and attractiveness of our Christian faith. As Hans Küng expresses all this:

> [T]he strength of [the Christian faith] lies in being able to justify and substantiate in detail an attitude to life, a way of life and a life-style, by pointing to a quite definite, authoritative, historical figure …. And … a historical figure is undoubtedly convincing in a way that is impossible to an impersonal idea, an abstract principle, a universal norm, a purely ideal system. Jesus of Nazareth is himself the **personification** of this new way of life.[204]

The Letter to the Hebrews connects the human Jesus, our salvation, and our following of this human Jesus: "[I]t was fitting that [God] … in bringing many children to glory, should make the leader to their salvation perfect through suffering" (Heb 2:10). This is the famous argument *ex convenientia*, indicating that it was entirely **fitting and appropriate** for God to determine that Jesus, the author of our salvation, should become "perfect through suffering." This kind of argument regarding our salvation in Jesus is not found anywhere else in Scripture; it seems to be an innovation in the Bible.[205] This argument *ex conveniencia* offers us an interpretation of Jesus' way of salvation and helps us appreciate God's involvement in our human suffering. To understand it, we'll take one phrase at a time.

---

204 Hans Kung, *On Being a Christian* (NY: Doubleday and Co. Inc., 1976), p. 546 (emphasis added).

205 See C. Spicq, *L'Epitre aux Hebreux, 2 vol.* (Paris: Etudes Bibliques, 1952-53), vol. 2, 36.

It was fitting. It was entirely fitting and appropriate for God to determine that Jesus, the author of our salvation, should become "perfect through suffering." The same argument from the perspective of our human experience might be expressed similarly: It is appropriate that we humans who are caught up in a history of suffering should be saved by someone who personally identifies with our suffering. This kind of argument offers a new interpretation of Jesus' way of salvation. Even more significantly, it offers a unique insight into why God decided that our Savior would save us precisely by his suffering and death. That is what we hope to prove here.

God made [Jesus]. What is described here is the plan of God: that Jesus as Savior would actually suffer greatly and, by his faithfulness in suffering, complete his commitment to God's plan of salvation. With that complete commitment in the most trying of circumstances, Jesus attained his moral perfection. God wanted Jesus to bring about our salvation by means of his free human life, including all that would happen to him as a result of the great opposition that was bound to occur, resulting in his death. Thus, God chose to bring about human salvation, not only by the public life and teaching of Jesus, nor even by his divine power evident in Jesus' life, but rather by Jesus' entire human life and passion, which included his great suffering and death. In that sense, Jesus' suffering and death are essential to God's way of salvation.

Bringing many to glory. Bringing to glory means effecting eternal salvation. God's purpose was to bring human beings to eternal salvation. And his plan included the suffering and death of Jesus as the instrument of our salvation. The way God brings many to glory is similar to the way Jesus came to glory; just as Jesus fulfilled his work of salvation by voluntarily suffering his passion and death, so those who follow him must voluntarily suffer all the trials of human living.

Leader of salvation. God not only decided that Jesus would suffer the ordinary trials of human existence during his lifetime and in his passion, but also that he would suffer AS the leader of salvation and the model for his followers. As the example of obedience to God and his way, Jesus epitomizes complete faith and confidence in God. All those who **follow** Jesus must necessarily suffer the various forms of suffering that are the necessary part of human life. It is appropriate for them to follow one who can completely sympathize with their weakness because he "has similarly been tested in every way" (Heb 4:15). By accepting those trials and following this human model, they too can become perfect through suffering and come to salvation.

Perfect through suffering. That is, Jesus himself became complete and morally mature through suffering.[206] In chapter five, Hebrews explains this connection more fully: Jesus "… learned obedience from what he suffered; and when he was made perfect, he became the source of eternal salvation for all who obey him …" (5:8-9). What is meant by perfection here, involves Jesus' complete faithfulness to God who sent him, especially by the voluntary acceptance of his suffering and death. So, by means of his obedient acceptance of all his suffering, he became perfect. Similarly, the most difficult form of obedience for us human beings is found in accepting suffering and trials.

What can we conclude, then, from this argument *ex conveniencia*? First, it tells us that God chose to grant us eternal life not by his almighty power or by a magical fiat, but by the real human life of Jesus, who had to suffer all the varieties of human experience, including the terrible suffering of the cross. Second, it teaches that God intended that Jesus, as the leader of our salvation, should come to his human perfection though suffering. Third, it is fitting that God should choose this way

---

206 B. F. Westcott, *The Epistle to the Hebrews* (London, 1909), p. 49: "…to the full moral perfection of his humanity."

of salvation, by the entirely human life of Jesus, who by his very suffering throughout his life and passion should become complete in his commitment. Fourth, just because Jesus is the leader of salvation and the model for his followers, it is fitting that he became perfect through suffering, because all those who follow him must suffer endless forms of human suffering as an entirely natural part of human life. By imitating Jesus' way of suffering and commitment to God, they too can become perfect and gain salvation. Fifth, because Jesus was taught in the school of suffering and was "tested in every way," he can sympathize with our weakness. Finally, it gives us a new appreciation of God's involvement in our human suffering, for Jesus is God's wondrous sign to console us in all our human trials, who can really say, "I know how you feel; I've been through that myself."

It would help to add, here, the connection between this argument *ex convenientia* and the one and only commandment of Jesus: "… [L]ove one another as I love you" (Jn 15:12). It seems to me that most of Jesus' suffering throughout his public life came from others, from trying to teach them, serve them, and accept them with all their imperfections, rejection, and enmity. And most of our suffering comes from trying to live out his command of love of others. That is, if the sum of Christian living is to love as Jesus loved, then his kind of love of neighbor demands some suffering, requires a denial of self-interest, and entails a constant giving of self. For we cannot be thoughtful of others without thinking a little less about self; we cannot help anyone without some personal effort; we cannot be kind to them unless we overcome our personal preferences or aversions; we cannot be patient unless we control our anger; we cannot deal with their unchristian attitudes and actions without some pain. And when we learn to do all of these things in imitation of Jesus, we become more complete and mature. So following Jesus as our model of suffering and love leads necessarily to mature Christian living and some degree of completeness.

Finally, consider how one man followed the human Jesus in love of others, and so came to fulfill his life. Albert Schweitzer, as a young man, was already known as a genius—as well as a concert soloist, an outstanding philosopher, a respected historian, and a reputable theologian. At the age of twenty-one, he promised himself that he would pursue art and science until he was thirty years old. Then he would devote the rest of his life to working among the needy in some direct form of service. He decided to do this because of his deep faith in Jesus. One of the influences that inspired him was his meditation on the parable of the rich man and Lazarus in Luke's Gospel (Lk 16:19-31), along with the moral spoken to the rich man: "[R]emember that you received what was good during your lifetime while Lazarus likewise received what was bad; but now he is comforted here, whereas you are tormented" (v. 25). Albert Schweitzer described that transforming moment: "It struck me as incomprehensible that I should be allowed to live such a happy life while so many people around me were wrestling with…suffering." Then, on his thirtieth birthday, he informed his family and friends that he was going to become a doctor and then go to Africa to work among the poor as a missionary doctor. His family and friends thought his plan was foolish and unreasonable. They argued with him that he was only burying his immense talent; he could do so much more by lecturing and developing scientific knowledge.

But he was determined to spend his life helping the needy. He got his degree in medicine at the age of thirty-eight. At the age of forty-three, he left for Africa, where he opened a hospital on the edge of the jungle. Throughout the rest of his life, he dedicated all his talents and skill to relieving the suffering of the poor in Africa. In 1952, he was awarded the Nobel Peace Prize. Two years earlier, he was internationally acclaimed as the "man of the century." He died in what was then called Equatorial Africa in 1965, at the age of ninety. He fulfilled his life by his extraordinary service and love of the people of Africa as his way of following Jesus.

REFLECTIONS

1. Were you surprised to learn that theologians concede that Jesus was ignorant about certain things? Do you see how Jesus' freedom as a human being would have been compromised if he knew precisely what the future had in store for him?

2. Apply the following thought to your own life experience: Following Jesus as our model for suffering and love leads necessarily to mature Christian living and some degree of completeness.

3. Albert Schweitzer was so moved by Jesus' parable about the rich man and Lazarus (Lk 16:19-31), that he devoted his life to the needy. Consider how you too help the needy.

CHAPTER 24

Jesus on His Terms

If we Christians follow a way of life that is identified with the person, teaching, and way of life of this human Jesus, then we need to know just what kind of leader we are following. What kind of leader was he? What was his cause? Where does he fit in the possible categories of religious leaders?

People in our modern world have so many different views of the person of Jesus: some secular historians see him as a good and wise Jew; people of other faiths see him only as a prophet; some people without any religion limit his influence to that of a do-gooder; socialists consider him as a friend of the poor or a social revolutionary; politicians often portray him as one who supports their political views; rationalists depict him as a preacher of morality; for idealists he is the epitome of humanity; and, finally, some fiction writers make him merely a character in a novel.

For 2,000 years, Christians have seen Jesus in one role or another, and that role determined to a large extent the form that Christianity took for them. History suggests many different answers to this question about Jesus as a religious leader, but Hans Küng reduces most of them to four general answers.[207] Most essential for us is to carefully add the picture of Jesus as developed in Scripture.

Very often in history, Jesus has been appealed to as the **foundation for the establishment.** That is, many times he has been depicted as the reason for maintaining the religious or political status quo. The Holy Roman Empire dominated the whole western world for centuries and was the sovereign church and state in one. It believed that it ruled according to the will of God and Christ. Also, in later centuries, in endless ways

---

207 Hans Kung, *On Being a Christian*, p.546 (emphasis added).

Christian rulers, political parties, ethnic groups, traditions, and laws were defended as in keeping with the plan of Christ.

But Jesus was not that kind of religious leader at all. He was not a supporter of the religious or political establishment of his time. The historical Jesus was neither a priest nor a supporter of the religious leaders. Nor was he a Sadducee, who respected Roman sovereignty in order to maintain their power as a priestly aristocracy. And more generally, he was not concerned with the political Roman rule, or even with the Jewish hierarchy, but only with the kingdom of God, now and at the end of time. His message was simply one of forgiveness, justice, freedom, and love in the kingdom of God.

Second, Jesus has often been seen as a **social or political revolutionary.** He is presented as one who wanted the social order overthrown, either gradually or suddenly. This is how he was misjudged in his own time, even by his own disciples. The Jews expected a messiah who would be the long-awaited one to restore their country and bring freedom to them. They looked for a descendent of David who would establish the political kingdom of God and destroy the godless rule of Rome. Indeed, one clear fact of Jesus' passion is that he was condemned by the Jewish leaders as a false messiah and by the Roman rulers as the "king of the Jews," which is a Roman equivalent of messiah.

But Jesus was not a social revolutionary at all. Nowhere does he speak of restoring David's kingdom; never does he proclaim any kind of theocracy or political rule; not once does he ever indicate any political objective, hope, or strategy. In fact, he personally avoids titles such as messiah and Son of David, because they might be misinterpreted in a political sense. On the contrary, the point he made constantly with his apostles was that he was not a social liberator or political messiah, but one who saves by his suffering and death. This was the "messianic secret" that his own followers could not understand or his contemporaries accept.

Third, Jesus has often been considered a **religious ascetic,** as one who retreats from the world. He is presented as one who dissociates himself from the world, as a religious leader who wants to form an exclusive group of holy people separate from the world, similar to many Hindu or Buddhist holy men who taught renunciation of the world as the way of holiness. Many Christian zealots over the centuries have taught that the only proper way to follow Jesus was by severe ascetic practices, with exclusive groups, rigid rules, and retreat from the world. In a more moderate fashion, some Christian monks taught that retreat from the world into hermitages was the only way to holiness. Much of medieval spirituality was tainted with this view of Jesus, to the degree that it taught that monastic spirituality was the superior way to follow Jesus and maintained that "contempt of the world" was necessary for holiness.

But Jesus was not an ascetic monk who turned away from the world or opted out of ordinary life. He seems to have had no connection with the Jewish spiritual community of Essenes of his time, who isolated themselves from the world and sought salvation in a special group with numerous religious laws, ascetic practices, and monastic-like spirituality. Their Qumran Community was an outstanding example of this way. In the 1950s, the original Dead Sea Scrolls were discovered in the caves near Jerusalem; they presented a vivid picture of the ascetic way of life of the Qumran Community. However, in Scripture, Jesus did not demand sacrifice for the sake of sacrifice or renunciation of all material possessions. Nor did he require of his followers special vows, practices, rituals, or rules of living separate from the rest of the world.

Finally, Jesus is often considered **a moralist,** as a teacher of righteousness. Some perceive him as a prudent compromiser who teaches that right living consists of careful observance of God's laws along with pious practices, while living in the world. This view of Jesus' teaching has often been the simplistic summary of Christian living, especially in previous centuries.

That is, Jesus started a moral renewal movement with a set of wondrous ideals, but also with an understanding spirit. But Jesus cannot be categorized as a moralist at all, for he did not proclaim a kingdom that would be brought about by the exact fulfillment of laws and strict morality. We need only look at the Scribes and Pharisees to see that Jesus' way was quite different. The Scribes joined a rigid traditionalism with practical realism; that is, they insisted on the law, while providing all kinds of excuses and dispensations. And the Pharisees found righteousness, not in basic attitudes, dispositions, or commitments, but in a complex casuistry of detailed good actions and religious observances. All of them were very concerned with minute laws and practices, with careful casuistry. Jesus condemned them severely, because they found their righteousness before God in their own complex blueprint of rites, ascetic practices, Sabbath observance, and pious casuistry. Jesus insisted that we are saved only by God's mercy, and that God rewards us according to our good works, but not strictly because of our goodness.

Therefore, Jesus fits none of the ordinary categories for a religious leader; he was not a supporter of the establishment, not a social revolutionary, nor one who retreats from the world, nor a moralist. Rather, Jesus is entirely unique in his teaching. What did he stand for? What kind of leader was he? His cause is simply the kingdom of God, that **his will be done** on earth: "/As is written of me … /Behold, I come to do your will, O God" (Heb 10:7). In John's Gospel, Jesus proclaims this cause again and again: "My food is to do the will of the one who sent me and to finish his work" (4:34); "… I do not seek my own will but the will of the one who sent me" (5:30); "… I came down from heaven not to do my own will but the will of the one who sent me…" (6:38); "I glorified you [God] on earth by accomplishing the work that you gave me to do" (17:4).

And this same cause of doing the will of God is what Jesus again and again taught us. The central part of the one prayer

Jesus taught us is: "/[Y]our kingdom come, / your will be done …" (Mt 6:10). The way to the Kingdom of heaven is: "… [O] nly the one who does the will of my Father in heaven" (Mt 7:21). Our commitment to the will of God does not require a retreat from the world or a narrow form of asceticism. It requires only that we do God's will by accepting the reality of our lives just as it comes to us.

There is one incident in Jesus' life that captures this one requirement for us to carry out. It is found in all three synoptic gospels; in Luke's Gospel, it occurs twice. In Luke's Gospel, Jesus' mother and brothers are standing outside, while Jesus is inside a house surrounded by a crowd of people. "He was told, 'Your mother and your brothers are standing outside and they wish to see you.' He said to them in reply, 'My mother and my brothers [and sisters] are those who hear the word of God and act on it'" (Lk 8:19-21). This incident is supremely important for the synoptics. In fact, it is the primary passage for Matthew, Mark, and Luke to describe our intimacy with Christ. For Jesus asserts here that there is something more blessed than to be a blood relative of his. He assures us that if we "hear the word of God and act on it" by trying to live it, then we are more blessed than those who are physically related to him; we are his beloved brother or sister. This one incident can inspire us to follow Jesus not just as a great leader but also as our intimate brother.

What all this means is that the cause of Jesus himself is simply to fulfill the will of God in his life. That does not require retreat from the world or great asceticism or strict morality. It only requires that he fulfill the will of God by proclaiming his kingdom and carrying out the way of suffering and death that came to him as a result of his ministry. For us too, it means that we are not required to choose any extreme forms of asceticism, retreat from the world, or rigorous morality. We, like Jesus our leader, have only one cause: to "hear the word of God and act on it." In practice, this is entirely unique for each one of us; it consists of accepting all that happens to us naturally in the spirit of Jesus. This cause of Jesus becomes concrete for us in the person of Jesus himself, who is our "way," our model for living. We try to live our individual life according to the virtues and motivation of Jesus. As disciples, no matter what our circumstances, we try to live according to the model of Jesus our leader, to commit our lives to Jesus as our leader.

One unusual example of committing his life to God comes in the person of a leading politician. Charles Colson had an office next to the president of the U.S., along with a six-figure income, a yacht, a limousine, and a chauffeur. But he realized, finally, that he was an unhappy man; as he put it, he had a "gnawing hollowness" deep inside him; something was missing from his life. Then, one August night in 1973, he talked to his friend, Tom Phillips, who had gone through a similar experience in his own life. He explained to Charles Colson: "I saw what was missing [from my life]. It was Jesus Christ. I hadn't ever turned my life over to him." The more Colson listened to Tom Phillips, the more he became convinced that he had put his finger on the cause of his "gnawing hollowness" and had some insight into what he could do. Driving home that night, he suddenly stopped his car, pulled over to the side of the road, and began to cry. He described what happened next: "I prayed my first real prayer, 'God, I don't know how to find you, but I'm going to try; ...somehow I want to give myself to you.... Take me.'" That insight and commitment was the beginning of a religious conversion that surprised not only the White House staff but also the whole country. The so-called "hatchet man" of the Nixon administration underwent a real conversion. To this day, Colson travels around the country preaching the gospel, especially in prisons and on college campuses.

REFLECTIONS

1. Would you agree that Jesus was not a political revolutionary? Does it bother you that he was indifferent

to politics in general? Do you see any connection between his strong moral stance for individuals and the actual improvement of society and political reform?

2. Christians and non-Christians have endless ways of evaluating what kind of leader Jesus was. What was your image of Jesus our leader? Has your image of Jesus changed?

3. Make a list of descriptive words or adjectives about Jesus, as you know him. Begin the list with the phrase, "Jesus, our leader, is ...."

CHAPTER 25

Jesus Our Model

Have you ever noticed that, in the Synoptic Gospels, Jesus never asks his followers to "imitate me?" Never once does Jesus encourage all his followers to imitate his lifestyle. But he does invite us often to **follow him**. The central invitation in all the synoptic writers is: "Whoever wishes to come after me must deny himself, take up his cross, and follow me" (Mt 16:24). In fact, 19 times in the gospels we hear this invitation of Jesus, "follow me" (and the verb, "to follow" appears seventy times in the New Testament). What is the exact meaning of Jesus' call to all of us Christians?

When Jesus spoke these words in his lifetime, I don't think he was referring to his own crucifixion, which was not known yet. Rather, he was probably referring to a common expression of Jewish and Greek leaders of his day. From Plato's time down to Jesus' day, "take up [your] cross, and follow me" implied "be ready to offer your life for my cause."[208] So for Jesus it meant: be willing to live or die for the cause of the kingdom of God; it meant a thorough commitment of one's whole life to the way of Jesus. By the time Matthew wrote his Gospel, around 80 AD, his readers certainly read it with Jesus' death in mind, and perhaps with their own persecution already a reality in the Greco-Roman Empire. But during his lifetime, Jesus was simply making it clear for all his followers that following him involves more than believing in him intellectually or having a lukewarm attachment to him and his way. Rather, Jesus meant that any Christian should be ready to commit his life for Jesus and his kingdom.

So, the general sense of Jesus' call to all his followers involves sharing his cause throughout our lives, wherever it

---

208   See Edward Schillebeeckx, *God Among Us, The Gospel Proclaimed*, pp. 202-03. Also see the footnote in Chapter 20, above.

leads us. But what does this call of Jesus mean in practical terms? Karl Rahner has his own way of describing Jesus' call: "The Christian, every Christian, follows Jesus by dying with him." He calls it "dying by installments." This does not mean seeking out suffering, for throughout his life, Jesus did not seek out suffering; he merely accepted it. The sufferings he endured were a part of his human condition, not a part of personally chosen asceticism. Bearing the cross of Jesus, then, means bearing our personal crosses, just as they come to us naturally; it means accepting what we would like to avoid; it means steadfast loyalty to the way of Jesus in all our daily living. These are the crosses that weigh heavily upon us; they are our individual way of "dying by installments." So in simplest terms, conformity to the cross of Christ is entirely individual and unique for each one of us; it is accepting the will of God as seen in the ordinary daily life that comes to us humanly.

In **Luke's** parallel passage, this becomes even clearer: "If anyone wishes to come after me, he must deny himself and take up his cross **daily** and follow me" (Lk 9:23, emphasis added). By adding the one word, "daily," Luke makes it clear that he refers to our everyday life. He would have us all be ready to **live** each day for Jesus and his cause; he teaches us that Jesus' radical challenge includes our following in his footsteps and living "the way" each day. In practical terms, then, Jesus' call to all of us does not demand a particular lifestyle; it does not require a retreat from the world or a monastic existence; it does not require an elitist way of life. It is simply a call to all of us to follow Jesus by loving others and accepting the unique human life that comes to us. This is how we "carry our cross" and offer our life for the cause of Jesus our model.

Paul's clearest expression of imitating Jesus is found in his famous hymn to Christ:

Have among yourselves the same attitude that is also yours in Christ Jesus, Who ... emptied himself, taking the form of a slave, coming in human likeness; … he humbled himself, becoming obedient to death, even death on a cross … (Phil 2:5-8).

Here Paul challenges us to follow "the same attitude" and example of Christ in humility and selflessness. Similarly, Paul connects Jesus' love and his dying for us as an example for us: "… [T]he love of Christ impels us …. He indeed died for all, so that those who live might no longer live for themselves but for him who for their sake died and was raised" (2 Cor 5:14-15). He suggests here that the example of Jesus "impels us," urges us, pushes us, draws us to live "for him who for their sake died."

Peter might be the clearest of all the Scripture writers in urging us to imitate the sufferings of Jesus: "… [T]o this you have been called, because Christ also suffered for you, leaving you an example that you should follow in his footsteps" (1 Pt 2:21). Here Peter is speaking to slaves and encouraging then to put up with unjust masters. But his teaching would apply to all of us, his disciples. We have all been called to follow the example of the suffering Jesus.

In **John's Gospel,** we do find two wonderful instances of Jesus' referring to himself as a model for us to follow. They both occur just before his passion. The **first instance** is found in chapter 13, after Jesus washed the feet of his disciples. He clearly explains why he performed this figurative action: "I have given you a model to follow, so that as I have done for you, you should also do" (Jn 13:15). That is, Jesus wants them to see that this figurative, humble action should serve as a **model of humble service** that they should imitate by serving their fellow Christians. Later in this same chapter, Jesus offers a second and more involved explanation for this foot washing. He carefully tells Peter that he will only understand the deeper meaning of this symbolic action "later." "What I am doing, you do not understand now, but **you will understand later**" (Jn 13:7). He means that Peter will only understand this deeper meaning after Jesus' death. That is, only after his passion and death will Peter understand that this foot washing is also a symbol of Jesus' supreme model of service and love for his disciples in dying for love of them: "I give you a new commandment: love one another. As I have loved you, **so you also should love one another**" (Jn 13:34). He means that his death is the ultimate example and the most intense model for them to follow in their love for one another. And Jesus introduces all this by referring to his **new commandment.** How is this a new commandment? Raymond Brown explains that this is a new commandment in two ways. First, it is new because it is the basic stipulation of the **new covenant.** God had promised that new covenant to Jeremiah: "... I will make a new covenant with the house of Israel ..." (Jer 31:31). And God fulfills that promise here at the Last Supper: "This cup is the **new covenant** in my blood ..." (Lk 22:20). So this new commandment—"As I have loved you, so you should love one another"—is central to our new covenant with God. Second, it is a new commandment because it has a **new model.** Jesus' love, proven by his passion and death, is the model for us Christians to follow. To fulfill that commandment of love, we have the supreme model of Jesus' selfless love for us, which we try to follow in all our Christian living.

The **second instance** is found in the parallel passage of chapter 15: "This is my commandment: Love one another as I love you" (Jn 15:12). This wording is similar to that in chapter 13—with two changes: 1) In chapter 13, Jesus mentions the new commandment; 2) In chapter 15, Jesus adds a direct reference to his sacrificial death: "to lay down one's life for one's friends" (15:13) But in both quotes, Jesus offers his love as the **model** for the disciples' love: "[L]ove one another as I love you." The connection between "love one another as I love you" and "lay down one's life for one's friends" in verses 12-13 here, was later understood as a justification for Christian martyrs who died for Christ. But these two verses are also seen as a more general model of selfless love for all Christians.

Let me summarize how Jesus, in chapters 13 and 15 of John's Gospel, urges us to take him as the model for our Christian life and love:

1. 13:15a, "I have given you a model to follow ...." Jesus washes the feet of his disciples as a figurative model of humble service to others.

2. 13:7b, "... [Y]ou will understand later." After Jesus death, the disciples will understand the deeper meaning of the foot washing as a symbol of the supreme model of service and love in his dying for our salvation.

3. 13:34, "I give you a new commandment:" Jesus' new commandment of love is exemplified by Jesus.
   a. Cf. Lk 22:20, "This cup is the new covenant in my blood, which will be shed for you:" His commandment of love is new because it is the basic stipulation of the new covenant in his blood.
   b. 13:34b, "As I have loved you, so you also should love one another:" His commandment is new because Jesus himself is the new model for that love.

4. 15:12b, "... [L]ove one another as I love you:" Jesus' general commandment is to love one another after his example.

5. 15:13, "No one has greater love than ... to lay down one's life for one's friends:" Jesus' model is the extreme example of his "laying down his life for his friends."

Notice that all these quotes from Scripture suggest that we should follow Jesus in his suffering, his humble service, and his selfless love. Why all this emphasis on suffering? It's true that our lives are filled with all kinds of human experiences; many are joyful, some are very troubling. Most of us would admit that suffering is only a moderate part of our lives. Yet, almost all of us have a major trial at some time in our life: the death of a parent or child, an illness that threatens us, a divorce that destroys our family, a child who distresses us, an addiction that crushes us, or a loss of job. In all of such trials, the strong language of Jesus in Scripture does not seem extreme at all. And even when we reflect on the other parts of our life that include all the ordinary human activities, we are happy to hear Jesus graciously describe our minor ills and trials as our simple way of imitating his life of service and suffering. Besides, we don't have any hesitation to offer all the satisfying and joyful events of our life to Jesus as a part of our Christian living.

For some people, however, some constant trial dominates their life. For example, the very poor who constantly struggle for the bare necessities of life; the disabled whose lives are filled with daily limitations; the single parent who constantly worries about raising her children alone; the children whose parents died from AIDS and must survive without their support; the children who were abused physically or sexually by their parents and have to live continually with those scars; the starving people in so many ravaged parts of our globe; and the displaced or persecuted people in many war-torn countries of our world. For all of these people, the example of Jesus' suffering can be very real and powerful, and might help them to repair their broken lives.

One real-life story seems appropriate here. In 1981 Peter Cropper, the British violinist, was invited to Finland to play a special concert. As a personal favor to him, The Royal Academy of Music lent him their priceless 285-year-old Stradivarius for use in the concert. This rare instrument takes its name from the Italian violinmaker, Antonio Stradivari. It is made of eighty pieces of special wood and covered with thirty coats of clear varnish. Its beautiful sound has never been duplicated. But when Peter Cropper brought this violin to the music hall, he accidentally tripped and fell, and the violin broke into several pieces. Peter was in a state of shock over the incident, yet he could do nothing but fly back to England.

A master craftsman named Charles Beare agreed to try to

repair the violin. He worked endless hours on it and finally got it back together again. Peter Cropper returned to Finland and was asked to play the repaired violin. With his heart pounding, he picked up the bow and began to play it. Those present could hardly believe their ears. Not only was the violin's sound excellent, but it actually seemed better than before. In the months ahead, Cropper took the violin on a worldwide tour. Night after night, the violin everyone thought was ruined forever drew standing ovations from concert audiences.

How does this story relate to real life tragedies? For me, it illustrates that no tragedy is so terrible that we cannot survive it; no disaster is so destructive that we can't pick up the pieces and start over again—in one form or another. When we believe that our life is ruined forever, we need to turn to Jesus. Like the master craftsman who fixed the violin, Jesus can help us repair our broken life in some way.

* * * * *

One of the best presentations of Jesus as our human model is found in the writings of St. John of the Cross. Those who are familiar with John of the Cross know that most of his teaching on the spiritual life centers on God the Father; they actually wonder why he doesn't focus more on Jesus Christ. But one outstanding example of his emphasis on Jesus is found in his *Ascent of Mount Carmel:*

> A man makes progress only through imitation of Christ,
> Who is the Way, the Truth, and the Life. No one goes
> to the Father but through Him, as he states himself in
> St. John. [Jn 14:6]... Accordingly, I should not consider
> any spirituality worthwhile that would ... run from the
> imitation of Christ.[209]

---

209 John of the Cross, *Ascent of Mount Carmel, II,* 7,8 From The Collected Works of St. John of the Cross. p. 124.

This quote, in John 14:6, is variously interpreted by Scripture scholars, as we will see in the next chapter. But for John of the Cross, Jesus is the way, the truth, and the life for us because he is our **model**; he is the model we are to imitate. In the quote above, John interprets these words of Jesus Christ as referring to the **imitation of Christ** and adds, "I should not consider any spirituality worthwhile that would ... run from the imitation of Christ."[210] Also in the very next paragraph he adds: "Christ is the way .... For He is our model and light."[211] Notice also, that when John of the Cross counsels us near the beginning of *The Ascent of Mount Carmel*, his first norm is this: "First, have a habitual desire to imitate Christ in all your deeds by bringing your life into conformity with His ... in order to ... behave in all events as He would."[212]

So, John of the Cross puts primary emphasis on Jesus as **the way**, as the example we are to imitate. Later, in the *Spiritual Canticle*, John indicates how this imitation of Christ culminates in being transformed into Christ. He comments on the profound words of St. Paul, "... I live, no longer I, but Christ lives in me" (Gal 2:20):

> In saying, I live, now not I, he meant that, even though he had life it was not his, because he was transformed in Christ, and it was divine more than human. He consequently asserts that he does not live, but that Christ lives in him. In accord with this likeness and transformation, we can say that his life and Christ's were one life through union of love.[213]

John of the Cross notes how Paul's love of Christ transforms him anew, so that his self is lost in Christ, and a symbiosis or intimate living together results between Paul and Christ. John's

---

210 Ibid.
211 Ibid. 9. (p. 124).
212 Ibid. (p. 102).
213 *Spiritual Canticle*, 12, 8. (p. 456).

exegesis of Paul here is very accurate, for Paul refers to a vital union and incorporation into Christ, a mutual belonging; he says that his self is lost in Christ; he speaks, acts, and lives with Christ. Then he applies these words of Paul to the soul that is being transformed into Christ, however imperfectly.

Then John takes these words of Paul and applies them to us in some degree. He does not refer to the mystical life here,[214] but rather to our faith and love of Jesus, which form a certain likeness and union to Jesus in us. However, he qualifies that union and likeness to Jesus by noting that, at this stage, our knowledge and love of him are imperfect, so that the image of Jesus is only **"sketched"** in us:

> [S]ince the knowledge of [the truths of faith] is imperfect, [the soul] says they are sketched. Just as a sketch is not a perfect painting, so the knowledge of faith is not perfect knowledge .... Over this sketch of faith is drawn in the will of the lover the sketch of love .... Love produces such likeness ... that one can say each is the other and both are one .... Thus each one lives in the other and is the other, and both are one in the transformation of love.[215]

What John means is that once we have come to this stage of faith and love of Jesus, there is an outline of Jesus formed in us. In simple language, he tells us that our faith and love in him, as the way "produces such likeness ... that one can say each is the other and both are one."[216]

To sum up what all these Scripture writers and John of the Cross tell us about Jesus: he is our model, not in the sense of how he physically spent his life, but in the sense of his service to others, his love for all, his acceptance of suffering, and his way of treating others in his ordinary daily living. This seems to

---

214 This stanza 12 comes before his treatment of contemplation.
215 Ibid. 7. (p. 455).
216 Ibid.

include his values, his attitudes, and his motivation. Jesus' own summary is: "As I have loved you, so you also should love one another" (Jn 13:34).

People have been inspired to follow Jesus in all kinds of ways. One of my favorite stories is that of a boy named Neil. When he was fifteen years old, he was driving with his father past a tiny airport in Ohio. Suddenly a low-flying airplane spun out of control and nose-dived into the runway of the airport. Neil saw this accident and yelled to his dad, "Dad, stop the car!" Minutes later, he was pulling the pilot out of the plane, who was just twenty years old and a student pilot. He was desperate to help him, because he was his friend; they both were trying to get their pilot's license. But the young friend died in his arms.

When Neil got home, he cried for a long time. He was too shocked to eat supper, so he went to his room and threw himself on his bed. Neil's parents wondered what affect his friend's death would have on his dream of becoming a pilot, but they were willing to let him decide. Two days later, his mother went to his room and brought him something to eat. She noticed a notebook that he had kept since his childhood. Across the top of the page was written, in big letters, "The Character of Jesus." Beneath it was listed some of the qualities of Jesus: "sinless, humble, unselfish, devoted to God, and a champion of the poor." His mother realized that Neil was turning to Christ for guidance. Neil told his mother, "Mom, I hope you and dad will understand, but with God's help, I **must** continue to fly." That is just what he did for most of his life. The boy was Neil Armstrong. On July 20, 1969, he became the first human being to walk on the moon.

A final word of encouragement for those of us who will never walk on the moon or accomplish great renown while trying to follow our human model, Jesus. An incident in the life of Mother Teresa of India can help us all not to be discouraged at our inadequacies and failures in following Jesus. One day a reporter was interviewing Mother Theresa and sincerely questioned her about her difficult work with those who were suffering and dying in terrible conditions: "How can you continue to care for these sick and dying people day after day, when you never see an end to their misery and dying? How can you not get terribly discouraged, because of so little success and constant failure?" Mother Theresa answered him simply, "God does not require me to be **successful**; he only asks me to be **faithful**." I believe, she would remind all of us Christians that God does not require us to follow our model Jesus with complete success, but only with trying to be faithful to him with all our limitations. None of the qualities that the world recognizes as success are important to Jesus: not achievement, status, advancement, popularity, or social recognition. The only quality Jesus looks for is the central quality of his own life: doing the will of God. And for us Christians, that means accepting the reality of our life just as it comes to us; it means being faithful to the way of Jesus, despite our many personal limitations and frequent failures. "God does not require me to be successful; he only asks me to be faithful."

REFLECTIONS

1. Jesus often says, "Follow me." Compose a prayer to Jesus, asking for his help and telling him you want to follow him.

2. We all need to learn how to approach the problem of suffering in life. In what ways has Jesus shown us how to learn from and share his suffering? How can our relationship with Jesus help in suffering?

3. What do you think about Mother Teresa's response to the reporter: "God does not require me to be successful; he only asks me to be faithful"?

CHAPTER 26

The Way, the Truth, and the Life

One of the most familiar of all the claims of Jesus is from John's Gospel: "I am the way and the truth and the life. No one comes to the Father except through me" (Jn 14:6). For John, it is almost a summary of his entire Gospel. What does John mean here? What is Jesus telling us about our relationship to him? How is he "the way and the truth and the life" for us, according to Scripture scholars? The critical problem for understanding this quote is the **relation** of these three nouns to one another.

Throughout history, the fathers of the Church and Scripture scholars have related these three nouns in every possible way, emphasizing one or other of them, or making one of them primary and the others secondary. For example, the ancient Greek Fathers understood that **the way and the truth** were the means leading to eternal life, while many of the Latin Fathers understood that **the way** leads to both truth and life, considered as eschatological, heavenly realities. Today, some scholars consider the way as the primary predicate and the truth and the life are **just explanations of the way**. Even though there are myriad ways that the Fathers and Scripture scholars **relate** these three nouns, they all agree that Jesus **is** the way, truth, and life for us Christians.

The best treatment of this question, I believe, is that of Raymond Brown as found in *The Anchor Bible Commentary, Vol. 29A*.[217] After he mentions all the various alternative explanations offered for these three nouns, he then chooses this explanation:

> [T]*he way* is the primary predicate, and *the truth* and *the life* are just explanations of the way. Jesus is the way because he is the truth and the life .... He is the way because he is the truth or revelation of the Father ... [And] he is the way

---

217   Raymond Brown, S.S., *The Gospel According to John, 13-21*, pp. 618-636.

because he is the life ... the channel through which the Father's life comes to [all people]."[218]

He gives two reasons for seeing "**the way**" as dominant: 1) in verse 4, Jesus asserts, "you know the way;" and verse 5 continues with Thomas' question, "how can we know the way?" So "the way" is the **focus** of the entire exchange between Jesus and Thomas; 2) the last part of verse 6 only mentions Jesus as the way: "No one comes to the Father except through me." So Raymond Brown concludes:

> These verses simply explain how Jesus is the way to the Father. He is the way because he is the truth or revelation of the Father, ... so that when [the disciples] know him, they know the Father (v. 7). ... [And] ... he is the way because he is the life; [that is,] since he lives in the Father and the Father lives in him (vv. 10-11), he is the channel through which the Father's life comes to [us].[219]

A. JESUS AS THE WAY

According to this exegesis, the **dominant** claim of Jesus is that he is **the way;** "he is the channel through which the Father' life comes to us." So the truth and the life are just explanations of the way. According to this explanation, then, Jesus is **not primarily** presenting himself as a moral guide, or as a leader for his disciples to follow. Rather Jesus is presenting himself as the only **avenue of salvation** for his followers. There is a strong parallel to Jesus' claim earlier in John's Gospel: "I am the gate. Whoever enters through me will be saved ..." (10:9). Clearly here, Jesus is the gate leading to salvation. All the sheep must pass through the gate, that is Jesus, to be saved. He came as the channel to bring life to the sheep: "I came so that they may have life and have it more abundantly" (Jn 10:10). In John, then, all the emphasis on Jesus as the way is found in his being

---

218 Ibid. p. 621 and 628.
219 Ibid. p. 628.

the gate to eternal life and the channel of grace leading to salvation.

What about Jesus, the way, in the sense of him as the **model** for us to follow? Are Christians wrong in understanding Jesus' words, "I am the way" as the image for us to imitate, the model for our Christian living? Let us try to answer that question carefully. Admittedly, there is no example in the Hebrew Scriptures of the absolute use of "the way" as the summary of keeping the laws of the Old Covenant. But there are several passages in the Hebrew Scriptures that spoke of the "way of truth" as a way of life in conformity with the Mosaic Law (see: Ps 119:30; Tob 1:3; Wis 5:6). Then, in the time of Jesus, the Qumran community of faithful Jews designated itself absolutely as "the Way"; the Dead Sea Scrolls described the Qumran members as "those who have chosen the Way;" and the regulations of community life were "regulations of the Way." So for Qumran, "the Way" consisted of the strict observance of the Mosaic Law as interpreted by the great Teacher of the community.[220] More significantly, in the Acts of the Apostles, the Christian community looked on itself as "the Way" (Acts 9:2; 19:9; 22:4; 24:14 and 22). The sense seemed to be that they were following a way of life commanded by Jesus. So when Raymond Brown interprets John 14:6, he argues that there is a **secondary meaning** to Jesus' words, "I am the way:"

> … John 14:6 reflects [the] whole chain of usage of the imagery of "the way," originating in the O T, modified by sectarian Jewish thought illustrated at Qumran, and finally adopted by the Christian community as a self-designation. It is not unusual for the Johannine Jesus to take terminology once applied to Israel … and to apply it to himself.[221]

We can validly conclude, then, that Jesus is the way for us because he is the model for us to follow, the image we are

---

220   Ibid. p. 629.
221   Ibid.

to imitate. So Jesus is the way in a twofold sense; the primary sense is that he is the mediator of salvation and the channel of salvation; the secondary sense is that Jesus is the norm or model of life for us to imitate.

We should also take note of the final sentence of John 14:6: "No one comes to the Father except through me." In the past, some scholars interpreted this sentence to mean that **no one at all** can reach salvation without following Jesus as the way. But Joseph Fitzmyer and some other scripture scholars point out that Jesus, here, is not referring to all those who lived before Jesus' time, or those who never heard of him, or those who follow other religions; rather, he is speaking to his own disciples. Fitzmyer then adds the clarification that Scripture does not consider the salvation of peoples of **other** religions that are not influenced by Christianity; "That question is more properly addressed to a systematic theologian, because it is not within the perview of New Testament writings."[222]

Nevertheless, this sentence is really absolute in affirming that **for us Christians** he is the **only way**, the only avenue of salvation. There are two reasons for this conclusion: The first part of this sentence is so emphatic in using the definite article before each of these three nouns, which seems to imply that Jesus is the only way to the Father for his followers; and the second part of this sentence—"no one comes to the Father except through me"—must at least be true for his followers.[223]

B. JESUS AS THE TRUTH

In John's Gospel, then, Jesus is the way because he is the truth and the life. How does John's Gospel present Jesus as **the truth**? In chapter 8, Jesus clearly claims to be the light of the world as the one who reveals the truth about God to the world: "I am the light of the world. Whoever follows me will not walk

---

222   Joseph Fitzmyer, SJ, *A Christological Catechism*, Mahway, NJ: Paulist Press, 1991, p. 111.
223   Ibid. p. 631.

in darkness, but will have the light of life" (Jn 8:12). When the Pharisees challenge his claim with the question, "Who are you?" he responded, "... [T]he one who sent me is true, and what I heard from him I tell the world ... I say only what the Father taught me" (Jn 8:25, 26, 28). The Johannine idea of truth, revealed throughout his Gospel, is the divinely revealed reality of God, manifested in the words and the person of Jesus Christ. This is the ultimate, supreme truth for John. To reveal this truth is the entire purpose of Jesus' life: "For this I was born and for this I came into the world, to testify to the truth" (Jn 18:37). Whoever **believes** the truth that Jesus speaks has eternal life: "... [W]hoever hears my word and believes in the one who sent me has eternal life ..." (Jn 5:24). Whoever **sees** Jesus, sees the Father: "Whoever has seen me has seen the Father" (Jn 14:9). Whoever **knows** Jesus and what he tells them about "the only true God" can gain eternal life: "Now this is eternal life, that they should know you, the only true God, and the one whom you sent, Jesus Christ" (Jn 17:3).

Hans Küng summarizes this very well:

> ... [T]he *true man* Jesus of Nazareth is for faith the real *revelation* of the one *true God.* This is what John's Gospel especially makes clear. [S]ince ... the Father and the Son are one, it follows that whoever sees the Son sees also the Father. ... In him therefore God shows himself, shows who he is. ... The man Jesus ... might almost be called the *visage* or *face of God* or—as in the New Testament itself— the *image* or *likeness of God.* The same thing is expressed also in other terms: when Jesus is called the *Word of God.* ... All these metaphors are meant to express ... his significance as God's revealer for the salvation of the world.[224]

When Jesus proclaims, "I am the truth," we understand that the human Jesus is God in his self revelation; he is the **unique, final, complete revelation of God**; he is God inasmuch as

---

224 Hans Küng, *On Being a Christian*, p. 444 (emphasis added).

he reveals himself; he is the best way of knowing what God is like. The man Jesus, by his words, actions, suffering, and entire life, is the unsurpassable definitive word of God's affirmation of himself to our world. The revelation of God is a person, Jesus Christ: "[In Christ] dwells the whole fullness of the deity bodily" (Col 2:9; notice also the older translation of this verse: "In him the fullness of God's nature lives embodied").

In a similar way, Vatican II affirms that Jesus Christ "perfected revelation," and adds that Jesus Christ is himself "the Mediator and ... the fullness of all revelation."[225] Still, we can inquire **how** Jesus Christ personally is the fullness of revelation. Jacques Dupuis answers:

> [T]his fullness is not to be understood **quantitatively**—as though after Christ everything related to the divine mystery were already known and there were nothing further to learn—but **qualitatively.** It is owing to his personal identity as Son of God that Jesus Christ is, properly speaking, the pinnacle and culmination of the revealed word.[226]

By "qualitatively," Dupuis means that no revelation of the mystery of God can match the depths of what occurred when the Son of God lived in a human form and communicated the mystery of God to human beings. Jesus speaks the word because he is the Word. This fullness of revelation is of a singular intensity, but it does not exhaust the mystery of God. Even though it is unsurpassable, it remains unfinished until the final days, the eschaton. Indeed, *Dei Verbum* teaches that "... as the centuries succeed one another, the Church constantly moves forward toward the fullness of divine truth until the words of God reach their complete fulfillment." So, the qualitative fullness does not rule out "... the continuation of a divine self-revelation also through the prophets and sages of other religious traditions. Such ongoing self-revelation of God has taken place

---

225 *AAS*, 1966, 818; *Dei Verbum*, 2.

226 Jacques Dupuis, S.J., *Christianity and the Religions*, p. 129.

in history and continues to take place."[227] Jesus, then, is the pinnacle and culmination of God's revelation to our world; he is himself both the mediator and the perfector of revelation; his word is unsurpassable because he is the Word.

No one has expressed this better for me than the Mystical Doctor, John of the Cross. He begins by quoting Hebrews 1:1-2: "In times past, God spoke in partial and various ways to our ancestors through the prophets; in these last days, he spoke to us through a son .../ who is the refulgence of his glory, / the very imprint of his being."

Then he responds to anyone who would desire some personal vision or revelation, by imagining what God might answer such a person:

> If I have already told you all things in My Word, My Son, and I have no other word, what answer or revelation can I now make that would surpass this? Fasten your eyes on Him alone, because in Him I have spoken and revealed all, and in Him you shall discover even more than you ask for or desire .... For He is my entire locution and response, vision and revelation, which I have already spoken, answered, manifested, and revealed to you, ... Hear Him, because I have no more faith to reveal nor truths to manifest. ... [F]ix your eyes on Him, and you will discern hidden in Him the most secret mysteries and wisdom, and the wonders of God, as My Apostle proclaims: "... [in Christ] are hidden all the treasures of wisdom and knowledge ...." One should not, then, inquire of God in this manner, nor is it necessary for God to speak any more. For, since He has finished revealing the faith through Christ, there is no more faith to reveal ....[228]

C. JESUS AS THE LIFE

---

227 *AAS*, 1966, 821; *Dei Verbum*, 8.

228 *The Collected Works of John of the Cross*, pp. 180-81.

Jesus is also the way for us because he is **the life.** How does John's Gospel present Jesus as **the life?** The **primary** sense of "life" in John's Gospel is that of **eternal life;** when Jesus speaks of life in John, he almost always means eternal life. For example: "I came so that they may have life and have it more abundantly" (Jn 10:10). His mission is to bring people to eternal life; the final destination of his followers is life with the Father, eternal life. Often, Jesus teaches that his followers obtain eternal life through faith in him: "… [E]veryone who believes in him may have eternal life …" (Jn 3:15; see also 3:36; 5:24; 5:40; 6:47; 6:54; 6:68). Through hearing Jesus they come to believe in God and gain eternal life: "[W]hoever hears my word and believes in the one who sent me has eternal life …" (Jn 5:24). For the words of Jesus are the source of life: "The words I have spoken to you are both spirit and life" (Jn 6:63). And that life is eternal and assured: "I give them eternal life, and they shall never perish" (Jn 10:28; 17:3). He even proclaims to be the resurrection and the life: "I am the resurrection and the life; whoever believes in me, even if he dies, will live" (Jn 11:25).

However, the life that Jesus brings also relates to this **present life.** When Jesus speaks of the Eucharist, he proclaims, "Whoever eats my flesh and drinks my blood remains in me and I in him" (Jn 6:56). Surely remaining in Jesus means possessing life now. And in the next verse: "Just as the living Father sent me and I have life because of the Father, so also the one who feeds on me will have life because of me;" he is speaking about his life now and the life of his followers.

In a similar way, when Jesus speaks of himself as the vine, he adds, "Remain in me, as I remain in you. Just as a branch cannot bear fruit on its own unless it remains on the vine, so neither can you unless you remain in me. … [W]ithout me you can do nothing" (Jn 15:4-5). He clearly means that we must remain on the vine in order to have life in him **now.** Throughout this entire parable of the vine, Jesus requires that we "remain" in him, especially by loving him and keeping his commandments: "Remain in my love. If you keep my commandments, you will remain in my love ..." (Jn 15:9-10).

There is another way that Jesus gives us life **now**; it is by means of his Spirit dwelling within us: "... I will ask the Father, and he will give you another Advocate to be with you always, the Spirit of truth ... it remains with you and will be in you" (Jn 14:16-17). Nineteen times in John's Gospel, John uses the expression *manein en* (meaning to remain, abide, or dwell in). He means that God remains in us individuals by his Spirit (see Jn 14:15-24). To paraphrase his theology here: the Spirit is the presence of Jesus in our lives now, after Jesus has gone to the Father ("another Advocate to be with you always"). This is how Jesus can say, "I will come to you ... and you will live ... and you are in me and I in you" (Jn 14:18-20).

By way of summarizing what Jesus in John's Gospel means when he proclaims: "I am the way and the truth and the life," here is a schematic form:

- Jesus is **the way:** 1) This is Jesus' dominant claim; "the truth and the life" are explanations of the way; Jesus is the way because he is the truth and the life; 2) Jesus is the way primarily because he is the **channel of salvation,** the avenue of salvation with God for his followers; 3) Jesus is the **model** for us to follow, the image we are to imitate; 4) For us Christians, Jesus is the **only** way of salvation: "No one comes to the Father except through me."

- Jesus is **the truth:** 1) The divinely revealed **reality of God is manifested** preeminently in the words and person of Jesus; to reveal this truth is the entire purpose of Jesus' life; 2) Whoever sees, hears, and believes in Jesus, sees, hears, and believes in God the Father and will possess eternal life; 3) Jesus is the unique, final, and **complete revelation** of God; by his words, actions, suffering, and entire life, he is the unsurpassable, definitive word of God to the world; 4) The revelation of God is a person, Jesus Christ.

- Jesus is **the life:** 1) The primary emphasis, here, is on Jesus as the source of **eternal life;** the words of Jesus lead to faith in God and eternal life with God; 2) Jesus is "the resurrection and the life;" 3) Remaining in Jesus now means possessing **life now;** we remain in Jesus by our love; only by remaining in him can we bear fruit; 4) The **Holy Spirit** is the presence of Jesus in our lives now, after Jesus has gone to the Father.

REFLECTIONS

1. Jesus assures us, "… [W]ithout me you can do nothing" (Jn 15, 5). Does that metaphor of the vine mean that for us Christians all grace, all life comes from him?

2. What is your primary image of God? If Jesus is the best way of knowing what God is like, how does he give you a more personal image of God?

3. If we affirm that Jesus is "the fullness of revelation" about God, does that exhaust the mystery of God? Can there still be many other continuations of divine revelation by other prophets or religious leaders?

CHAPTER 27

The Appeal of the Person of Jesus

Hans Küng has an insightful way of describing our following of Christ as our way, our truth and our life:

> [Our] *following* of Christ is what distinguishes Christians from other disciples and supporters of great men, in the sense that Christians are ultimately dependent on this person, not only on his teaching, but also on his life, death and new life. …. For Christians then Jesus is certainly a teacher, but at the same time also essentially more than a teacher: he is *in person the living, archetypal embodiment of his cause*…. [Following Christ in the New testament means] binding oneself to him in the same spirit of allegiance and discipleship, of joining him permanently and making him the measure of one's own life. This is what following means: *getting involved with him and his way and going one's own way*—each of us has his own way—*in the light of his directions.*[229]

Then, in the following pages,[230] he shows how Jesus is the personification of this new life. He argues persuasively that the whole Christian message and way of life is much more convincing and inviting than any possible set of principles, norms, values, or ideals. The strength of our Christian faith, he maintains, lies in being able to justify and substantiate an attitude of life and way of life by pointing to a quite definite and appealing historical figure, Jesus Christ. By describing the words, actions, virtues, life, death, and person of Jesus, he presents a thoroughly human way, truth, life, and model for all his followers. Kung mentions several ways in which the person of Jesus is more engaging and inviting than any set of ideals, principles, rules, and abstract visions.

---

229 Hans Kung, *On Being Christian,* p. 545 (emphasis in original).

230 Ibid., et seq.

First, **the person of Jesus is much more appealing** than ideas, principles, and abstract systems:

> A concrete person ... does not merely stimulate thinking, critical-rational conversation, but also continually rouses fantasy, imagination and emotion, spontaneity, creativity and innovation: in a word, appeals to the whole man, of flesh and blood. ... Only a living figure and not a principle can *draw* people, can be "attractive" in the most profound and comprehensive sense of the term: *verba docent, exempla trahunt,* words teach, examples carry us with them.[231]

Jesus, our model, does that by being a "shining example," inspiring us with new meaning to human life. We all have to face the threat of limited lifetime and death, the threat of nothingness and meaninglessness, the threat of despair and chaos, the actuality of suffering and evil. In the face of all this, we have a choice. Without Jesus and his truth about God, we find no rational explanation for the beginning of this immense cosmos; we cannot rule out the possibility that our world is under threat of chaos and despair; we face human life as very limited in time, and death as an absolute end; we see no primal meaning and value to this world; we can find no positive meaning to suffering; and we face death as an absolute end. On the other hand, with Jesus and his truth about God, we know that this immense cosmos is a benign world; we can reason that reality is sensible, reasonable, with primal meaning and value, with an ultimate source and goal; and we know that our human life is most valuable now and will lead to eternal life. We cannot pick and choose among these alternatives. If we choose the first alternative, we can only try to find some value to human life by whatever temporary value we can put on it. If we choose the second, then with Christ our life has ultimate meaning, value, sense, hope, and a goal.

---

231   Ibid. pp. 546-47.

Second, a concrete, historical person **can relate to us personally** by calling us, inviting us, summoning us, challenging us. Norms, principles, systems can do none of that. The following of Jesus is based essentially on being summoned by his person and way. All the gospels include many calls and invitations by Jesus to follow him, and in the Acts of the Apostles, those who accepted his invitation were known as people who followed the Way. And his call is still operative in our world today. Not only do women and men religious follow a special vocation, but also all Christians can feel called to their particular Christian vocation as parents, teachers, professional people, tradesmen, or social workers. And we know we are each individually called by name—by a Christian name—in baptism. Also, we maintain our personal friendship with Jesus by receiving the sacrament of the Eucharist, which is our means of a regular, external sign of friendship with Jesus.

Third, the whole **public life of Jesus** displays an excellent and imitable ideal of ethics that goes far beyond other systems of ethics. In Jesus' time, there was an ethics of some of the Jewish leaders that included sophisticated casuistry and ossified ritualism, and there were Greek ethical systems of Stoicism and Platonic universal ideas. In our day, our world includes so many national ethical systems that are without clear norms of gender equality, freedom of activity, or economic systems that have little respect for persons. On the other hand, Jesus exemplifies an attitude of respect for all persons that includes equality of all, and even a preference for the poor and needy. It is easy for us to respect ourselves when we are capable, successful, and popular. But when we no longer accomplish much, or are sick, or dependent on others, or are poor, or physically or mentally disabled, then we may no longer be convinced that we are valuable and worthy of respect. Don't we have an absolute value that doesn't depend on our accomplishments? Isn't our very person valuable and good, no matter what our condition? Jesus answers yes; he assures us that we are uniquely and absolutely valuable no matter what our condition. We are sons and daughters of God who are loved unconditionally, irrespective of any action or accomplishment of ours. That is an ethic that was preached and lived by Jesus, our real, human model.

Fourth, Jesus does not offer a universal ideal, a complex, external system of conduct, but rather **influences human life and conduct from within;** following him means a change of heart. Jesus' way does not impose human uniformity, but seeks to fashion a new person individually by offering challenging examples, significant deeds, concrete values, and model cases. He gives constant witness that we have all we need in order to become whole human beings in the midst of the uncertainties and struggles of our human existence. That is, we need to know that our world is a benign world not an evil one; Jesus assures us that our creator is a loving Father. We need to know what God is really like; Jesus offers us a tangible, understandable image of God. We need to know that it is possible to be kind, accepting, just, and understanding in our sometimes cruel world; our human Savior was such a man and affirmed, "I am the way." We need a motive that is strong enough for us to love even difficult people; Jesus is himself that motive: "... [L]ove one another as I love you" (Jn 15:12). We need a constant encouragement to try to build a world that is more just, peaceful and loving; Jesus assures us, "... [T]ake courage, I have conquered the world" (Jn 16:33). Finally, we need a hope that is real, a destiny that is worthy of us, to be worked out now and continue after death; Jesus has established that hope for us: "... Christ has been raised from the dead ... so too in Christ shall all be brought to life ..." (1 Cor 15:20, 22).

Fifth, the historical Jesus exemplifies norms and values for human living; he is **a living model** of mature human living. He is even a model regarding material possessions and pleasures. Contrary to popular estimates, Jesus was not an ascetic; he never demanded sacrifice for the sake of sacrifice. He shared the ordinary life of men and women of his time; he came "eating and drinking" (Mt 11:19). He took pleasure in friends. For him there was nothing unclean about marriage. He did not demand the renunciation of material pleasures in order to follow him. Though he warned that riches could easily corrupt one, he never condemned riches outright.

Jesus was clearly a model for dealing with human suffering. He did not deal with it by denying it or doing away with it. He did not offer a chimerical or impossible human life, but a life filled with the normal pains of human existence. He certainly did not promise that, if we were good, we would not suffer. Some of his sufferings he just worked through or alleviated: thus, he overcame misunderstandings by slowly instructing his followers. He overcame loneliness by making some friends and attaching disciples to himself. He dealt with illness by curing some and teaching others courage. He worked through the many inconveniences of his ministry by realizing the value and small success of his work. But there was a lot of suffering he could not overcome or work through, he simply had to undergo it; for example, his rejection by many, especially the religious leaders of his time, the sense of failure towards the end of his life, the agony in the garden, and his crucifixion. These sufferings at the end of his life led to the ultimate limit of his endurance; they were his hardest and most repulsive trials. Yet it is especially these sufferings that won our salvation.

The most engaging attitude of Jesus, constantly exemplified by him in his public life, was that of universal acceptance of all kinds of people; his approach to people was catholic; he showed no preference for any group of people, no superiority or dominance over others. He was amazingly involved with those who were left out of the dominant society of his time: the poor, the sick, the needy, women, and the oppressed. He showed a profound sense of kindness and compassion, forgiveness without end, simple honesty, individual responsibility, and freedom of conscience above the law. In all of his living, he exemplified a superior human model for all his followers.

Finally, Jesus offers us **new values, new motives for action,** in the midst of our world of hate, prejudice, injustice, and war; such motivations cannot be engendered by external laws, rules, norms, or ideals; they can only come from our hearts and human commitments. The deepest human question is: Why should we be honest, just, kind, and forbearing, even when we are made to suffer as a result of the actions of others? Why should we love and not hate? Why should not our norm for living with difficult or brutal people be "an eye for an eye?" Jesus answers such questions in Matthew's Gospel (5:38-48). First, he rejects the law of *talion* or retribution as it appears in the Hebrew Scriptures.[232] Instead he counsels a response to personal injury that is non-violent, that does not seek retribution at all. This principle of Jesus is one of those that distinguish Christianity from pagan or merely rational morality—in fact, from many other religions. But Jesus went beyond the common denominator of some other religions or ethical norms: "Do unto others as they do to you." Jesus here tells us that we cannot reciprocate in kind; we cannot let our decency depend on another's conduct. We cannot meet evil with evil, hatred with hatred. We must be willing to break the cycle of injustice in our world. Jesus insists that we must follow his ideal of love of enemies: "… [I]f you love those who love you, what recompence will you have? … Do not the pagans do the same? …" (Mt 5:46-47) "But I say to you, love your enemies, and pray for those who persecute you …." (Mt 5:44). What **motivation** does Jesus offer for us to love our enemies? His motive is deceptively simple: "… [L]ove your enemies … that you may be children of your heavenly Father, for he makes his sun rise on the bad and the good, and causes rain to fall on the just and the unjust" (Mt 5:44-45). That is, God sends his natural gifts of rain and sunshine to all people equally. We might add that God also offers his grace and forgiveness to all and provides possible eternal salvation equally to all. If God is most generous to "the good, the bad, and the ugly," then we

---

232   Ibid.

should imitate God and love even our enemies. Such teachings of Jesus were extreme in his day and seem just as extreme for us today. One modern writer summarizes such teachings of Jesus as a **social revolution**, one that turns social relations upside down:

> Jesus' sayings, especially those that were collected into the Sermon on the Mount, were subversive of almost everything his contemporaries took for granted. He spoke of turning the other cheek instead of taking revenge, of loving one's enemies instead of hating them, of doing good to those who hate you, and of forgiving them all seventy times … That alone would have revolutionized social relationships … as wellas relationships between different groups and classes ….[233]

In all honesty, you and I would probably admit that we do not always carry out these teachings of Jesus about loving our enemies. But we must admit that Jesus himself lived this ideal and invites us to follow him.

We Christians might agree that the essence of our Christian life is simply love; for the only command of Jesus, that he appropriates as his own, is this: "This is my commandment: love one another as I love you" (Jn 15:12). This is not exactly a command, for no one can command love. It is rather the appeal of a lover. But when we look at his actions, we see how his love was selfless and mature. Jesus' love was so understanding of human nature; see, for example, Lk 7:36-50, in which he showed great understanding for both the Pharisee and the sinful woman. His love was respectful of all kinds of people; he ate and associated even with the pariahs of his society—the poor, the outcast, the sinners, and the irreligious. Jesus' love was one that showed great concern, sympathy, and kindness. And his love was actively responsible; he responded to the needs of those

---

[233] Albert Nolan, *Jesus today: A Spirituality of Radical Freedom* (Maryknoll, NY: Orbis Books, 2007), pp. 50-51.

around him by curing some, feeding many, showing empathy for their suffering. Peter summarized very simply and accurately how Jesus lived: "He went about doing good…" (Acts 10:38).

Raymond Brown has a great insight regarding Jesus' love for others and how his love can become a driving force for us personally:

> … [I]n his life Jesus must have impressed people as extraordinary. But the tone of the following of Jesus in the ministry involves more than that—even more than religious awe and veneration. Jesus was remembered as one who exhibited love in what he did and was loved deeply by those who followed him.[234]

But then he asks a crucial question about love for Jesus long after he died:

> How did the following of Jesus, which involved love for him, survive after he died? The answer, I suggest, is that it survived only because love for Jesus was looked on as an ongoing element, even among those who never knew him during his ministry.[235]

Even the letters of Paul do not fill in the person of Jesus, the face of Jesus. He reasons that Paul did not know Jesus in the flesh and so did not vividly describe the kind of person Jesus was and why people followed him so intensely. Then Raymond Brown suggests that John's Gospel is the best portrayal of Jesus' individual love for us and draws us to love him in return, even though we "never knew him during his ministry."

Here are some of the ways that John's Gospel emphasizes our **individual** relationship to Jesus. First, even when John uses collective images of the vine and branches, and the shepherd and the flock, there is a decided concentration on the relation

---

234   Raymond Brown, *The Churches the Apostles Left Behind,* p. 97.
235   Ibid.

of the individual believer to Jesus. That is, even within these images, it is very important for each person not only to believe in Jesus, but also to remain attached to him. Thus, Jesus insists, "Whoever remains in me and I in him will bear much fruit …" (Jn 15:5), and then adds, "As the Father loves me, so I also love you. Remain in my love" (Jn 15:9). Second, in the so-called Last Supper discourses (chapters 14 to 16), Jesus speaks very intimately to the disciples: "… [W]hoever loves me will be loved by my Father, and I will love him and reveal myself to him" (14:21). And his one commandment is that of love, after the model of his love for them: "… [L]ove one another as I love you" (15:12). Also, only here does he call his disciples "friends:" "I have called you friends, because I have told you everything I have heard from my Father" (15:15). Jesus also provides for his friends, even though he will soon die: "I will not leave you orphans" (14:18); he promises them the Holy Spirit, "the Spirit of truth … to be with you always" (14:17 and 16); "… he will teach you everything and remind you of all that [I] told you." (14:26) "… [and] guide you to all truth" (16:13). All of these expressions of Christ's love are related to his disciples—and to us—**individually,** and they invite all of us disciples to be attached to Jesus in a loving relationship. Third, in an oblique way, John's Gospel teaches us how important Jesus considers such mutual love, for this gospel emphasizes the extraordinary personal love for Jesus of the **beloved disciple**. And because of this love, the beloved disciple is presented as the ideal and the hero of the Johannine community. He is never named—even though we used to think of him as John himself. But throughout this gospel, there is a consistent and deliberate contrast between the beloved disciple and Peter the apostle. Thus, at the Last Supper the beloved disciple rests on Jesus' chest, while Peter has to signal to Jesus (13:23-24). During Jesus' trial, the beloved disciple accompanies Jesus into the high priest's palace, while Peter only enters with his help (18:15-16). Most important, at the foot of the cross, we find the beloved disciple standing there, but Peter and the other disciples have abandoned Jesus (19:26-27). Then, in the early Easter event, the beloved disciple outruns Peter to the tomb and only he is said to believe the evidence he sees there (20:3-8). Finally, when the risen Jesus appears to them on the shore, the beloved disciple is the first to recognize him and he tells Peter that it is the Lord (21:7). This one-upmanship of the beloved disciple over Peter indicates that he is quicker to believe in Jesus and closer to him in love. And this whole comparison between Peter and the beloved disciple proves that for the Johannine community, our individual love for Jesus is all important. And just because all of these expressions of Jesus' love are related to his disciples—and to us—**individually**, they impel all of us disciples to be attached to Jesus in a loving relationship.

We conclude this chapter as we began it; Jesus proclaims: "I am the way and the truth and the life. No one comes to the Father except through me" (Jn 14:6). These three nouns are not theological ideas, they are Jesus' practical way of describing how he, by his words, actions, life, and death, is the channel leading to eternal life, and by the life he lived he is a model for all his followers. Jesus himself is the standard, the way leading to eternal life. For us Christians, there is no other way, no other model, and no other truth that leads to our heavenly Father. "Come follow me …." Most of all, we are each impelled to love him as he loved us.

REFLECTIONS

1. In the beginning of this chapter, Hans Kung taught that Jesus is unique as a religious leader, because he alone is the very embodiment of his cause, the very model of our Christian way of life. Do you know of any other religious leader who makes himself the concrete expression of the ideal way of life?

2. If Jesus were not entirely human, could he honestly claim to be a real human model of the Christian way?

3. Of all the norms and values for human living that Jesus exemplifies, which values mean the most to you?

CONCLUSION

In the introduction of this book, I promised a realistic and yet positive view of Catholicism in the twenty-first century. You can now judge how well this was done. The view of the institutional Church was **realistic** in several ways:

- Vatican Council II attempted to reform the life of the institutional Church. Many reforms regarding Scripture, religious freedom, and liturgy were not only declared by the council, but actually took root in the universal Church. These changes amounted to one of the most significant reforms in the 2,000-year history of the Church.

- Despite the efforts of the council fathers for *aggiornamento* and openness throughout the Church, the pope and Curia remained very authoritarian and controlling. The bishops, and even the conferences of bishops, were placated in some documents, but then were relegated to less influential positions, even in their own national settings.

- Though the Church had been slow to accept literary criticism, it finally permitted scholars to interpret Scripture according to modern forms of scriptural criticism. In the past sixty years, we have gained a thoroughly new and inspiring understanding of Scripture.

- Theologians and moralists continued to be investigated often, even without due process, and many were forbidden to teach or to write.

- Questions regarding Christology and Trinity continue to be explored with the hope of expressing them in modern terminology.

- In terms of ecumenism, there has been greater openness to the value of other religions to lead people to salvation.

- Rome did not permit public questioning of non-dogmatic questions; often "authentic" teachings were treated just as sacrosanct as dogmatic teachings.

So, the effort throughout this first half of the book was to evaluate those matters in a realistic but not condemnatory fashion. Problems with authority and change in the Church have distressed many post-Vatican II Catholics, so that they are now on the periphery of the Church or have opted out, at least in terms of their active participation. The problems of change in the Church have also disturbed many traditional Catholics, so that they are often confused, insecure, or angry with the Church. Certainly this human Church is far from the ideals of Jesus as found in Scripture. She has made mistakes in some changes; she continues to be authoritarian and centralized. The sober, everyday reality of this human Church is that it is finite, flawed, unresponsive, and burdened with history. We admit the faults of the institutional Church, the inadequacy of its members, and their failures throughout history. Yet we are bound together in Jesus, for there is no other way to follow him except by means of the Word, the sacraments, and the community of Christians.

The second half of this book presented a more **positive** view of the Church and our faith. It dealt with aspects of our Catholic life that were centered on personal faith—that faith which was so revitalized by the great advances made in the last fifty years, because of the Vatican council and the explosion of Scripture knowledge. Then, we pointed out a new lay spirituality that is no longer seen as inferior to monastic spirituality. It concentrated on our friendship with Jesus through union with him in the Eucharist and through regular prayer. The person of Jesus is our model for living an individual, free, loving, and inspiring Catholic life, that need not be restricted and dominated by the institutional Church. We understand that our faith is based on truths, laws, sacraments, and the community of believers. But in this twenty-first century, the focus of our faith is the human and historical Jesus who is the best revelation of God for us. By his ministry, teaching, life, death, and resurrection, he is the image of God. In Jesus we see God, we know God, and we believe in his plan of salvation. In terms of the ultimate religious question, Jesus is the medium or mediator of God. For our Christian faith and living, Jesus is our model; he is our way, our truth, and our life.

GLOSSARY

AGGIORNAMENTO
This Italian word means "bringing up to date." Pope John XXIII meant that he wanted to open up the Church to the way of renewal.

BELOVED DISCIPLE
There are five references to him in the last chapters of John's Gospel. He is not John the apostle but an unknown, real idealized model for the Johannine Church.

CONSTITUTIVE ROLE
Means that Jesus has established the way of salvation for all Christians.

CURIA
Includes all the formal Roman congregations that deal with specific ministries of the Church, along with their members.

DEAD SEA SCROLLS
Manuscripts found near the Dead Sea from 1947-1954 at a place called Qumran gulch. Many of them were scrolls written by the Essenes for their sect.

DOCETISM
A third century teaching, rejected by the Church, that Jesus was divine but not truly human.

DOXOLOGY
Doxa is Greek for "glory." Thus, a prayer of praise to God.

ECUMENISM
The movement that seeks to achieve the unity of Christians, and ultimately of all religions throughout "the whole wide world" (the literal meaning of the word).

ECUMENICAL
Fostering ecumenism.

ECUMENICAL COUNCIL
A Catholic council including bishops of "the whole wide world."

ESCHATON
From the Greek word meaning "last things." It refers to the end of the world and the second coming of Christ.

ESCHATOLOGICAL
Related to the eschaton or the events associated with it in religious expectation.

ESCHATOLOGICAL CHRISTOLOGY
Christian faith that focuses primarily on the next world and eternal life.

ESSENES
A strict Jewish sect that created a community near the Dead Sea. They flourished from second century BC to 68 AD, but were not mentioned in the Gospels.

EXEGESIS
The explanation of a text of Scripture or the scientific study of Scripture texts.

EXEGETE
Professional scholars who interpret Scripture.

FORM CRITICISM
An approach to Scripture that focuses on the literary forms of the texts, such as proclamation history, sermons, parables, canticles, allegories, poetry, or legends.

FUNDAMENTALIST
There are many meanings to this term. Here it refers to a rigid, literal sense of each text of Scripture, without comparing it to similar quotes.

HIERARCHICAL
A theological mentality that emphasizes the role of ecclesiastical officers in the teaching of the Church.

HIERARCHY
The body of ordained ministers of the Church (pope, Curia members, bishops), especially the leaders in Rome.

HISTORICAL-CRITICAL METHOD
Understanding a Scripture text in its historical context; that is, what it meant to the original hearers or readers.

HOMOIOUSION
"Ousia" means "substance" or "being". *"Homoi"* means "similar" or "subordinate." The entire term means "of similar (subordinate) being as the Father."

HOMOOUSION
"Homo" means "same." The entire term means "of the same substance as the Father" or equal to the Father.

HYPOSTATIC UNION
"Hypostasis" refers to the person of the *Logos*. The entire term refers to the permanent union of the divine and human natures in the one divine person of the Word in Jesus Christ.

HYPOSTASIS
The Greek word means "person." It refers to the personhood of Jesus or his identity with the divine *Logos*.

INCARNATIONAL CHRISTOLOGY
Christian faith that focuses primarily on following Jesus in this world as our model.

INSPIRATION OF SCRIPTURE
Vatican II says that God speaks "through men in human fashion" so that careful attention must be given "to what the sacred writers really intended."

JOHANNINE
Pertaining to all the writings of the Bible that are attributed to "John" or those influenced by him (Gospel, plus three Epistles, plus the Apocalypse).

LECTIO DIVINA
Latin for "divine reading." Refers to meditative reading of Scripture.

MAGISTERIUM
The teaching authority of the Church, which belongs by office to the pope, the Curia, and the bishops. Theologians contribute to the teaching mission.

MANDATE
A formal authorization from Rome to teach in Catholic universities.

METAPHYSICAL
Philosophical reflections on the nature of being and truth. Abstract thinking about the essences of beings.

MODALISM
A theological explanation of the Trinity that describes the three persons as different modes of the one God.

MONOTHEISM
Belief in one God.

MOTU PROPRIO
Latin for "by his own motion or decree." An apostolic letter signed by the pope, issued solely on his authority, and of less moment than an encyclical.

NIDATES
From the Latin for "builds a nest." It refers to the fertilized ovum attaching itself to the womb of the mother after a few days.

NIDATION
The state of the fertilized ovum after it nidates and is implanted into the womb.

ONTOLOGICAL
Related to the essence or being of something or the nature of a being.

PARACLETE
Greek for "called to the side of," meaning to intercede for or give assistance. In John's Gospel, it refers to the Holy Spirit who is the guide and helper Jesus promised the apostles and us. The Latin equivalent is Advocate.

PAROUSIA
Greek for "presence" or "appearance." In the NT it usually refers to the eschatological or second coming of Jesus at the end of the world.

PATRISTIC
From the Greek word for "Father." It refers to the early period of theologians or Fathers of the Church (100 to c. 500).

PAULINE CORPUS
The 13 letters attributed to Paul, including the seven considered authentic and the six not-clearly authentic letters.

PERITUS
Latin for "expert." It refers to theologian-advisors to the bishops at Vatican II.

PNEUMATOLOGY
"*Pneuma*" is Greek for "spirit." Pneumatology is the theology regarding the Holy Spirit.

POSITIVISM
A system of morality not resting principally on the natural law but rather on independent or church authority.

PROCLAMATION HISTORY
The gospels are an account of God's saving message by means of the life and preaching of Jesus. They are similar to a Greco-Roman biography.

PROSOPON
Another Greek word for "person," synonymous with hypostasis. It refers to the one, metaphysical subject that is the Lord Jesus Christ.

Q SOURCE
"*Quelle*" means "source" in German. It refers to the material common to Matthew and Luke yet not found in Mark. So the Q source plus Mark's Gospel supply most of the material used by Matthew and Luke.

QUMRAN
The community of the strict Jewish sect of Essenes near the Dead Sea. Many of their writings (Qumran Scrolls) were discovered between 1947-1954 and were a great archeological find, describing their "way" and teachings.

REDACTION CRITICISM
Analysis of how a text was put together by an editor or redactor from existing sources. Vatican II teaches that the Evangelists selected "some things from the many that had been handed down by word of mouth or in writing, reducing some of them to a synthesis."

RESSOURCEMENT
French word meaning "a return to the sources." Thus, church renewal must include the three great early sources of Christianity: the Bible, the liturgies, and the Church Fathers.

SCHEMA
An outline or plan, which gave direction to one session of the council or to the discussion regarding a particular doctrine.

SCHOLASTICISM
The dominant way of developing theology from the Middle Ages on to the last century. Instead of emphasizing the commentary on biblical texts and the writings of the early Church Fathers, it began with dogmas and argued systematically and philosophically.

SOTERIOLOGY
From the Greek word for "savior." The study of Christ as Savior. The theology of how Christ brought about our salvation.

SOURCE CRITICISM
One source hypothesis is that Matthew and Luke used the Gospel of Mark and another source, called "Q," when they wrote their gospels.

SUBORDINATIONISM
An early Church heresy, which held that Jesus was less than the Father and created by him.

SYNOPTICS
The first three Gospels, Matthew, Mark and Luke, called "synoptic" because they are similar in structure, content, and outlook.

SYSTEMATIC THEOLOGY
Dogmatic or doctrinal theology, as distinguished from scriptural or moral theology. It is systematic because it tries to see all the various doctrines in relation to one another.

THEOLOGY FROM ABOVE

Theology, especially Christology, that unfolded "from above," beginning with the exalted Christ in the Gospel of John, and then descending thru incarnation.

THEOLOGY FROM BELOW
Theology, especially Christology, which began with the human Jesus as seen in Scripture, and continued beyond his death to his glorification.

TORAH
A Hebrew word meaning "law" or "teaching." The Torah (or Pentateuch) consists of the first five books of the Hebrew Scriptures.

TRITHEISM
Belief in three gods, which is not the faith of Christians, who believe in three persons in one God.

ZYGOTE
From the Greek for "joined together." It refers to the human joined ovum and sperm. More broadly, it can refer to the developing individual in its early stage.